Tradition and Transformation in Medieval Romance

From the insular romance of the twelfth century (vital to an understanding of the literary and historical context of medieval English literature) to the era of the printed book, romance challenges generic definition, audience expectation and established scholarly approaches. This third volume of papers from the regular conference on Romance in Medieval England uses a broad range of material and methodologies to illuminate the subject. Topics include the strategies and audiences of crusading romances, the deployment by Chaucer and Gower of romance theme and style, a re-evaluation of the text of *Gamelyn*, and the shifting generic boundaries between romance, exemplum and legal narrative. Other papers explore the transformation of traditional material on the revenant dead and the divided family from ancient literary texts to the prose romances of the sixteenth century.

Dr ROSALIND FIELD teaches in the Department of English at Royal Holloway, University of London.

Tradition and Transformation
in
Medieval Romance

EDITED BY
ROSALIND FIELD

D. S. BREWER

First published 1999
D. S. Brewer, Cambridge

ISBN 0 85991 553 0

D. S. Brewer is an imprint of Boydell & Brewer Ltd
PO Box 9, Woodbridge, Suffolk IP12 3DF, UK
and of Boydell & Brewer Inc.
PO Box 41026, Rochester, NY 14604–4126, USA
website: http://www.boydell.co.uk

A catalogue record for this book is available
from the British Library

Library of Congress Cataloging-in-Publication Data
Tradition and transformation in medieval romance / edited by Rosalind
Field.
    p.   cm.
Includes bibliographical references (p.   ) and index.
ISBN 0–85991–553–0 (hardback : alk. paper)
    1. English literature – Middle English, 1100–1500 – History
and criticism. 2. Romances, English – History and criticism.
3. Rhetoric, Medieval. I. Field, Rosalind, 1945–   .
PR321.T7   1999
820.9'001–dc21   99–17690

This publication is printed on acid-free paper

Printed in Great Britain by
St Edmundsbury Press Ltd, Bury St Edmunds, Suffolk

Contents

Contributors

Elizabeth Archibald is an Associate Professor of English at the University of Victoria, British Columbia. She is completing a study of the incest theme in medieval literature.

Nancy Mason Bradbury is an Associate Professor at Smith College in Northampton, Massachusetts. She is the author of *Writing Aloud: Storytelling in Late Medieval England*.

Helen Cooper is a Tutorial Fellow in English at University College, Oxford, and Professor of English Language and Literature at the University of Oxford.

Jeremy Dimmick is a Research Fellow at Gonville and Caius, Cambridge. He recently completed his thesis on John Gower's *Confessio Amantis* and is currently working on Middle English Troy and Alexander narratives and on late medieval transformations of Ovid.

Joerg O. Fichte of the University of Tübingen, has published books and essays on Chaucer, the medieval drama, Arthurian romance and medieval literary theory.

Rosalind Field is a Senior Lecturer at Royal Holloway, University of London. She has published on medieval romance, alliterative poetry and Chaucer.

Phillipa Hardman is a Lecturer in the Department of English and at the Graduate Centre for Medieval Studies at the University of Reading. She has published articles on Middle English romances, Chaucer, Lydgate and the manuscript context of medieval English literature.

Stephen Knight is Professor of English at Cardiff University. He has written books on Chaucer, the myth of Arthur, and crime fiction and has recently published a study and edition of the Robin Hood tradition.

Noël James Menuge is completing her doctorate at the Centre for Medieval Studies, University of York. She currently works as a landscape historian in Cambridge. She has published on landscape history, medieval romances and the law.

Diane Speed is a Senior Lecturer in the Department of English at the University of Sydney. As well as medieval romance, her research interests include the Anglo-Latin *Gesta Romanorum*, Gower's *Confessio Amantis* and medieval biblical art and literature.

Contributors

Robert Warm received his doctorate from the University of Leeds in 1996. He is now in charge of Research and Development for Leeds Education 2000, a radical campaigning charity which orchestrates innovative programmes in inner-city Leeds.

Judith Weiss is a Fellow and Tutor of Robinson College, Cambridge. She has translated and introduced an anthology of Anglo-Norman romances, *The Birth of Romance*, and has recently published an edition and translation of Wace's *Roman de Brut*.

Elizabeth Williams lectured in medieval English at the University of Leeds until she took early retirement in 1991. Her main studies are now in medieval romance, folk-tale and ballad.

Abbreviations

ANTS   Anglo-Norman Text Society
CFMA   Classiques français du moyen âge
CR   *Chaucer Review*
EETS ES   Early English Text Society, Extra Series
EETS OS   Early English Text Society, Ordinary Series
JEGP   *Journal of English and Germanic Philology*
Manual *A Manual of the Writings in Middle English: 1050–1500, I,*
          Romances, ed. J. B. Severs (New Haven, CT, 1967)
MÆ   *Medium Ævum*
PMLA   *Publications of the Modern Language Association of America*
Readings *Readings in Medieval English Romance,* ed. Carol M. Meale
          (Cambridge, 1994)
SAC   *Studies in the Age of Chaucer*
SATF   Société des anciens textes français
Spec   *Speculum*

All references to the works of Chaucer are to *The Riverside Chaucer*, ed. L. D. Benson (Oxford, 1987)

Introduction

These papers originated at the fifth biennial conference on Romance in Medieval England, held at Royal Holloway, University of London, in April 1996. In accordance with the custom of these conferences the focus of the material is the insular romance (in any of the languages of medieval England) and non-Arthurian: this in effect occupies some of the most problematic and neglected areas in romance scholarship.

To some extent the problem of comprehending the insular romances has for long been solved by a silent conspiracy of exclusion. Now, however, the familiar canon of romance, specifically of Middle English romance, has been enlarged significantly in the last decade or so, and these papers reflect and continue this process. As with its two predecessors,[1] there is no single or preferred approach in this volume to the subject of romances in England: it is a collection which reflects the interests of a variety of scholars, not the programme of a compiler. But what emerges strongly from this collection is the willingness to attend to often marginalised areas: twelfth-century Anglo-Norman/Latin narrative, later verse and prose Charlemagne romances, narratives concerned with cross-dressing or dubiously grateful dead – the fluidity and protean shape of insular narrative are very apparent here. So, as the title of this volume indicates, most of these papers are concerned with change as well as with relating the particular work to traditions, historical or generic; the development of a narrative under the pressure of political events, the transformation of popular idiom, metre and material at the hands of a major poet, or the sensational changes, in fortune, form or gender, within the narrative itself.

A chronological starting point is provided in Judith Weiss's paper, which provides a context, of audience and occasion as well as literary exchange, for one of the major works of the twelfth-century flowering of insular narrative. In reconstructing the relationship between the Anglo-Norman *Romance of Horn* and the East-Anglian Hereward tradition, her paper confirms how insular narrative at this date is confined neither by locality nor language. The transformation of traditional tale and legend into courtly romance relates to the demands of a particular historical context.

Gamelyn has always attracted historicist readings, but Stephen Knight demonstrates the need to return to the text, long neglected and misunderstood, in order to establish the poem's stature. Once rescued from the

---

[1] Maldwyn Mills, Jennifer Fellows and Carol Meale, eds, *Romance in Medieval England* (Cambridge, 1991); Carol M. Meale, ed., *Readings in Medieval English Romance* (Cambridge, 1994)

distortions of poor-quality transmission, the text of *Gamelyn* reveals literary sophistication, dramatic structure, and a verbal matrix shared with such different works as *Piers Plowman* and the ballads of Robin Hood. Knight's view of the likely audience for *Gamelyn* is consistent with Noël James Menuge's procedure of reading that poem as one of a group of wardship romances and examining its language and subject matter in relation to texts of a different discourse, the legal documents pertaining to wardship and guardianship. Romance can offer alternative resolutions, not just to familiar social and emotional dilemmas, but to precise legal failures to protect the vulnerable from the predatory and the powerful.

Diane Speed's paper is another which questions generic boundaries, in this case between romance and exemplum, by investigating the nature of the relationship between Middle English romances and the *Gesta Romanorum*. She provides a resource for identifying and comparing a range of treatments of similar material, and suggests further areas of enquiry into the reception of medieval romance, the uses of allegory, the relationship between texts in Latin prose and vernacular verse. This is a rich field for further research, and, as with other papers in this volume, her enquiry moves into the era of printing, when the activities of Caxton and de Worde in translating and printing both romance and exempla collections, blur the practical distinction between the genres for a fifteenth-century reader.

Elizabeth Williams's enquiry into the disturbing inconsistencies in the conventionally labelled 'Grateful Dead' tale uncovers connexions between romance, folktale and biblical apocrypha. Assumptions about folktale motifs and romance classification that have remained largely unexamined for a century or more are, as this paper shows, ripe for re-assessment. Williams's analysis, linking as it does the *Book of Tobit* with *Sir Gawain and the Green Knight*, offers further confirmation of the need for the alert reader to recognise the narrative and cultural complexity behind texts which are more than they seem.

As the focus of the Romance in Medieval England conferences is primarily, if not exclusively, on non-Arthurian material, they have provided the opportunity to give more attention to those other Worthies, Alexander, Charlemagne and Godefrey de Bouillon, and this volume contains three papers on Charlemagne and crusading romances. Phillipa Hardman returns to the Thornton MS and the *Sege of Melayne* and addresses the three main problems posed by this poem: its lack of an extant ending (she offers a reconstruction of events), its apparent partisanship on behalf of the French during the Hundred Years War, and Bishop Turpin's castigation of the Virgin. She responds to these with a close contextual reading drawing on popular and learned religion, nationalist appropriation of French heroes, and the manuscript context of the poem. Robert Warm places the *Sege of Melayne* in the company of the non-Thornton Charlemagne romances, and also in the context of events in the east. He sees the Charlemagne romance transformed from a nationalist text to a supranationalist one in which Christendom is favoured at the expense of the emergent nation-state. The text gathers up its medieval audience into the crusading experience: it reveals to the modern reader the all-too-familiar features of the fault-line at the eastern fringes of Europe, both medieval and modern, where Europe constructs its identity. Joerg Fichte's study of Caxton's *Godeffroy of Boloyne* shows the changes brought about in the century between Thornton and Caxton; a century in which the Turkish threat came closer, and the mass market provided by printing was ready for romances which provided exemplary figures for a unified Christendom. The *chanson* tradition had been newly transformed into a text for the times, its heroes the new men needed by Europe, its audience the stay-at-home crusaders, for whom literature offered a form of participation.

It is a measure of the coherence, as well as the development, of insular romance that the twelfth-century *Romance of Horn* also presented a crusading hero, and addressed an audience which would find their current interests fictionalised within the narrative. The similarity and the differences are equally instructive: medieval romance requires the presence of the 'other', the world of Saracen adversaries, to define itself and its protagonists and to offer self-definition to its audience. This becomes increasingly evident as the crusading romances of the fifteenth century problematise the tension between national identity and the supra-national identity of Christendom.

A deepening understanding of the range and effectiveness of the romances can serve to cast light on even the most securely canonical authors. Nancy Mason Bradbury's reassessment of Chaucer's debt to popular romance is made possible by the rehabilitation of popular romances such as that provided for *Gamelyn* by Stephen Knight. Bradbury, like Knight, offers close attention to verbal patterning, and identifies two obstacles to an assessment of Chaucer's relationship to the romances: *Sir Thopas*, seen as a devastating and destructive parody, and the modern embarrassment over formulaic language. This has implications for the reception and interpretation of Chaucerian narrative, especially *Troilus and Criseyde*; the study of Middle English romances may well create more responsive readers of Chaucer's greatest poem.

Jeremy Dimmick, in his study of Amans as a consumer of romance, also demonstrates the value of the resources offered by romance for the major authors of the fourteenth century. He shows how the structural cohesion of the *Confessio Amantis* is aided by the interrelationship of tales linked through generic patterning. Romance provides a unifying structure, leading to closure and the social integration of sexuality. The romances offer an affirmative philosophy, although one that can be negated by the disappointed expectations manipulated in the tale of Jason and Medea – this looks towards Helen Cooper's reading of the development of romance in the fifteenth century and beyond.

Interest in late medieval prose narrative has grown in recent years, and the studies by Helen Cooper and Elizabeth Archibald show that concealed within the lengthy cycles of the prose romances are oddly challenging episodes, even whole narratives, that see romance still maintaining its subversive quality and novelty. Elizabeth Archibald's study of the Ide episode in *Huon of Burdeux* – another off-shoot of the Charlemagne cycle – shows how the traditional narrative patterns of the Flight from the Incestuous Father are transformed by the superimposition of the heroine's cross-dressing, which requires divine intervention to re-gender the narrative and achieve a traditional closure. We may suspect that the effectiveness, surprise and entertainment value of this to its readers, medieval or modern, relies on the denial of the 'horizon of expectations' established by the preceding centuries of chivalric *roman d'aventure*.

Helen Cooper discusses how the prose romance shifts away from the generic expectations of romance in a move that apparently baffled readers of the following generations as well as modern scholarship. The story of *Valentine and Orson* provides an example of the strong anti-romantic tendencies of the prose romance, which, she argues, are best understood in the context of early Renaissance composition. The formal change to prose is not just a change of medium, but implies a change of focus towards disaster, even tragedy, and a world view from which providence is absent or ineffective. The generic pull of the romance towards the happy ending reasserts itself in later versions, through a process of abbreviation, censorship and mindless optimism. From the fifteenth century through to the nineteenth, the story of Valentine shows the varied transformations of romance along the full trajectory from tragedy to banality.

It has become axiomatic in the discussion of narrative fiction to consider audience reception, and this is evident in these studies of separate romances. The combined effect of these papers is to suggest that the audiences of medieval romance must have been prepared for anything – with their generic expectations existing only to be confounded. They were flattered, cajoled, mirrored, exhorted to prayer, crusade or almsgiving, titillated by hints of transgressive sex, spine-chilled by ghouls, given responsible reflections on family law, and, if fortunate enough to encounter the works of Chaucer or Gower, would recognise the style and stories of popular fiction transformed by an author of genius.

It has recently been claimed, rather despairingly, that 'the scholarly study of romance ends up by disenchanting the very idea of romance that draws us to it'.[2] But perhaps it is becoming evident that in resisting the lure of the ur-romance of the imagination, modern scholarship has revealed more of the fascinating actuality – of audience, of inter-textuality, of a variety of purpose, material, style and language, and of the existence of a lively and confident body of narrative fiction. The quest may not lead to mysterious lands – what scholarly quest ever did? – but it can still turn up buried treasure.

It is a long way from a sumptuous Dublin Christmas in 1171 to the printing

---

[2]   John M. Ganim, 'The Myth of Medieval Romance', *Medievalism and the Modernist Temper*, eds R. Howard Bloch and Stephen G. Nichols (Baltimore, 1995), p. 155

press of Caxton, but the path is remarkably direct. The romances of medieval England have moved out of their position as a chorus line to the virtuoso performances of Chaucer and the *Gawain*-poet into a tradition stretching from the Conquest to the printed text: a tradition indeed, that renews itself through transformation.

Thomas and the Earl: Literary and Historical Contexts for the *Romance of Horn*

JUDITH WEISS

THERE is no argument nowadays about the stature of the Anglo-Norman *Romance of Horn*. Once dismissively regarded as a mannered French elaboration of a good plain English story, it is now recognised, not just as the greatest of the Anglo-Norman romances but as one of the best, as well as one of the earliest, of all the romances of Britain. Considering its date, which could be anywhere between 1154 and 1170,[1] its artistry is remarkable, as is its successful combination of features from both *chanson de geste* and romance.[2]

Unfortunately, we know nothing of the author of *Horn* – one 'Thomas' – nor its audience and sources. The poet himself took care to advertise both his and his son's names (the latter is called 'Willemot'), and, in addition, the poems that they had apparently finished and were about to write. Pope, *Horn*'s editor, concluded from a study of the composite language of the poem that Thomas might be the son of immigrants from the Loire valley. Clanchy thinks this composite language is one adopted and constructed by Thomas as appropriate to his theme and audience rather than necessarily his own, and believes that he may well have been 'a native English speaker'.[3] Certainly, Thomas's use of English, extending to wordplay on the hero's name (ll. 4206–10, and see oath of *witegod*, l. 4013), suggests, in turn, an audience with some knowledge of, and alertness to, that language.

In outline, this paper advances two surmises. The first concerns context and audience. I believe that Thomas composed and delivered his romance in Dublin, at Christmas 1171–2, to an audience comprising Henry II, Richard FitzGilbert, Earl of Clare (alias Strongbow), and other Anglo-Norman

---

[1] As will become clear, I prefer the latter date. See Mildred K. Pope and T. B. W. Reid, eds, *The Romance of Horn*, 2 vols, ANTS 9–10 (Oxford, 1955–64), II, pp. 12–14. Hereafter referred to as *Horn*.

[2] The *Horn* would seem to demonstrate Sarah Kay's argument that we should not think so much of a 'shift' or 'development' from one genre to the next as of a fruitful co-existence: Sarah Kay, *The Chansons de Geste in the Age of Romance* (Oxford, 1995), ch. 1.

[3] *Horn*, II, p. 122; M. Clanchy, *From Memory to Written Record: England 1066–1307* (London, 1979), p. 164.

barons who had come to Ireland at the request of the king of Leinster. The second surmise, much more hypothetical than the first, concerns the sources of Thomas's material. The written *escrit* to which he refers[4] could have been influenced by stories of Norman-Cambrian dissidents in the eleventh and twelfth centuries, and has a curious and as yet unexplained relationship with the *Gesta Herwardi*.[5]

Horn and Ireland

The Horn story appears to be at its outset a familiar insular one. Its kernel is as follows:

> A hero is exiled from his home and kingdom. He travels to a country where he helps a king against his enemies. That king rewards him by offering him his daughter, his land and help to regain his own patrimony. He returns home and secures it. He goes back to the other country to rescue his bride from an unwelcome marriage, and marries her himself; happy ending.

As we find it in the *Romance of Horn* (and in the English *King Horn* and *Horn Childe*), this story has undergone duplications.[6] The most important of these is that instead of two countries being involved – Horn's home and the other kingdom – there are now three. Horn is exiled from A, travels to B and is exiled again to C. This change entails duplication of princesses, bridegrooms and rescues (though the villain remains single throughout). In B, Horn and a princess love each other; on account of their affair he is exiled to C; in C another princess loves him, but before he accepts her he has to return to B to rescue the first princess. Before marrying her, he has to return to A to regain his patrimony; that done, he has to return to B to rescue princess no. 1 for the second time. The duplication of exiles, princesses, bridegrooms and rescues was probably already in Thomas's source, his *escrit*; certainly the 'Man with Two Wives' motif, as it is often called (a hero is loved by two women and marries one or both), was a popular one in twelfth-century narrative, as illustrated in a variety of insular and continental texts: the *Gesta Herwardi*, Marie de France's *Eliduc*, *Ille et Galeron*, *Boeve de Haumtone*, the Tristan story.

---

4 Line 192; note also references to *la geste*, l. 1644, *la letre*, l. 1656 and *le parchemin*, ll. 2933 and 3981.

5 As Ward, I think, first suggested: H. L. D. Ward, *A Catalogue of Romances in the Department of Manuscripts in the British Museum*, 3 vols (London, 1883–1910), I, p. 449.

6 Several early critics who studied the Horn story believed its extant written English and French texts show a doubling of the early kernel: M. Deutschbein, *Studien zur Sagengeschichte Englands* (Cöthen, 1906), pp. 3–5; G. H. McKnight, 'Germanic Elements in the story of King Horn', *PMLA* xv (1900), pp. 221–32, p. 223; and Joseph Hall, ed., *King Horn* (Oxford, 1901), p. lv. They also believed that Ireland was the 'original' country of exile. Though they may all have been influenced by the prevailing critical fashion for 'primitive simplicity' in narrative, their views should not on that account be quite discounted.

In Thomas's *Horn*, country C is Ireland. It was probably so in his source too, influenced by the *Gesta Herwardi* (see p. 12), but I suspect Ireland in the ur-*Horn*, the kernel, originally took the part of country B, that is it was the single, only, country to which the hero was exiled. I shall return to this possibility later. Meanwhile, I suggest that the Irish location suited Thomas very well when he came to revive this particular story for the entertainment of his audience. An assembly of small details, each probably insignificant in itself, suggests to me that Thomas might have known Ireland at first hand. I was bolstered in this supposition by Domenica Legge, who first advanced the idea that *Horn* was written for Henry II's Christmas feast in Ireland.[7] Investigating the possibility, I was struck by the history of the man who spearheaded the Anglo-Norman invasion of Ireland and eventually held Leinster under the English Crown: Richard FitzGilbert of Clare, known as Strongbow. The Irish section of *Horn* seemed to fit him rather well; recited at that Christmas feast, it would have seemed appropriate. Here is a summary of the Irish section:

> Horn, in bad odour with the king of Brittany, travels to Ireland and attaches himself to the two sons of Gudreche (or Gudred)[8] the king. When two 'Saracen' kings (with the Germanic names of Hildebrand and Herebrand) invade, Horn helps to fight and overthrow them. In the process Gudreche's two sons are killed. He offers his daughter and heir, Lenburc, to Horn and promises him the kingdom after his death. Horn does not accept them because at that moment a messenger arrives with the news that his first princess (the Breton Rigmel) is about to be forcibly married, so he departs to rescue her.

Strongbow's history runs as follows: having supported Stephen against Matilda in the civil wars after Henry I's death, he was unsurprisingly in the bad books of Matilda's son, Henry II. Thus when Henry came to the throne in 1154, though he allowed Strongbow Chepstow and other estates inherited from his father Gilbert, he would not give him his Norman lands or allow him Gilbert's title of Earl of Pembroke.[9]

Meanwhile, the king of Leinster, Dermot Mac Murrough, for thirty years intermittently overlord of Dublin, was defeated in 1166 by an alliance of Irish and Norse chiefs. He sought Norman support in Wales and from the late 1160s Norman-Welsh allies went over to Ireland to help him. Dermot was

---

[7] M. Domenica Legge, 'The Influence of Patronage on Form in Medieval French Literature', *Stil-und-Formprobleme in der Literatur*, ed. Paul Böckmann (Heidelberg, 1959), pp. 136–41.

[8] MS C: Gudreche/Godreche; MS O: Gudere[c]che; MS H: Guddret/Gudred; MS F2: Gudrike.

[9] Giraldus Cambrensis, *Expugnatio Hibernica; The Conquest of Ireland*, ed. and trans. H. B. Scott and F. X. Martin (Dublin, 1978), p. 299, n. 64; M. T. Flanagan, *Irish Society, Anglo-Norman Settlers, Angevin Kingship* (Oxford, 1989), pp. 114–17 and 'Strongbow, Henry II and Anglo-Norman intervention in Ireland', *War and Government in the Middle Ages: Essays in Honour of J.O. Prestwich*, eds John Gillingham and J. C. Holt (Cambridge, 1984), pp. 62–4.

introduced to Strongbow and asked for his help; in return, he promised him his daughter Aife and the kingdom of Leinster after his death.[10]

In 1170 Strongbow followed his Welsh allies to Ireland to help Dermot against his foes – a mixture of Irish, Norse and Danes. Having taken Waterford for Dermot, killing its two Norse leaders, he was married to Aife in the autumn. She was by this stage the only surviving legitimate heir, her brother Conchobar having been killed by Dermot's enemies that year.[11]

When Dermot died in 1171, and Strongbow declared himself king, there was a rebellion against him, and several sieges of Dublin. In particular, a huge fleet arrived, commanded by Hesculf (or Haskulv) MacTurkil, previous Norse ruler of Dublin, and John 'le Devé' (the Mad), nephew of the king of Norway. The attacks were repulsed and Haskulv was beheaded.[12]

When Henry II, alarmed at the possible creation of a rival Norman kingdom, visited Ireland in person in 1171, Strongbow was made tenant-in-chief of Leinster. His fortunes had recovered: from having only 'a great name, rather than great prospects',[13] he became 'celebrated for wealth and great prosperity in England and Ireland'.[14] He died in 1176.

I think it possible that Thomas was at that Christmas feast in Dublin, 1171–2,[15] perhaps as a member of Strongbow's household, and entertained Strongbow, Henry and others[16] with a story in which a Briton comes to seek his fortune in Ireland, helps the king there, and, after the male heir has been killed, *nearly* marries the king's daughter, and acquires the kingdom. It was an old story which nearly fitted the facts. To update it a little, Thomas added to his version many small details. These suggest to me that he knew Ireland, though probably only the area around Dublin, and knew some details of the recent fighting there.

---

10 Giraldus, *Expugnatio*, p. 27; *The Song of Dermot and Earl Richard FitzGilbert*, ed. Denis J. Conlon (Frankfurt am Main, 1992), ll. 327ff; G. H. Orpen, *Ireland under the Normans* (Oxford, 1911), I, pp. 144–9, 181–200; Flanagan, *Irish Society*, pp. 87–92; Richard Mortimer, *Angevin England 1154–1258* (Oxford, 1994), pp. 143–4.

11 Flanagan, *Irish Society*, p. 103. Strongbow does not seem to have been married before, although Martin mysteriously mentions, without further evidence, a first marriage: F. X. Martin, 'Allies and an Overlord 1169–72', *A New History of Ireland. Vol. II, Medieval Ireland 1169–1534*, ed. Art Cosgrove (Oxford, 1993), p. 80. On the other hand, he would seem to have had two illegitimate children. One daughter, Aline, was married to William FitzMaurice in 1174, another nameless one to Robert de Quenci. See G. E. Cokayne, *The Complete Peerage*, eds H. A. Doubleday, Geoffrey H. White and Lord Howard de Walden, 12 vols (London, 1910–59), X, p. 356, note f. and Appendix H, pp. 102–3.

12 *Song of Dermot*, ll. 2255–2466; Orpen, *Ireland*, pp. 239–44.

13 Giraldus, *Expugnatio*, p. 55.

14 William of Newburgh, *Historia Rerum Anglicarum*, ed. R. Howlett, *Chronicles of the Reigns of Stephen, Henry II and Richard I*, 4 vols, Rolls Series, 82 (London, 1886), I, p. 169.

15 Which was obviously memorable because sumptuously celebrated; see Giraldus, *Expugnatio*, p. 97 ff. and Roger of Hoveden, *Chronica*, ed. William Stubbs, 2 vols (London, 1869), II, p. 32.

16 These are likely to have included Hugh de Lacy, William FitzAudelin, Humphrey de Bohun, Bertrand de Verdun and Robert FitzBernard.

For example, he gives 'Westir' as the alternative name for Ireland; it was known to the Vikings as 'Westland'. He knows that its port is not far from the city of Dublin, and he depicts that port as marked by a solid rock ('une roche naal', l. 2175) and calm waters: 'Ja nef k'i enterra de ored n'avra mal' ('no ship entering there is ever damaged by wind', l. 2177).[17] Dublin stands, of course, on the Liffey, just by a tributary, the Poddle; its harbour 'was one of the few sheltered havens on the east coast of Ireland'[18] and perfect for beaching ships. All around this area were the flat and marshy lands known as the Staine (or Steine), which took the name from a large standing stone, some twelve to fourteen feet high, put up when the first Vikings took possession of the site, and which survived till the seventeenth century. Ships had to heave to at the Long Stone.[19]

Thomas also knows that Dublin has a cathedral: he mentions a 'metropolitan' church with an archbishop, both of which the city acquired in 1152.[20]

Much to the disgust of Horn (who would rather be up and fighting), the Irish court when not at war is a cultured one given to peaceful pursuits. It is perhaps unfair to remember Giraldus Cambrensis's contemptuous remark (he thought the Irish were barbarians) about the Irish being 'given only to leisure and devoted only to laziness'![21] On the other hand, Giraldus also comments on certain Irish skills: they are 'quicker and more expert than any other people in throwing stones' and have 'incomparable skill' at musical instruments especially the harp.[22] The skill of the Irish with stones, notably the 'Champions' Hand-Stones', is mentioned in many early Irish texts.[23] So when Thomas depicts the Irish court engaged in serious contests of putting the stone, he is perhaps not just merely imitating one of the details which Wace added to the account of the festivities of Arthur's court. As for skill on the harp, there is of course a long and justly famed passage in *Horn*, when the harp goes round amongst the nobility who 'all knew how to play the harp well' and who are only outdone (naturally) by Horn (ll. 2776–844). It is

17 Translations from my *Birth of Romance* (London, 1992).

18 Peter Somerville-Large, *Dublin: the first Thousand Years* (Belfast, 1988), p. 16.

19 Edmund Curtis, 'Norse Dublin', *Medieval Dublin: The Making of a Metropolis*, ed. Howard Clarke (Dublin, 1990), pp. 98–109, p. 102: 'the river came up to D'Olier Street and all between the College and Ringsend was a marsh'. For maps showing the Long Stone, see *Dublin c.840–c.1540: The Medieval Town in the Modern City* (Dublin: Ordnance Survey, 1978), prepared by Howard B. Clarke. I am most grateful to Dr Alan J. Fletcher for his help here.

20 Ll. 3557, 2559, 4069. See Cosgrove, *A New History*, p. 54.

21 Gerald of Wales, *The History and Topography of Ireland*, trans. and with an introduction by John J. O'Meara (Harmondsworth, 1982), p. 102.

22 *History and Topography*, pp. 101, 103–4. The illustration to the latter passage, in MS 700, National Library of Ireland, shows a harper. Judging from his long, detailed and enthusiastic description of Irish harping, Giraldus was most impressed.

23 E. O'Curry, *On the Manners and Customs of the Ancient Irish*, ed. W. K. Sullivan, 3 vols (Dublin, 1873), I, p. ccclvi, II, pp. 263–83.

likely that Thomas invented these episodes; they are certainly absent from other versions of the story.

When the peacetime pursuits are interrupted by the 'Saracen' invaders, Thomas supplies details of the conflict reminiscent of the sieges of Dublin in 1171. Though the pagans fight and talk in many respects like the Muslims, traditional enemies in the *chansons de geste*,[24] their location and behaviour remind us of Haskulv and John le Devé. Landing at the port, they pitch their tents on the seashore, which is also called *marage*, 'marsh'. When they are defeated, they flee towards their ships, but Horn's forces cut them off and most of them drown; the rest close ranks and make a shield-wall (l. 3446). According to the contemporary *Song of Dermot and the Earl* (dated soon after 1176),[25] the forces of Haskulv and John landed at the Steine and encamped there on the marshy ground left by the tidal Liffey. Defeated by the Normans, they fled towards their ships, but were cut off, and drowned. Haskulv was beheaded, like the Saracen prince Rollac in *Horn*, both said to be arrogant of speech.[26] All these details incline me to think that Thomas elaborated the story of Horn, already in circulation, with what he picked up during his stay in Ireland.[27] I think, too, that his version of the Horn story was intended as a kind of compliment to Strongbow, casting, as it were, Strongbow as Horn, and it is possible he was actually in Strongbow's entourage. One of Thomas's rather odd embellishments of his story is that he gives Horn a great-grandfather who is Emperor of Germany, which may seem strange in a hero who otherwise seems very British, though Boeve de Haumtone has as uncle a German bishop and acquires the Emperor of Germany as stepfather, and one of Waldef's sons acquires the Imperial throne. But this may be a result of Thomas perhaps being one of Strongbow's retainers when the latter (along with the putative patron of *Boeve*, William II of Albini) escorted Henry II's daughter Matilda to Germany in 1167 to marry Henry of Saxony.[28] There would be thus some slight but favourable knowledge of Germany, the

---

[24] As Diane Speed has pointed out in 'The Saracens of King Horn', *Spec* 65 (1990), pp. 564–95.

[25] *Song of Dermot*, p. x.

[26] Somerville-Large, *Dublin*, p. 12; *Song of Dermot*, ll. 2473–82, 2469; *Horn*, ll. 3208, 2989.

[27] I have not given prominence to two other interesting details which may be entirely coincidental or of too general occurrence to be of note. Horn and his friends present the heads of the defeated pagans to king Hunlaf and king Gudreche (ll. 1541, 3211); Giraldus, *Expugnatio*, p. 37 and the *Song of Dermot*, ll. 776–8 mention 'two hundred' and 'eleven score' heads of his enemies being presented to Dermot. And Giraldus also mentions (*Expugnatio*, p. 113) a dream of wild swine, presaging Irish treachery, supposedly dreamed by Griffin, a nephew of FitzStephen and Maurice FitzGerald: compare Rodmund's dream in *Horn*, ll. 4644–53. I wonder how widely Griffin's dream was known – or is it artistic licence on Giraldus's part?

[28] *The Historical Works of Master Ralph de Diceto*, ed. W. Stubbs, 2 vols, Rolls Series 68 (London, 1876), I, p. 330; Judith Weiss, 'The Date of the Anglo-Norman *Boeve de Haumtone*', *MÆ* 55 (1986), pp. 238–41. An ancestor, Roger FitzGilbert of Clare, had escorted the earlier Matilda, daughter of Henry I, to Germany in 1110.

Emperor (Frederic Barbarossa) suggesting the right, splendid lineage for the hero.

Thomas's Sources

Having suggested an Irish context and inspiration for the first appearance of *Horn*, I want to return to the question of the narrative material available to Thomas and to his source. This is not clearly discernible, partly because the poet himself has falsified the traces. This is true of the story of Aalof, Horn's father. It is possible he may have had by this date a story of his own, as an allusion to his *geste* in the thirteenth-century *Waldef* suggests,[29] but Thomas's own account of Aalof's life, which emerges piecemeal throughout the poem, is distinctly suspect, because it does not add up to a coherent or consistent story, but only appears to exist as a duplication of Horn's. Following the details Thomas gives us of Aalof's life, it can be reconstructed as follows.

> Aalof is born in Suddene of a German mother and an unnamed king of that land. He is 'found', along with his friend Hardré (later father of Horn's friend Haderof), by king Silauf, who becomes his foster-father and brings him up. He fights pagans for Silauf and is accused of an unspecified crime by Denerez, ancestor of the villain Wikele who accuses Horn of sleeping with Hunlaf's daughter. No consequences follow this accusation: Aalof never leaves Suddene, and indeed marries Samburc, Silauf's daughter. He succeeds to the throne and rules the country for ten years before dying at the hands of invading Saracens.

Awkward questions about this plot abound. Why are Aalof and his friend 'found', presumably in their own land, when they do not seem to have ever been exiled? It can surely only be to prefigure and parallel Horn – found with his best friend on the Breton coast by Hunlaf. And why is king Silauf, who 'finds' them, now inexplicably king of Aalof's own land? What happened to Aalof to turn him into a foundling? Are we to assume Denerez later accused him of the same crime of which Wikele accused Horn? in which case, why were there no consequences?

Whatever tale may have been told of Aalof at the time when Thomas used his name, I doubt it was as full of holes as this one. But the details accord with Thomas's passion for prefiguration and duplication, which is such that at the end of *Horn* he promises a third romance (by 'Willemot') about Horn's son Hadermod – whose career will proceed on similar lines. All this convinces me that Thomas's 'Aalof' romance is a false predecessor: it was not part of the

---

[29] *Le Roman de Waldef*, ed. A. J. Holden, Bibliotheca Bodmeriana, Textes V (Cologny-Geneva, 1984), ll. 39–54; see also Mills's interesting speculations: Maldwyn Mills, ed., *Horn Childe and Maiden Rimnild* (Heidelberg, 1988), pp. 60–8, and his scepticism about Thomas's version of the Aalof story, p. 61.

material available to him, and I doubt his audience heard it in this unsatis-factorily reconstructed form from his lips.[30]

But where did he get the name Aalof from? This takes me further back, to the question of what was Thomas's *escrit*, the written source to which he refers, and the sources that *escrit* might have drawn upon. The kernel, the ur-*Horn* story which I referred to at the start of this paper, may well have been formed around the end of the eleventh century or the beginning of the twelfth, influenced by the stories of the numerous English, Welsh and Norman dissidents who, deprived of power in Britain, travelled to Ireland looking for help.[31] The story of Gruffyd ap Cynan, king of Gwynedd (d.1137), in particular, has some interesting details in common with the Horn story: he spent twenty-five years as an adventurer pursuing his legiti-mate claims to his kingdom, principally with Irish aid; he received help from Godred (Crovan) Meranach, king of Man and of Dublin (1090–4); finally he recovered Gwynedd and kept it until his death at eighty-two, much mourned. The name Ragnhild/Ranult/Ragnailt (cf. Horn's Rigmel/Rimignil/Rigmenil) was his mother's and his daughter's (though admittedly it occurs several times in other Hiberno-Norse genealogies; Godred Crovan's granddaughter, for instance). He, like Horn, was reportedly very interested in music, possibly attempting to reform and improve Welsh music by importing teachers of Irish music.[32]

It is possible Gruffyd's story may have influenced the formation of the ur-*Horn* story, but it is certain that this story carried, from the beginning, the name of its eponymous hero. As Morgan Dickson has shown, in a study of horns in *Horn*, the hero's name is inseparably tied to a crucial element in the story, the moment when, in disguise, he rescues his bride from a forced mar-riage, she serves him drink, and he makes riddles linking his name with the

---

30 At the beginning of the Oxford MS of *Horn* (missing in the Cambridge MS, Ff. 6.17 and the fragments F1 and F2) Thomas tells his audience that they have heard the verses of the parchment on how Aalof died ('oi avez le[s] vers del parchemin,/ Cum li bers Aaluf est venuz a sa fin' [ll. 1–2]). The use of the perfect tense may imply they have just heard this, or they heard it a while ago; the lines could refer to Thomas's own reconstruction (as has been gen-erally assumed), but could equally well refer to another document, recounting Aalof's death.

31 For details, see Flanagan, *Irish Society*, pp. 57–69, who remarks upon a 'pattern of indi-viduals seeking, or deprived of, power in Britain, looking to Ireland as a recruiting-ground for mercenaries'.

32 On Gruffyd ap Cynan see his Welsh life, composed in the 1160s, a close translation of an non-extant Latin one: *Hanes Gruffyd ap Cynan*, ed. and trans. Arthur Jones (Manchester, 1910) and D. Simon Evans, *A Medieval Prince of Wales: The Life of Gruffud ap Cynan* (Felin-fach, 1990). See also George Broderick, 'Irish and Welsh Strands in the Genealogy of Godred Crovan', *Journal of the Manx Museum* viii (1980), pp. 32–8 and, for Gruffyd's inter-est in music, Thomas Stephens, *The Literature of the Kymry* (London, 1849), pp. 65–71 and J. Loth, 'Remarques sur les vieux poèmes historiques gallois', *Revue Celtique* xxi (1900), pp. 28–58, p. 56.

horn from which he drinks.[33] The name, in other words, is invented to fit the plot[34] and the very rarity of the name Horn in Scandinavian, German, Anglo-Saxon and Norman usage tends to support this idea.[35]

The name 'Aalof', on the other hand, occurs in the *Gesta Herwardi*. Is this where Thomas or his *escrit* took it from? It has often been pointed out that there seems to be a close relationship between the stories of Hereward and Horn, but what exactly this consists of is very hard to say. It has been assumed that Horn borrowed from Hereward[36] but I think it more likely that each story borrows from the other over a period of some fifty years – that is, the borrowings are mutual and not one way. The *Gesta Herwardi* has been dated between 1109 and 1131, at least fifty years before Thomas's romance.[37] So surely it cannot borrow from *Horn* or that poem's immediate source? Yet the *Gesta* clearly yokes legendary-cum-historical exploits of a real outlaw to a fabulous *enfances*, bearing all the hallmarks of having been added later, as *enfances* usually were, and heavily influenced by romance material, above all by the kind provided in *Horn*.

Where *Horn* and the *Gesta* are very close indeed, so close as to rule out coincidence, is in the account of the rescues from the wedding feast. In Horn's case, this is precisely the narrative crux we have discussed earlier: his first rescue of his Breton princess. In Hereward's case, it is his second rescue of the Cornish princess. There are other general similarities between the two stories – exiled, disinherited heroes, both skilful harpers, wooed by two women, using disguises – but these occur in other texts too. The rescues at the wedding feast have, on the other hand, matching scenarios and details which occur over one narrative sequence, and this cannot, it seems to me, be a coincidence.

---

[33] In 'Twelfth-Century Insular Narrative: The Romance of Horn and Related Texts', unpublished PhD dissertation, Cambridge, 1996, ch. 3.

[34] Dickson assembles evidence to show that in insular texts horns could be used as symbols of aristocratic or royal power. For horn used as metaphor for lord and patron, see also Proinsias MacCana, 'Irish *Buaball*, Welsh *Bual*, "Drinking Horn" ', *Ériu* xliv (1993), pp. 81–93.

[35] A Danish general called Horm (or Gorm) Enske or 'the Englishman' (killed 855 by Rhodri Mawr) has from time to time been hopefully mentioned in connection with Horn. See *The War of the Gaedhil with the Gael*, ed. and trans. J. Henthorn Todd, Rolls Series 48 (London, 1867), p. lxii; Saxo Grammaticus, *The History of the Danes*, ed. H. E. Davidson, trans. Peter Fisher, 2 vols (Cambridge, 1979), I, pp. 162, 294, and Mills, *Horn Childe*, pp. 58–9.

[36] Cyril Hart, *The Danelaw* (London, 1992), p. 635, but for the contrary view see James Dunbar Pickering, 'The Legend of Hereward the Saxon: An Investigation of *De Gestis Herwardi Saxonis*', unpublished thesis, University of Columbia, 1969, p. 135. I am indebted to Dr Dickson for this reference.

[37] Hart, *Danelaw*, p. 633.

THE RESCUE SEQUENCES IN *GESTA HERWARDI* AND *HORN* AND THEIR CONTEXT

Horn 1st exile: Brittany. Rigmel falls in love with hero by hearsay.

Gesta [1st exile of hero by own family to Gislebritus]
2nd exile: Cornwall, to prince Alef. Rescues Alef's daughter from Ulcus Ferreus.
She sends him to Ireland.

Horn 2nd exile: Ireland. Hero takes false name; he and the king's sons defeat enemies.

Gesta 3rd exile: Ireland, to king's son. War with duke of Munster. Hero and king's son defeat enemies.

Horn Hero harps skilfully.

Gesta Irish attack Cornwall.

Horn Message from Rigmel for help against forced marriage to Modin.

Gesta Message from Cornish princess to hero and king's son (to whom she is betrothed), for help against forced marriage to another Irish prince.

Horn Hero rescues her (Brittany): disguised as palmer, sits with poor at end of bench.

Gesta Hero rescues her (Cornwall): disguised with ointment as 'stranger from long distance', he sits in lowest seat at end of table.

Horn Rigmel suspects hero could be Horn. In 'custom of the land' bride serves drink.

Gesta In 'practice of the province' bride offers drink to guests and servants.

Horn Hero refuses drink from cup offered by bride; asks for horn.

Gesta Hero refuses drink from cup offered by damsel. Bride recognises him.

Horn Hero throws ring into horn and drinks half. Rigmel drinks other half and recognises ring.

Gesta Bride passes hero a ring.

Gesta Provoked by jester, hero harps and sings skilfully.

Horn Hero ambushes Modin and rescues bride.

Gesta Hero ambushes and rescues bride; takes her to betrothed, who marries her.

[*Horn* Before rescue of Rigmel, Irish king supplies hero with money and offers crown and daughter; hero refuses]

Gesta Irish king gives hero ships and equipment, and offers granddaughter in marriage; hero refuses.

Gesta   4th exile: Flanders. Hero assumes false name. Turfrida falls in love
with him by hearsay. Later she becomes a nun because another
woman woos and wants to marry him.

Horn's rescue of Rigmel at the wedding feast fits logically and coherently
within his story as a whole. Hereward's rescue of the Cornish princess does
not. This is because the love element is an essential feature of the Horn story
but only garnishing in the *Gesta Herwardi*. Hereward in fact rescues the
Cornish princess from unwelcome marriages twice, yet on neither occasion is
it for love. He acts on the second occasion merely as the agent for the Irish
king's son, said to be the princess's betrothed. This is because Hereward
cannot marry yet: he is destined for the resourceful Turfrida later in his
career.[38] Yet the rescue episodes fit very awkwardly into the *Gesta* narrative if
unmotivated by love, because inconsistencies are never explained. Why does
the Cornish princess load Hereward with gifts and 'desire him to remember
her'?[39] When she sends a letter to Hereward and the Irish king's son, to whom
she says she is betrothed, asking to be rescued from a second marriage, why
was this betrothal not mentioned in the preceding rescue, from the odious
Ulcus Ferreus, only a very short time before? And why is this second bride-
groom also an Irish prince? Why, above all, is it Hereward who rescues the
princess, whereas the betrothed fails, and Hereward to whom she gives a ring?
Yet he hands her over to her betrothed and leaves.

These incoherencies in the *Gesta* can only be explained by its author, the
monk Richard, or his immediate source,[40] using a version of the Horn story,
which must have existed at the start of the twelfth century, to add *enfances*
and excitement to the tale of the historical Hereward. For the sake of argument, I am assuming this ur-*Horn* was like the kernel I sketched earlier – that
is that it contained only two countries, Ireland and one that could have been
Cornwall. Horn's father, in this kernel, is called Alef and is the ruler of Cornwall; he has no independent story except, perhaps, that of his death which
drives Horn to exile in Ireland. Horn, after regaining Cornwall, returns to
Ireland to rescue his bride, punning on his name when she offers him drink,
and, perhaps, harps at the wedding feast.

The *Gesta* (or its source) borrows from this ur-*Horn* the details from the
rescue at the wedding feast, including the harping, but it cannot let Hereward
marry the bride, now cast as a princess in Cornwall, the country to which
Hereward is exiled. As Hereward's Lincolnshire parents and provenance are

---

[38] Turfrida is probably, though not certainly, the same as Gaimar's Alftrued, represented as
wooing Hereward and offering to marry him. See Geffrei Gaimar, *L'Estoire des Engleis*, ed.
Alexander Bell, ANTS 14–16 (Oxford, 1960), ll. 5586–94.
[39] *De Gestis Herwardi Saxonis*, transcr. and trans. S. H. Miller and W. D. Sweeting, *Fenland
Notes and Queries* iii (1895–7), p. 15.
[40] See John Hayward, 'Hereward the Outlaw', *Journal of Medieval History* 14 (1988), pp.
293–304 and Hart, *Danelaw*, pp. 627–34.

historical facts, the *Gesta* cannot make Alef Hereward's father, so it transfers the name Alef, and his country, to the father of the princess – so he is still king of Cornwall. At the end of the rescue-feast episode, it is anxious to keep *Horn's* scene where the Irish king offers him his daughter and ships with which to regain his patrimony.[41] On the other hand, Hereward cannot be allowed to accept the offer, because of Turfrida, so he has to refuse. The scene may be there to enhance Hereward further, but, again, it is awkwardly inserted. It has, though, however briefly, added a second princess to the narrative. It also (again for enhancement purposes?) has Hereward rescue the Cornish princess twice, that is, it introduces the Ulcus Ferreus episode.

We come now to the hypothetical *escrit*, source of Thomas. Around the mid-twelfth century, the 1150s to 1160s, say, its author gets to know the *Gesta*. The *escrit* borrows from it the second princess. In this it may also have been influenced by the two heroines in Marie de France's *Eliduc*, or by the Tristan story (two Iseults). Influenced by the *Gesta*, it duplicates the kernel story by giving Horn not only two princesses but two exiles, and by relegating Ireland and the Irish princess to his second exile. It invents a new country for his first exile, possibly Brittany, whose princess becomes Horn's real love and is (like the *Gesta's* Cornish princess) rescued twice; to that second rescue is removed the hero's harping. It can then borrow from the *Gesta* its hero's refusal to accept the Irish king's daughter – because of that first princess. To enhance its hero, and maybe for misogynistic reasons, it borrows from the *Gesta* the fact that two women woo the hero – and it makes those wooing women the two princesses.[42]

The following summarises the hypothetical links I have proposed between the Hereward and Horn stories, and adds some notes on each stage of the process:

(1) Ur-*Hereward* story: eleventh century.
The Ur-*Hereward* story is largely historical and is the basis for the second part of the *Gesta Herwardi*.

---

[41] It is possible other Irish elements in the *Gesta* are influenced by the ur-*Horn* story. As for Hereward's Irish hosts fighting the 'duke of Munster' (*De Gestis*, p. 15), Godred Crovan (see note 32) fought Muircheartach O Brien, king of Munster and was expelled by him from Dublin in 1094 (Broderick, *Irish and Welsh Strands*, pp. 36–7, n. 3). In 1114 Connacht began a long and bitter struggle against Munster dominance, which ended in 1119 with the death of Muircheartach: see D. O'Corrain, *Ireland Before the Normans* (Dublin, 1972), pp. 149, 152. Could the Hereward story have borrowed this detail then?

[42] In the wooing woman scenes it may also have been influenced, once again, by *Eliduc*; alternatively, it was Thomas who was responsible for similarities of detail here. It is also almost certainly Thomas who makes the harping perfunctory in the second rescue but gives it a prominent place in the peacetime activities of the Irish court.

(2) Ur-*Horn* 'kernel' story: end eleventh/early twelfth century.

The Ur-*Horn* has only two countries: A= Cornwall (?) and B= Ireland. Horn's father Alef, king of country A, is killed. Horn is exiled to Ireland and helps Irish king who offers daughter as bride. Horn secures patrimony with Irish help and returns to Ireland to rescue bride at a feast, which includes harping and references to horns, and marries her.

(3) *Gesta Herwardi* (or its immediate source): end eleventh/early twelfth century.

The *Gesta* (or its source) borrows from ur-*Horn* an *enfances* for Hereward, which comprises: rescue at wedding feast including harping; name of Alef – but as the Cornish princess's father – and Irish king's offer of bride and help. It also adds two rescues of same princess (Cornish); duplicates princesses: Irish bride, see above (refused by Hereward); duplicates wooing women: the wife of Earl Dolfinus later woos Hereward; and adds curious details of the Irish fighting the 'duke of Munster'.

(4) *Escrit* of Horn: 1150s/60s? (French? Latin? English?).

The *Escrit* is indebted to both ur-*Horn* and *Gesta*. It keeps Alef/Aalof as Horn's father, not the princess's; it duplicates the kernel by adding a new country (Brittany); it borrows from *Gesta*: the second princess and second wooing woman (here conflated), the refusal of the Irish princess (because Horn is promised to Breton one) and the second rescue of the same princess (now Breton.) The first rescue now becomes the crucial feast/horn scene: harping is relegated to the second rescue.

(5) Thomas, *Romance of Horn*: c.1170–1.

Thomas's *Romance* adds (among many other things) spurious details of Aalof's life and Horn's son Hadermod.

The framework of borrowings I have outlined here is wholly hypothetical and of course open to modification in numerous details. But it does make better sense of the curious first half of the *Gesta* than the two unlikely alternatives: a much earlier date for the Horn story or a much later one for the *Gesta*. Each, I think, fed off the other, but whereas in the case of the Hereward story this resulted in an inconsistent, and at times implausible, narrative, the Horn story was enriched by its borrowings and ultimately found its way into the hands of a masterly poet. Should further evidence reveal that his masterpiece had indeed received the royal and aristocratic audience that I have suggested, that would have been no less than it deserved.[43]

---

[43] I had already delivered this paper when Dr Rosalind Field kindly drew to my attention that a section of her DPhil thesis comes to the same conclusion, that Strongbow was Thomas's patron, and adds more useful information to support it: R. P. Wadsworth, 'Historical Romance in England', unpublished DPhil thesis, York, 1972, pp. 141–9.

'harkeneth aright': reading *Gamelyn* for Text not Context

STEPHEN KNIGHT

1

G AMELYN the character is a fugitive, driven by his grasping elder brother from the family home, respected for his brute force by ordinary people but treated with contempt by the learned. Then, through his own prowess and natural nobility as well as the support of an elderly yet still active retainer he re-establishes himself in honour, lordship and royal favour.

Gamelyn the text has been banished in a comparable way from the domains of literary authority. It has no separate status, being merely found in the cd* tradition of *The Canterbury Tales* manuscripts, usually as a spurious second Cook's tale. Even when seen on its own, it is thoroughly marginalised. Not mentioned in Derek Pearsall's influential article on 'The Development of Romance',[1] it is generically condemned to hover between modes, seen as a 'germanischen Romanze' by W. F. Schirmer, as an 'older and longer kind of ballad' by W. W. Skeat and even as a 'rebel romance' by Lee C. Ramsey.[2]

Equally faithful to the parallel between the history of the hero and the poem is the normal reception of the text by the 'lered' of our time. Their admiration is restricted to noting a few humble virtues, namely its representation of legal conflict in the period: the socio-legal historian Richard Kaeuper has written most closely and penetratingly on the text, and the bulk and weight of John Scattergood's recent essay is in the same contextual mode.[3] Informative as those accounts are, they bind *Gamelyn* to the pillar of historicity, just as the hero stood captive in his elder brother's hall. Now though, I

---

[1] Derek Pearsall, 'The Development of Romance', *Medieval Studies* 27 (1965), pp. 91–116.
[2] Schirmer is quoted in Dieter Mehl, *The Middle English Romances of the Thirteenth and Fourteenth Centuries* (London, 1968), p. 269, n. 17; Skeat's comment is in his edition of *The Tale of Gamelyn* (Oxford, 1884), p. vii; Ramsey, *Chivalric Romances* (Bloomington, 1983), p. 93.
[3] Richard W. Kaeuper, 'An Historian's Reading of *The Tale of Gamelyn*', *MÆ* 52 (1983), pp. 51–62; V. J. Scattergood, '*The Tale of Gamelyn*: The Noble Robber as Provincial Hero', *Readings*, pp. 159–94.

suggest, with the support of a faithful retainer in my own person, *Gamelyn* can reveal its true quality as a literary text of some sophistication and reclaim the honoured status which its creator, like Gamelyn's father, wanted it to have.

2

In one way scholars and critics can be forgiven for their misrepresentation of the text. The poem has not itself been fairly represented, and the version that all have had available to read is a poor one. Skeat decided to print *Gamelyn* as it was found in Harley 7334 (Ha4), that manuscript which seems so handsome and authoritative but it is in fact heavily and even whimsically edited.[4] The situation was not much improved when Neil Daniel re-edited the poem from the Corpus manuscript (Cp)[5] which, though a very early representation of *The Canterbury Tales*, is also here and elsewhere seriously fallible. In my edition for the volume *Robin Hood and Other Outlaw Tales*[6] I have used as base text the Petworth manuscript (Pw); this is known to be the 'head' of the *d* family of *Canterbury Tales* manuscripts, and in *Gamelyn* at least provides a text evidently superior to both Ha4 and Cp. Its quality shows up in part in the very few emendations needed: I have found only seventeen errors of all kinds in the poem of 898 lines, a sign of high quality scribal work and closeness to an excellent source. But there is a more general issue, more pertinent to this paper. Petworth provides a slightly but crucially different poem, one that lacks many of the extra syllables and has less frequent extra stresses than the processes of slack copying or casual editing have produced in Ha4 and Cp – and in the latter case have been handed down through most of the *cd** line. An example will indicate the difference: Skeat reads from Ha4:

> 'By my faith,' saide Gamelyn, 'now me thinketh neede;
> Of alle the harmes that I have I took never ar heede.
> My parkes been tobroken and my deer bireved,
> Of min armure and my steedes nought is me bileved.' (ll. 95–8)

Cp has exactly the same syllable count, with the variant 'ybroken' for 'tobroken' in line 97. Petworth, without the padding of an extra syllable in most half lines, moves more swiftly and gives a sense of the urgency of the speech, including the crisper 'yit' rather than 'ar' in the one line where Petworth has the same number of syllables, 96:

> 'By feithe,' seide Gamelyne 'now me thenketh nede;
> Of al the harmes that I have I toke never yit hede.

---

4 For Skeat's edition see note 2.
5 Neil Daniel, '*The Tale of Gamelyn*: A New Edition', Indiana University PhD, 1967.
6 Stephen Knight and Thomas Ohlgren, eds, *Robin Hood and Other Outlaw Tales*, TEAMS Series (Kalamazoo, 1997). Line numbers refer to this edition; Skeat's line numbering differs.

> My parkes bene broken   and my dere reved,
> Of myn armes ne my stedes   nought is byleved;'

This passage is a good index of the superior quality of Petworth, but there are many similar cases; in minor but cumulative ways it offers a distinctly better poem.

Largely as a result of poor-quality transmission, the metre of *Gamelyn* has been regarded as fairly clumsy, though not ineffective. Skeat said the poem worked well if read slowly and D. B. Sands recommended it be 'read aloud' for best effect; both felt it was basically a long line, which Sands describes as 'a seven stress affair.'[7] He and Skeat appear to have in mind a similarity with ballad metre (which would divide the lines at the caesura into an 'eight and six' quatrain with ABCB rhyme).

But as the sequence above shows, and as is clear elsewhere in the poem, the line is shorter than Sands suggests and is at basis a five stress line, which is often amplified with weak or half stresses and can at times carry an extra stress in either or, exceptionally, both half lines. This is far from ballad form; it is in fact the line found in alliterative poetry of the period, and *Gamelyn's* metric can be seen as an effective compromise between alliterative and rhymed techniques. Alliterative language, however, is not very common in the poem, and tends to operate only as a feature of occasional stress rather than a structural device within line or paragraph; the orientation is firmly towards rhyme in that respect.

Inherently romance-oriented as rhyme might be in this period, the character of the rhyme-words is remarkably English in its effect. It has been noted that this is the earliest outlaw tale in English, and although Skeat hypothesised a French original, the rhymes would suggest the text has come from oral into written English rather than from French. As F. Lindner noted[8] there are very few rhyme words of non-English origin: he found nine in all, with the name Gamelyn (possibly Flemish, though more probably Germanic) providing another six conceivable cases. More striking even than this is the remarkably small number of the English-originated rhyme words that are longer than one syllable. Apart from the occasional 'brother/other' called up by the plot and one or two of the 'sorowe/borowe' or 'reved/byleved' type, the rhyme has a remarkably direct and monosyllabic impact that might well be read as not naive clumsiness, but a conscious creation of a driving unelaborate tone appropriate to the tale – a decision which Chaucer appears to have taken in most of *The Reeve's Tale* for example.

It is equally striking that when romance words do appear in the rhyme they often have a malign import – 'trecherye/mangerye' (459–60) and 'trecherye/folye' (879–80), 'boure/traitour' (401–2) – as well as some referring to aspects

---

[7]   Skeat's comment is in his edition, p. xxvi; Sands's comments are in his edition (where he re-uses Skeat's text) *Middle English Romances* (New York, 1966), p. 156.
[8]   F. Lindner, 'The Tale of Gamelyn', *Englische Studien* 2 (1879), pp. 94–114, 321–43.

of what this story finds an unreliable legal system – 'delyveraunce/chaunce' (741–2) 'justise/assise' (865–6).

A sign that the poet has not stumbled by accident on some occasionally effective patterns of rhyming is found when the patterns of rhyme repetition are studied. It is quite common in the longer outlaw ballads or ballad-epics like the *Gest of Robin Hood* or *Adam Bell* for rhyme patterns to repeat in sequential stanzas, creating an effect a little like the *laisse* of Old French epic. Clearly an author working with a limited vocabulary will sometimes throw up the same rhyme more than once in a sequence largely by accident, but in this poem the phenomenon occurs on two occasions for emphasis (725–8 and 807–10) and it appears so often in the wrestling scene between 204 and 282 that there must be some idea of making a dynamic and drumming rhyme recur, such as right at the beginning of the sequence:

> 'I will yeve ten pound by Jesu Christ! and more,
> With the nones I fonde a man wolde handel him sore.'
> 'Good man,' sayde Gamelyn 'wilt thou wele doon,
> Holde my hors the whiles my man drowe of my shoon,
> And helpe my man to kepe my clothes and my stede,
> And I will to place gone to loke if I may spede.'
> 'By God!' seide the frankleyn 'it shal be doon;
> I wil myself be thi man to drowe of thi shoon,
> And wende thou into place, Jesu Crist the spede,
> And drede not of thi clothes ne of thi good stede.' (205–14)

And the sequence ends with the *laisse*-like repeated rhyme:

> Thoo that wardeynes were of that wrastelinge
> Come and brought Gamelyn the ramme and the rynge,
> And Gamelyn bithought him it was a faire thinge,
> And wente with moche joye home in the mornynge. (279–82)

Passages of phonic confirmation like that suggest that the poet can be defended as an effective oral technician within the limits of his mode and discourse; in this context, it is notable that when Scattergood finds that the poem contains 'awkward verbal repetitions'[9] he has a merely literary position, and that the repetitions to be found are just those that are required in an orally performed poem, as in a lecture or conference paper, to give clarity and emphasis. For example, the repeated references to 'rede' in 595–602:

> Gamelyn stode stille and loked hym aboute,
> And seide 'The shyref cometh with a gret route.'
> 'Adam,' seyde Gamelyn 'what bene now thi redes ?
> Here cometh the sheref and wil have oure hedes.'
> Adam seide to Gamelyn 'My rede is now this,

9 Scattergood, '*The Tale of Gamelyn*', p. 160.

> Abide we no lenger   lest we fare amys:
> I rede we to wode gon   er we be founde,
> Better is ther louse   than in the toune bounde.'

The technique is direct, even declamatory. This is recurrent in the poem; not found here or elsewhere is the elegant interweaving of rhyme-breaking and rhyme-linking, of the crossing and resolving rhyme and syntax to create patterns of mobility and occasional patterns of emphasis, that is so much a feature of Chaucer's work. And yet the passage is not without subtlety, especially in the vocalic repetitions of the last two lines which deepen the impact of Adam's proverbial wisdom.

In general then, in terms of language and style I would argue that, with a good text available, *Gamelyn* can be shown to be a highly effective poem working within a restricted discourse appropriate to its audience and context. It also exhibits more flexibility than has been noted, which is deployed both for emphasis and effective communication and occasionally for the more searching processes of semantic implication as has been shown in the passages discussed.

3

In terms of theme I want to make the same kind of argument, finding aspects of complexity where others have only seen banality and a useful terrain for historico-legal research. All have felt that at least there is a story that is effectively told. As the text has been so fugitive, it seems appropriate to resume the plot briefly.

Sir John of Boundes divides his property among his three sons on his death. The eldest makes Gamelyn, who is very young, his ward. Time passes. When Gamelyn is a young adult he realises his property has been either appropriated or ruined. He complains; the older brother abuses Gamelyn, then sets his men on him. The young hero defends himself vigorously with a large pestle and his brother flees to the loft. Then this young Sir John promises Gamelyn all, including being heir to all his brother's lands – but there is falseness in his heart.

Gamelyn wins a wrestling tournament and returns in triumph with many guests. The house is locked against him. He kills the porter with his fist, bursts in and feasts his friends. His brother watches from the solar. When the guests leave, his brother explains that he has vowed to tie Gamelyn up to avenge the porter's death, and Gamelyn agrees to be bound to avoid a breach of his brother's vow. The brother refuses to release Gamelyn and is going to exhibit him at a feast. Adam the steward agrees to help Gamelyn in part for the memory of his father, in part because he is promised land. At the feast, Gamelyn pretends to be bound and appeals to the assembled dignitaries for help. Led by the clergy they mock him. He and Adam beat them all, breaking his brother's back in the process; then they drive off a sheriff's posse.

When they hear the sheriff is coming with many men, they take to the woods. They are welcomed by the king of the outlaws who soon is pardoned, goes home, and leaves his title to Gamelyn. Hearing that he has been made outlaw, and that his lands and people have been repossessed by his brother, now the sheriff, Gamelyn goes to court to claim his own but he is seized as outlaw and imprisoned. His second brother Sir Ote appears and has him bailed, on Ote's own surety. Gamelyn returns to the woods. He comes back to court just in time, as Ote has been arrested in his place. With his 'young men' from the outlaw band he bursts into the court, kills the justice with a blow and after holding his own 'quest', hangs the twelve bribed jurymen and his brother. Gamelyn agrees to be Ote's heir to the inheritance and regains his own lands. The king makes Ote a Justice and Gamelyn Chief Justice of the Forest. He marries, lives happily and dies.

Gamelyn encounters no women at all until the final nameless wife; his tenants similarly have one mention of their spouses (709). There is much violence and much legal activity, most of it corrupt. The clergy (monks and friars only it seems) are enemies to Gamelyn. The underlying structure is the 'male Cinderella' story about the dispossessed younger son of folklore. Some have seen it as an outlaw poem but in fact the outlaws are only an instrument by which the youngest son regains his own, instead of his noble birth being magically revealed (as in *Havelok*) or powerful friends supporting him and his birth being revealed (as in Malory's *Tale of Sir Gareth*). Gamelyn makes his own way in the world by strength and fidelity to a form of generous lordship: various men support him and are honoured by him – his tenants, Adam the steward, the outlaws. A hands-on type of feudalism is behind the text; it both ideologises the antique possession of land and family and also embraces the common fourteenth-century reality of gaining property by your strong right arm – presumably how old Sir John gathered so much property in addition to his own inheritance. There is a focal structure that must appeal directly to both the realities and the ideologies of an expansive and less than blue-blooded gentry of the period. Kaeuper has described the audience as 'an amorphous social level of minor landowners, lesser knights and retainers'.[10] This grouping is also the audience identified by Holt as that for the Robin Hood ballads,[11] and while there is room for disagreement in that context, especially in seeing the Robin Hood ballads as having more complex and varied audiences including townspeople, there is no doubt that the parts of the *Gest of Robin Hood* that deal with the Knight (Fitts 1 and 4) appear to have concerns and a structure very like *Gamelyn*, so much so that it could be read as *Gamelyn* appropriated into the Robin Hood myth and told from the outlaw's point of view. The relation of these two texts seems in fact closer than that

---

[10] Kaeuper, 'An Historian's Reading of *The Tale of Gamelyn*', p. 53.
[11] See his chapter on 'Audience' in Holt, *Robin Hood* (London, 1980).

which has been hypothesised with *Fulk Fitz Warin*,[12] which is more elaborate in structure, at a higher social level and from an earlier period. We know the date of *Gamelyn* must be by the very early fifteenth century for it to be in Pw, Ha4 and Cp. Some have dated it to the mid-fourteenth century but C. W. Dunn's range of 1350–70 seems about right.[13]

But there is more to be said about the text than a general allocation of it to a place in what used to be called the sociology of literature. There are greater complexities within *Gamelyn*, often lurking inside its apparent simplicities. It could, for example, be analysed as a homosocial text. A reading focused in those gender-aware terms may well bring a rewarding explanation of some features, such as the wrestling sequence, emphasised as it is by rhyme, the stress on true and false fraternity, the absence of father-figures – as well as women. That approach is not my focus here, though it is well worth pursuing, and will I hope be developed as *Gamelyn* is drawn back into the mainstream of medieval poetry, as I believe it should be.

I want rather to look at two main areas of complexity in the text: first, how certain passages are directed and emphasised through language, especially figurative language, and secondly, how the structure of ideas and judgements as a whole works through the narrative to underline certain values.

4

Emphatic repetition can seem simple, but in effect be dynamic. Throughout the opening sequence of the poem there is a good deal of the repetition that some have found clumsy. The second half-line frequently draws attention to old Sir John's illness: 'sik ther he lay' appears at 11, 21, 25, 33 and 66 and 'ther he lay stille' at 23, and 50; as he dies it becomes 'he lay stoon stille' at 67, right after the last 'sik ther he lay' in 66. Variations of the idea of lying still and being ill appear in 41 and 52.

These indications of inactivity, though, are contradicted by the dying man's determined engagement with the future of his lands, and this is focused in a rhyme that plays on the repetitions. The local 'wise knyghtes' (17) who help him divide his land give it all to the two eldest and ignore Gamelyn:

> And whan thei had deled   the londe at her wille,
> They commen to the knyght   ther he lay stille   (49–50)

For all this static implication, he is not yet fully inactive. He appropriates their view of him as still, and returns it in action:

12 W. F. Prideaux, 'Who Was Robin Hood?' *Notes and Queries*, 7th Series II (1886), pp. 91–116.
13 C. W. Dunn, 'Romances Derived from English Legend', *Manual*, pp. 17–37, p. 32.

> 'For Goddis love neighbours   stondeth alle stille,
> And I wil delen my londe   after my owne wille.'   (55–6)

This rhyme focuses and makes appear quite conscious on the poet's part the interweaving dance of concepts through this opening sequence. As the knight grows both increasingly sick and still, his lands themselves become volatile – and the word 'londe/londes' itself also haunts the passage, appearing fourteen times (and once as the pronoun 'hem', 43). But it moves through the lines in an unstabilised way, only settling in the rhyme as the father finally speaks, with effort, his will. And then, with a proleptic view of the end of the poem, it provides the clinching rhyme for the donation of land to Sir Ote:

> 'And my myddelest sone   fyve plowes of londe,
> That I halpe forto gete   with my right honde'   (59–60)

and to Gamelyn himself:

> 'And I biseche you, good men   that lawe conne of londe,
> For Gamelynes love   that my quest stonde.'   (63–4)

The obsession with land that motivated men with and without property in the period, the deep contemporary concern with its transmission, these themes are both the focal point of the whole poem and are also condensed in the linguistic dynamics of the opening scene. There are strengths here beyond the crudities noted and sometimes admired by commentators.

Less far-reaching but similarly enriched sequences of figurative meaning occur throughout the text. As Gamelyn realises he has been mistreated he handles his beard for the first time, so indicating his new maturity and also, if his brother has been his guardian for sixteen years (356), indicating that he was a baby at his father's death, so giving force to Skeat's interpretation of the name as 'son of an old man'.[14] His brother's remark as Gamelyn stands there thinking about his lands, 'Is our mete yare?' (90), suggests that like Gareth in Malory's tale (which is without a source; perhaps Malory had heard *Gamelyn*) the male Cinderella is, like his female avatar, confined to the kitchen. That certainly seems implied as Gamelyn takes fierce vengeance in his new-found strength with a pestle, obviously a heroic version of the modern grinding implement. Not only does he win; the incident seems resonant late on when at line 319 as he brings his wrestling celebrants into the house he calls out 'I am our catour and bere our alther purs.'

He drives his brother up into the 'loft' (127), and this motif also recurs when Gamleyn returns from the wrestling when, in the reliable Petworth, the brother watches the feast from a 'litel torret' (327) or the 'solere' (349) – Ha4, like Cp and its followers, make no sense with 'cellar'. The curious motif

---

14 Skeat, *The Tale of Gamelyn*, p. viii.

of the isolated and elevated villain in part etches the separation of lord from lordship that was a feature of late-medieval social stratification and domestic architecture, but it also ironically foresees the brother's ending, swinging on a rope and, as the poet darkly remarks, drying in the wind – but then joined with his party of suborned justice and jurors.

Language, rather than visual suggestion, is the medium of intensification of meaning during the wrestling scene. Not only is this sequence worked up in terms of emphatic rhyme as was argued above, but it also, unusually for this poem and this register of English poetry, adventures an extended metaphor.

Arriving at the wrestling Gamelyn meets a franklin whose sons the champion threatens to kill. The hero undertakes the mission like any knight of romance facing a dragon to free an innocent – usually a young woman. But there is also a reminiscence of this scene in the *Gest of Robin Hood* where the knight, on his way back to repay Robin four hundred pounds, stops to help a yeoman receive the prize for a wrestling bout. While most commentators refer to Havelok's wrestling skill, the social level is much closer to the *Gest*.

But *Gamelyn* has its own subtleties not found in the *Gest*. As Gamelyn heads off he says:

> 'And I wil to place   gon to loke if I may spede.'   (210)

The familiar sense of 'succeed' seems the best translation for 'spede' here, but in the later part of the sequence it seems that the author might have had in mind its business sense of 'achieve a good profit'. After Gamelyn has beaten the champion the two 'gentile men', who own what seems to be an early commercial sports arena, speak in their own business-like register saying 'this fare is doon' (270): Gamelyn picks up both their word and their implication:

> And than seide Gamelyn   'So mot I wel fare,
> I have not halvendele   sold my ware.'   (271–2)

In the second rhyme line of the following three couplets the metaphor is confirmed. The champion says 'He is a fool that therof bieth   thou selleth it so dere' (274). The Franklin teases him in the same vein: 'whi lackest thou this ware?' (276) and ends 'Yit is it to good chepe   that thou hast bought' (278).

Sustained metaphors like this are as rare in *Gamelyn* as they are in Chaucer (except when he is translating from Italian or using sermon tradition as in the Prologue to that plain and sometimes fancy poem of violent vengeance *The Reeve's Tale*, which bears some tonal resemblance to *Gamelyn*).

There is however a closer parallel in the Robin Hood ballads and their avatars; it seems important that the hero, representing the natural and traditional values as he does, is shown both ignoring and mastering the values of the town. *Robin Hood and the Potter, Robin Hood and the Monk* have their critical action in the town and these forms (and in the Potter variant *Robin Hood and the Butcher*) make ironic use of commercial practice and language.

Defeating and parodying hostile values at their source seems an attribute often found in these muscular but by no means unsubtle tales.

Another sequence of mockingly triumphant language attends Gamelyn's routing of the oppressive clergy. Tied up to the post in his brother's hall, Gamelyn pleads for food and freedom, but only refusal and abuse is delivered by an abbot, then 'another' – presumably another abbot – and finally a prior, who is charitable enough to say 'It is grete sorwe and care   boy that thou art alyve' (484).

They will pay for this in blows and mockery. As before, the theme of the irony is revealed in advance: when Adam and Gamelyn plan the great scene, Gamelyn says:

> 'If we shul algate   assoile hem of her synne,
> Warne me, brother Adam,   whan we shull bygynne.'   (445–6)

The religious metaphor in 'asoile', supported by the friar-like irony of the only time Gamelyn calls Adam 'brother', calls up a register of language which is fulfilled when the poet implies a sense of a Christian mission in their brutality: as he says 'Gamelyn spreyeth holy watere with an oken spire' (499) he is playing on the two meanings of 'spire' as both club and asperge. Adam picks up the joke, combining Gamelyn's quasi-religious mission with his own sense of secular stewardship:

> 'Gamelyn,' seide Adam,   'for Seinte Charité,
> Pay good lyveré   for the love of me,
> And I wil kepe the door   so ever here I masse
> Er then bene assoilled   there shal non passe.'   (509–12)

Adam returns to Gamelyn's joke with grisly pleasure:

> 'Thei bene men of holy churche   drowe of hem no blode
> Save wel the crownes   and do hem no harmes,
> But breke both her legges   and sithen her armes.'   (518–20)

Having described how the two heroes club down the religious so they have to be taken home in carts, while respecting their tonsure in the distinctly literal way by only beating their bodies, the poet rounds up the sequence with his own joke: the religious are being laid side by side in carts so it can be said that 'Gamelyn made orders   of monke and frere' (529).

This is the kind of robust jesting that J. A. W. Bennett and Douglas Gray refer to as a 'touch of grimmer humour'[15] and not unlike the tendency in heroic poetry to humiliate your enemy in mockery as well as brute force. It is not dissimilar to the earthy proverbial touch with which when the sheriff's first and feeble posse are on their way Adam remarks:

---

15 J. A. W. Bennett and Douglas Gray, *Middle English Literature* (Oxford, 1986), p. 163.

'. . . we shul so welcome   the shyreves men,
That some of hem shal make   her beddes in the fenne.'   (583)

And the same salty simplicity is found in the narrator's remark when, after routing these foolish young men, Gamelyn and Adam decide wisdom is the better part of valour, since the sheriff is coming with a formidable party. They take off to the woods and so the sheriff finds the birds have flown – or, in Middle English, he discovers 'nyst but non aye' (606).

In these moments the poem makes verbally framed references to a repertoire of shared popular ironic wisdom, very close to proverbs, and similar language is used through the closing stages to assert how common and valid are the judgements being made: for example Gamelyn learns how 'the wynd was wente' (699), Sir Ote thinks Gamelyn's departure is 'a colde rede' (755) and that 'alle the carke   schal fal on my hede' (756), and Gamelyn's brother is 'honged by the nek   and not by the purs' (881).

On other occasions the poem has resource to other popular sources of value. The poet appears to refer directly to the Robin Hood materials – even though none have survived from this early period – at two crucial moments. The first is evidently referential:

Whan Gamelyn was crowned   king of outlawes,
And walked had a while   under the wode shawes,   (691–2)

In many ballads Robin first appears 'walking under wode shawes': his formulaic, even mythic, iconicity is surely touched on here. The same moment is recreated at the end of Gamelyn's outlaw life:

Gamelyn stode on a day   and byheeld
The wodes and the shawes   and the wild feeld,
He thoughte on his brothere . . .   (783–5)

And so the final sequence begins in which Gamelyn, touched with the glamour of the myth of an outlaw leader and backed up by hard-handed men from the forest, asserts his sense of true rights above the corrupted law.

That his ultimate success has never been in doubt has itself been strongly suggested by regular use of a narrow range of confident evaluative epithets. Gamelyn is consistently 'yonge' but from the time he feels first his beard and then the weight of the pestle, he is also 'bolde' – itself a significant Robin Hood epithet. The eldest brother is consistently 'fals' and often also 'fickle': he has neither truth nor constancy on his side. As in the *Gest*, *Adam Bell* and other texts with a colloquial register and a confident morality, a web of value-terms is opposed: Gamelyn is never false or fickle, his brother is never young or bold. The pattern may be simple, but it has undoubted strength and general assent.

5

A large-scale structural pattern of evaluation, generalised rather than verbally specific, as with 'bolde' and 'fals', can be found in the poem. It charts the way in which through the action Gamelyn's position rapidly weakens and then finally strengthens. This formation brings together the structures of evaluative language, figurative suggestion and the segments of narrative that create the sequence of this forceful and not unsubtle poem.

There appear to be four units of value which operate for Gamelyn and which need to be all present for his success. These are Strength; Family (including Friends); Status; and Law. In the opening sequence the child Gamelyn is weak and has no Strength, but has access to Family support through his father, Status as the future inheritor of his father's residuary estate, and Legal standing through that. It is notable however that this position is achieved with some difficulty as the 'wise knyghtes' whom his father at first appointed to divide his lands intend to strip Gamelyn of Status and, through their right to do so, of Law. The full value of Family, through the authority of the father, succeeds against that threatened deprivation.

In the second major sequence Gamelyn has gained Strength as he shows with the mighty pestle, but has now lost the support of Family and so his Status has gone. It seems that Law is also against him, though this is equivocal as he believes in his brother's honesty in promising him his lands and even in becoming his heir. Here apparent Family, in the context of real Strength, promise him both Law and Status.

However in the next main action his brother makes it clear that Family is now hostile and so, through the sheriff, is Law. So Gamelyn's Status is fully removed in spite of his Strength: this is his only remaining value. But suddenly the wheel turns and he acquires in Adam a Friend who is in fact quasi-Family and then achieves the new Status of King of the Outlaws. Though he still struggles for Status within Law, in these circumstances he also wins back Family support from Ote – that perhaps explains why that figure suddenly appears. With half his values back in place (still lacking Law and Status), Gamelyn is strong enough to overthrow bad Law: he holds his own quest before he hangs the jurors, justice and sheriff-brother; then he and Ote become justices, regaining Status with ultimate royal sanction.

Gamelyn has finally gained all the four features of value, and fully equipped now with Strength, Family, Status and Law the sequence of deficits is over. In these circumstances he marries and is honoured by the king. It is striking that he now accepts from Ote the offer that from his older brother proved false: he will be Ote's heir, and will eventually gain for himself all the lands his father once held. So Gamelyn can represent both the landless son, the *iuvenis* of Duby's account,[16] and also the re-established rightful inheritor.

---

16 Duby, 'Youth in Aristocratic Society', *The Chivalrous Society*, trans. C. Postan (London, 1977), pp. 112–22.

Most readers seem to think that Gamelyn simply fights for his lands and wins them: but Strength is by no means the only factor of value, and his personal prowess is shown to be in need of support by family, friends and the 'yonge men' who come from the forest to form his 'meynye'.

6

While it is a misreading to see this poem as just a testimony to joy through strength, it is also an error to think of it as a failed revolution. Maurice Keen spoke with apparent disappointment of the 'conservative' nature of the ending,[17] clearly feeling that Gamelyn's hatred for the church and the law should have led to some literary Peasants' Revolt. But unsophisticated as the poem might in some ways seem (though not in all ways, as this paper has argued) this is a gentry story and the restoration of true law is here, as in Langland, the only objective. Grisly as its final context is, with a whole jury swinging in the wind, the end of *Gamelyn* has a social-utopian theme and with its constant reference to the plain and direct and well-known ways of doing things properly, the text asserts a sense of rectitude that is at once combative and deeply rooted in a tradition both widespread and conservative.

The strangely marginal existence of the text, its inadequate transmission to the present, even its ghostly presence as a para-Robin Hood text and a much transformed source (via Lyly's *Euphues*) for *As You Like It* – these distractions have prevented readers from assessing the poem fairly. Neither multicultural like Chaucer, nor imitative of French lifestyles like most of the English romances, it moves in a serious, hard-handed and morally assertive world much like that of the colloquial alliterative poems such as *Winner and Waster* or even – including the rough humour, but excluding the learned spirituality – *Piers Plowman*. Gamelyn is a strong and well-founded poem, with a limited but skilful and highly effective capacity for poetic realisation of meaning in terms of metre, reference, imagery and thematic structure.

If, I suggest, we 'harkeneth aright', we can release the rough beast that most have found *Gamelyn* to be from the pillory where it has suffered the contumely of established scholarship. Through processes like this essay in critical stewardship we can re-establish it in its rightful place as a bracing, assertive, but ultimately imaginative and good-hearted distributor of a low-toned but highly effective form of literary authority.

---

[17] Maurice Keen, *The Outlaws of Medieval Legend* (London, 1961), p. 93 (a comment unchanged in the 1977 revised edition)

The Wardship Romance: a new methodology[1]

NOËL JAMES MENUGE

> Godrich þe erl was swiþe wroth
> Þat she swor swilk an oth,
> And seyde: 'Hwor þou wilt be
> Qwen and levedi over me?
> Þou shalt haven a gadeling . . .
> þe shal spusen mi cokes knave;
> Ne shalt þou non oþer loverd have . . .
> Tomorwe ye sholen ben weddeth
> And, maugre þin, togidere beddeth!
>
> . . . Or þou shalt to þe galwes renne,
> And þer þou shalt in a fir brenne.'
> Sho was adrad for he so þrette,
> and durste nouth þe spusing lette.
> But þey hire likede swiþe ille,
> þouthe it was Godes wille . . .

> (*Havelok the Dane*, ll. 1118–29, 1161–5)[2]

The proctor of Constance daughter of Walter del Brome, named proctor for the same Constance against William son of Adam Hopton . . . in the matrimonial case alleged between William the plaintiff . . . and the said Constance the defendant . . . Item he puts it that [the marriage took place] through fear, terror and force by the said Adam de Hopton, guardian of the same Constance and natural father of the said William, towards the same Constance [and William] who mutually objected and resisted and disagreed with the alleged contract [which was forced] by striking, holding and forcing and compelling them . . .

(Extract from CP. E. 62 [1348])[3]

---

[1]   I should like to thank Felicity Riddy, P. J. P. Goldberg and Rosalind Field for advice and comments on various drafts of this article.
[2]   Diane Speed, ed., *Havelok the Dane*, in *Medieval English Romances*, pt. 1, *Durham Medieval Texts* 8 (Durham, 1993). All line references are to this edition.
[3]   Held at the Borthwick Institute in York. This transcription and translation is by Lisa Howarth.

I begin with two types of narrative, one from a romance and one from a legal case, and although these would normally be regarded as belonging to different genres within different disciplines they are in fact remarkably similar. In the extract from CP. E. 62 we are introduced to the case of a young female ward, Constance, daughter of Walter del Brome of Skelmanthorp in North Yorkshire, who is defending a plea brought against her by Adam de Hopton, apparently her guardian. It appears he is related to Constance. Previously he had forced her, with physical violence, into a consanguineous union with his nine year old son, thus ensuring that Constance's property remain under his 'care'.[4] We do not know from this example how old Constance is, nor how old she was when joined with the infant William, although we may assume that she is above twelve (marriageable age for females),[5] as she is also claiming pre-contract with a certain William Boseville, as well as a previous marriage (with issue) to a John of Rotherfield (deceased). We may also assume that she is below twenty-one during the time of her wardship, although she has probably come of age by the time she defends this suit. We may assume that she is propertied, especially for her guardian to show such interest, and that her father, and probably her mother, are dead.[6] We know from the case itself that William de Hopton was the first cousin of Constance's first husband, John de Rotherfield, and that Adam de Hopton was therefore the uncle by marriage of Constance.[7] We know that at some time he had held her in care and custody, along with her land, and that he abused this one-time position of guardianship in an effort to keep her land within his own family, and, during the minority of his son, under his own care.[8]

With this slight evidence, I have been able to construct a narrative about Constance and her situation, which although in part only conjecture, does at least give us a clearer idea of her circumstances than is explicitly stated in the initial extract. By using what is known about contemporary legislation and custom, the social historian may construct such narratives which bring the

---

[4]   See notes 8 and 32 for further examples, explanations, and implications of the use of such force (known as 'force and fear') within marriage legislation, and especially within this case. 'Force and fear' is a legal term for any undue force which is brought to bear on one or both members of the potential marriage union in order for marriage to take place. In effect, it is to force one or both of them against their will(s) into marriage. See further p. 37 below.

[5]   According to Gratian a female must be able to procreate in order to marry, and this ability to procreate helped determine the age of consent, which although open to interpretation is generally accepted to have been the age of twelve. See Gratian, *Glossa Ordinaria* ad X 4.2.3, *Corpus Iuris Canonici*, ed. A. L. Richter & A. Friedberg, 2 vols, 2nd edn (Leipzig, 1922).

[6]   In the actual case her mother is not called as a witness; it seems likely therefore, that she is deceased.

[7]   See the deposition of Adam de Helay, CP. E. 62.

[8]   'Item . . . he [Adam de Helay] says that Adam de Hopton father of the said William once had custody and care of the said Constance and her land which Adam together with the consent of this Adam the witness compelled and drove the aforesaid William and Constance by force and fear to contract marriage . . .' CP. E. 62.

litigants, and their sometimes dry cases, to 'life'. I have chosen the words 'constructed' and 'narrative' deliberately. Legal cases in themselves are constructed narratives, and as such constitute a genre that can be read alongside other, more obviously literary, genres. Among these other genres is that of romance. One kind of romance which seems particularly appropriate to Constance's story is that which I term the 'wardship romance', owing to its obvious concern with the issue of medieval wardship. It is already plain that the romance heroine (Goldborough) of my first quotation is in a similar situation to Constance. She too is attempting to resist a marriage thrust upon her with the threat of 'force and fear'.[9] She too accepts the wishes of her guardian, because at this stage in her life she has no other option. Significantly, both girls are hovering in that nebulous period between puberty and legal adulthood, an extremely vulnerable place to be. Goldborough's guardian (in this case a friend of her late father's) is forcing the union so that he, as in the case of Adam de Hopton, may keep her inheritance. This is perhaps not simply a case of romance imitating litigation, nor of art imitating life. The similarities we find between wardship romance and wardship law have a more complex basis than this; in the remainder of this paper I shall attempt to explain why, and in so doing, offer a methodology which may help to unravel the complex nature of this relationship.

The approach of reading romances in the context of historical events is not a new one. *Gamelyn*, for example, has been studied in this way by Shannon,[10] Keen,[11] Kaeuper[12] and, most recently, Scattergood.[13] My approach is different from theirs. The type of study that I am suggesting is not simply a reading of the legislation into the relevant romances, nor a demonstration that the romance authors had a precise knowledge of legal procedures, although these approaches do have their merits. I am not only looking at the relationship between romances and law, but at the relationship between romances and legal cases. If we break down the distinct generic barriers which force us to view romance as literature and legal cases as law, and instead view both as related fictions with consciously constructed narratives and similar agendas, we may get closer to those issues which faced medieval wards and guardians.[14] What I am suggesting is a thoroughly interdisciplinary study of the two genres, reading them alongside and against one another. It follows that comparative provenance and dating of each genre has to be

9 See notes 4, 8 and 32.
10 Edgar F. Shannon, 'Medieval Law in *The tale of Gamelyn*', Spec 26 (1951), pp. 458–64.
11 Maurice Keen, *The Outlaws of Medieval Legend* (London, 1961).
12 R. A. Kaeuper, 'An Historian's Reading of *The Tale of Gamelyn*', MÆ 52 (1983), pp. 51–3.
13 John Scattergood, '*The Tale of Gamelyn*: The Noble Robber as Provincial Hero', *Readings*, pp. 159–94.
14 By the term 'legal cases', I am referring specifically to the set of documents which record the actual actions and words of the litigants and witnesses themselves when a legal action is brought. We have examples of these from all types of common and ecclesiastical law courts.

taken into account, and that both need also to be viewed on a specific, as well as on a broader, more general, scale. I have argued and presented these points elsewhere;[15] within this paper, as we have seen, there are obvious comparisons to be made between *Havelok the Dane* and CP. E. 62, both in terms of general dating and provenance, and especially in terms of specific content. Such a study must surely show us where the romances provide for their public an encounter with the legal system in which we may perhaps see the influential reflection and representation of each source within the other. The importance of this cannot be stressed too highly.

Through the romances we may also be able to see where the legal system failed wards and guardians, and where it served them justly; romances may be wish-fulfilment narratives with outcomes the law cannot provide for, outcomes to do with love, care and security. Through the similarities between the situations of characters in romances and participants in legal cases, we may see medieval people responding to legal situations in terms defined for them by imaginative literature.

It is the nature of romances to have plots, narrative voices, dialogue and a structure which moves towards a resolution of the conflicting issues and interests that arise during the plot. So too is the nature of legal cases. The purpose of courts of law is to resolve conflicts. Legal cases are themselves plots with resolutions, or at least narrative discourses which move towards resolution, a resolution which in theory attempts to redress the legal balance. These resolutions might not always be recorded: sometimes we have situations and narratives, yet no conclusion. The wardship romances offer us possibilities for conclusion. One might argue that legal cases concern actual historical figures and events, whereas romances are, even if based on historical events, apparently fictional; their characters are not real. Whilst agreeing with the obvious truth of this statement, my argument is that what is essentially lacking from legal documents may be found in romances, and vice versa. The romances convey certain social ethics, certain ideals (such as morality, the need for justice, and so on) which although not necessarily facts in themselves are as important to a society as is factual evidence. The legal cases on the other hand, provide us with the so-called missing 'facts' which the romances cannot actually prove; the facts which prove that the issues (and ideals) at stake within the romances were at stake within actual human lives.

The works which I have chosen for study within this wardship romance

---

15 See N. James Menuge, 'In the Name of the Father: English Wardship in Romance and Law c.1200–c.1420' (unpublished DPhil thesis, University of York, forthcoming); 'Female Wards in Romance and Law: A Question of Consent', *Young Medieval Women*, ed. K. J. Lewis, N. James Menuge and K. M. Phillips (Stroud, 1999); and 'A Few Home Truths: The Medieval Mother as Guardian in Romance and Law', *Medieval Women and the Law*, ed. N. James Menuge (Cambridge, forthcoming).

grouping are the *King Horn* group, to which belong *King Horn* (south-western or south-Midland, c.1225–1300) and *Horn Child and Maiden Riminild* (Yorkshire, c.1320),[16] *Havelok the Dane* (Lincolnshire/north-east Midland, c.1280–1300), *Beues of Hamtoun* (Southampton, c.1300),[17] *William of Palerne* (south-west Midland, c.1350–61)[18] and *Gamelyn* (north-east Midland, c.1350–70).[19] In some way, all of these chosen romances address the various issues that concern the medieval ward and guardian, issues which may be found in any number of legal cases which concern wardship. I have chosen these particular romances because of the variety they offer within the similarity of their shared theme. They draw on a range of source material, have varied provenance, and each romance illuminates a different aspect of the wardship topic, whilst largely keeping sympathy with the ward. All of these romances are concerned with the issues of (dis)inheritance and fosterage, and to a certain extent exile and abandonment;[20] with the exception of *Gamelyn*, they all share the connected themes of wardship marriage, marriage abuse and disparagement. All use abduction in their plots (although not necessarily by would-be guardians), and all cover the issue of guardianship abuse. In addition to these topics, *Havelok the Dane* deals with the issue of willed, or testamentary, guardianship, whilst *Gamelyn* emphasises the corrupt nature of legal executors and the Church, as well as introducing the topical issue of partible inheritance versus primogeniture. *William of Palerne* gives us an extremely detailed, if at times somewhat fantastic, insight into the issue of foundlings and *de facto* guardianship. Issues such as custody, care, nurture, inheritance, property rights, personal rights, waste,[21] kinship structure, abuse and marriage control occur frequently within both romances and legal cases. Indeed, my overall study of wardship cases (those found within feudal, ecclesiastical and borough law) suggests the three most commonly occurring wardship case

---

[16] Rosamund Allen, ed., *King Horn*, Garland Medieval Texts 7 (New York and London, 1984), an edition based on Cambridge University Library MS Gg.4.27(2); Maldwyn Mills, ed., *Horn Child and Maiden Rimnild*, Middle English Texts 20 (Heidelberg, 1988). All line references are to these editions. I have not included *King Ponthus* in this particular grouping because of its prose nature, and because of its much later date (c.1400–50).

[17] *Bevis of Hampton*, ed. E. Kölbing, EETS ES 46, 48, 65 (London, 1885–94; rptd as one vol. 1975). All line references are to this edition.

[18] G. H. V. Bunt, ed., *William of Palerne: An Alliterative Romance* (Groningen, 1985). All line references are to this edition.

[19] Walter Skeat, ed., *The Tale of Gamelyn* (Oxford, 1893). All line references are to this edition.

[20] The early exile-and-return tale which *Horn*, *Havelok* and *Beues* in particular have in common lends itself quite well to a medieval wardship re-writing as a way of updating it. This reason for the recognisable wardship content within each of these romances should not be overlooked; it is certainly possible given that the dates for the Middle English versions of these romances do coincide to some extent with relevant (English) wardship legislation. See below note 24 for this legislation.

[21] Waste was a fairly common action brought against guardians by wards within the courts. See also p. 39, below, for an example of waste as it occurs within *Gamelyn*.

types are those that involve custody, waste and marriage. These are the three most central issues within the wardship genre. Thus reading these two sources alongside one another reveals the ways in which issues relating to the parentless child were debated, imagined, administered and legislated for in the later Middle Ages. Romances explore areas of action which legal narratives cannot reach; legal narratives define for us the contexts in which these issues were understood.

In this discussion I am concerned primarily with cases and depositions, as they constitute the main source of the legal narrative that I put alongside the romances in a wider study which continues beyond this paper.[22] The case example with which I have opened this paper is taken from the statement of Constance's defence proctor in the case brought against her by William, son of Adam de Hopton. The case itself is made up of the usual statements of prosecution and defence, and of depositions from witnesses. The wider legal framework within which I have based this specific discussion may be divided into two main generic categories: legislative material and case material. The legislative material is in itself largely formulaic, and provides an essential background to the understanding of the case material. The legislative material may be divided into the further categories of treatises,[23] statutes[24] and writs.[25] Treatises are, by and large, accounts of past law. They are discursive and philosophic, their aim is explanatory, and they are at times obscure. Statutes are law which has been passed; they are blunt and to the point. Writs are highly formulaic documents, and are useful in determining who has brought a case, and what its subject matter will be; they serve mainly as documentary templates. The case material provides a more useful and discursive source for the study of the 'human dimension' of the law, and may be divided into records of the pleadings,[26] and into depositions and cases.[27] Whilst the records

---

[22] See note 15.

[23] Especially G. D. Hall, ed., *The Treatise on the Laws and Customs of England, Commonly Called Glanvill* (London, 1968), (c.1190), and G. E. Woodbine, ed., *Bracton de legibus et consuetudinibus Angliae* (Cambridge MA, 1968) (early thirteenth century).

[24] *Statutes of the Realm, 1101–1713*, 11 vols (London, 1828), reprinted 1963. The most important statutes concerning wardship and guardianship are *Magna Carta* (1215) c. 6 (*Statutes* 1:3), the Statute of Merton (1236) (*Statutes* 1:3), the Statute of Marlborough (1267) (*Statutes* 1:23–4), Westminster I (1275) (*Statutes* 1:33), Gloucester (1278) (*Statutes* 1:40), and Westminster II (1285) (*Statutes* 2:16).

[25] *Glanvill* (see above note 23) is an important source for writs, as are the rolls and writ files of the various eyres, such as M. T. Clanchy, ed., *The Roll and Writ File of the Berkshire Eyre 1248* (London, 1973).

[26] See the various and numerous Yearbooks and Letterbooks, amongst which are the *Yearbooks of Edward II* (beginning in 1307), in several volumes, published by the Selden Society from 1903.

[27] Many sources contain cases and depositions: King's Bench, *Curia Regis* Rolls, Pipe Rolls, Eyre Rolls, Manor Court Rolls and Borough Customs are amongst the sources I have used in my wider study. Some of these are as follows: M. Bateson, ed., *Borough Customs* (London,

of the pleadings are often dry and bald in terms of personal detail, they do provide us with a record of cases, litigants and basic subject matter, which is complemented by the often rich detail of the cases themselves. It is this case material which at least gives us an entrance into the lives and worlds, as well as the words, of the litigants themselves, as may be shown by an exploration of the statements and depositions within CP. E. 62. Any of the depositions within this lengthy case (it comprises seventeen separate pages of statements and depositions) will testify to this. An example of this detail may be found in the deposition of Adam de Helay (the third page of the document), where he says (through the written words and Latin of the clerk, naturally) that:

Adam de Hopton father of the said William once had custody and care of the said Constance and her land which Adam together with the consent of this Adam the witness compelled and drove the aforesaid William and Constance by force and fear to contract marriage with much sacrifice and crying with the said Constance objecting and refusing so much that when Adam de Helay aforesaid recited the words of matrimony the said Constance would not dispute nor rightly recite the same words of marriage. And he says that the said Constance at no time consented to the said William in any way and did not cohabit with him except in as far as the said Adam [de Hopton] held her by her care [which implies that consummation – a necessary criterion for a marriage to be valid – did not take place].

Even the statement issued by the prosecution on behalf of William de Hopton hints at the vehemence with which Constance denies the suit brought against her. She denies, and does not believe 'as put', any of the seventeen clauses of the case, most of which stress that the marriage between Constance and William de Hopton took place voluntarily, and 'by words of mutual and present consent', and without violence. Such excerpts, although given through the necessary barriers of language, legal formulae and time, bring to us an immediacy of distressing personal circumstance, an immediacy which is often lacking in the formulaic language of the legislative material. Where the cases and depositions are most detailed, and even sometimes where they are not, they are generally the most telling source we have in terms of human nature and narrative content. Many of them read like romance plots, and the incidental material about the lives of litigants, which cases sometimes provide, is indeed a rich source of detail which may help us to understand the social and cultural mores of the type of society we find in the wardship romances.[28]

1906); William Pailey Baildon, ed., *Select Cases in Chancery: A.D. 1364–1471* (London, 1896); George O. Sayles, ed., *Select Cases in the Court of the King's Bench: Edward I–Edward III*, 5 vols (London, 1936, 1938, 1939, 1955, 1958). *Bracton's Note Book*, edited by F. W. Maitland, 3 vols (Cambridge, 1887) is also a good source for recorded cases. Amongst the unpublished cases I have used that are held in the Borthwick Institute of Historical Research, York, are CP E. 62, CP. E. 76 and CP. E. 89.

[28] See Carol M. Meale, ' "gode men/ Wiues maydnes and alle men": Romance and Its

The five romances that constitute the wardship romance genre have, at the very least, more than a hint of legal knowledge, and, at the very most (as in *Gamelyn*), a detailed understanding and representation of procedure.[29] We may therefore infer that their audiences, whoever they were, would have had at least a glancing understanding of legal procedure (and perhaps legislation) as well. It seems therefore plausible that such literature expressed discontent with certain legal proceedings, and was capable of offering alternative resolutions within the plot which the legal system was perhaps unable to supply. It is certainly true that formal justice is frowned upon and subverted within *Gamelyn*. This subversion is justified within the plot as we are shown that the legal system could not deal, or did not deal adequately, with the needs of its recipients.[30] *Havelok* shows us that formal guardianship procedures may have ensured guardianship for fatherless children, but it also shows us that these same procedures failed to ensure adequate care, and that they were readily open to abuse. *William of Palerne* hints at the same, and *Horn Childe and Maiden Rimnild* demonstrates an implied awareness through the words of King Haþeolf that the property of wards was often open to waste. After a battle in which the fathers of his son's friends are killed, Haþeolf emphatically states that 'Ward no kepe Y non' (132), and refuses to take advantage of their respective inheritances. *Beues* favours guardianship, but decries the role of the step-parent:

> 'Fals knyght [Beues to his stepfather],what dooste thou here?
> Why haste thou slayn my fader dere?' (325–6)

and [Beues to his guardian uncle]

> 'Bete I haue my stepfader!
> With my staff I smote hym on the hede,
> That I lefte hym all ffor dede!' (346–8)

as does *William* [Alphouns telling his tale of enchantment]:

> [his stepmother] . . . with wichecraft to a wolf him schaped;
> but sche of þat sclaunder excused hire algate,
> and seide þe child was in þe see sunken ful ȝore. (4044–6)

Audiences', *Readings*, pp. 209–27, for a discussion which helps to define who, within a medieval audience, would be receiving the messages presented within these romances.

[29] See Scattergood 'The tale of *Gamelyn*', who recounts and discusses the entirety of legal proceedings and practice within *Gamelyn*; he also reviews the discussion of these procedures in Shannon, Keen, and Kaeuper.

[30] See the many examples Scattergood gives of similar contempt for, and subversion of, the legal system as it was actually practised during the time of *Gamelyn*. Some of these cases are uncannily similar to the often violent action which takes place within *Gamelyn*. Scattergood, pp. 169–74, especially.

Let us then consider some other of the issues as they are presented within the romances. I return to the quotations with which I opened this paper. The second quotation, from CP. E. 62 (1348), concerned a case of a marriage brought about by 'force and fear'. According to Church law a ward was not legally bound to marry the partner chosen for him or her in marriage, but had the right, in certain circumstances, to refuse the union.[31] In the eyes of the Church the consent of the ward to marriage was vital for any such union to take place, and after the passing of the statutes of Merton (1236) and West-minster II (1285) guardians were forced to recognise this individual right. If such a union was still forced upon a non-consenting ward (or indeed, upon any minor with access to legal recourse) then the marriage could be annulled upon the grounds of 'force and fear', an opportunity which was offered by the Church courts if the marriage had been brought about with 'metus qui cadere potest in constantum virum/mulierum' ('the fear that can fall upon a constant man/woman').[32] CP. E. 62 is itself such a case. Provision was also given for wards to annul or refuse marriages if they were disparaging. A disparaging union is any union below the station of the ward; in this instance a ward may refuse the union, within reason. Guardians did have the right to sell their wards and their ward's marriages (for profit), although Magna Carta c. 6 (1215), the Statute of Merton c. 7 (1236) and the Petition of 1258, c. 6 all stipulate that the marriage must not be of a disparaging kind.[33] This points to the fact that disparaging marriages were indeed taking place, and this to the inevitable disadvantage of the ward. In *Havelok the Dane* we have a striking literary example of such a union, a union which also encompasses the threat of 'force and fear'. It is the voice of the ward Goldborough's guardian who is speaking:

> . . . 'Hwor þou wilt be
> Qwen and levedi over me?
> þou shalt haven a gadeling . . .
> þou shalt spusen mi cokes knave;
> Ne shalt þou non oþer loverd have . . .
> Tomorwe ye sholen ben weddeth
> And, maugre þin, togidere beddeth![34]

---

[31] Scott L. Waugh, *The Lordship of England: Royal Wardships and marriages in English Society and politics 1217–1327* (Princeton, 1988), pp. 216–17.

[32] See Richard Helmholz, *Marriage Litigation in Medieval England* (Cambridge, 1974), pp. 90–4. From this legal statement comes the legal phrase 'force and fear' which is used in legal records to describe how a forced marriage is brought about. If indeed the marriage has been brought about by 'force and fear' (as in the case of CP. E. 62), then a case may be brought to have the marriage annulled.

[33] See note 24 above for references to the relevant legislation.

[34] There is a further legal implication here concerning marriage, and also abduction. If the marriage is consummated, as Godrich threatens, then to annul it will be the more difficult. In some rape-abduction cases this same issue is forced to ensure that an elopement or an abduction will be legally recognised as a valid marriage. Godrich must recognise this, as

> . . . Or þou shalt to the galwes renne
> And þer þou shalt in a fir brenne.'

(*Havelok the Dane*, 1120–9, 1161–2)

In this passage Goldborough, heiress to the throne of England, is forced into what her guardian believes is a disparaging marriage, by the use of 'force and fear', so that he may retain custody of her property and her throne for the benefit of himself and his offspring. Goldborough's guardian, Godrich, Earl of Cornwall, has sworn to carry out the will of Goldborough's father (oath-taking was an initial part of a guardian's duties)[35] to marry her when she is 'tuelf winter old' (192), (legally recognised as marriageable age for females)[36] to 'þe beste, fayreste, þe strangest' (200). However, he chooses instead to prolong his profit from her property by incarcerating her without adequate food and clothing until she is 'Tuenti winter hold and more' (259), just before her legal coming of age, and to marry her instead to a kitchen boy (as he believes Havelok to be), thus effectively tying her to a male who has no claim upon her inheritance:

> He wende þat Havelok wer a þral;
> Þerþoru he wende haven al
> In Engelond, þat hire rith was.   (1098–1100)[37]

Although by marrying Constance to his own son, Adam de Hopton attempts to keep her wealth 'legally' within his family, the similarities between this example of romance narrative and legal narrative are obvious.

Havelok suffers even worse horrors at the hands of his guardian, the Earl Godard, 'þe kinges oune frende' (375), who imprisons Havelok and his two sisters in a castle without proper food or clothing, and breaks his oath to carry out his duties as Havelok's testamentary guardian ('He ne yaf a note of hise oþes' [419]). He does not stop at this abuse of custody rights, but proceeds to

---

must his audience. Goldborough surely does. Constance and her prosecutors do as well; a large part of their case is to prove that the marriage between William and Constance was consummated in order to prove it valid; a large part of Constance's defence is to prove the marriage unconsummated, and therefore invalid (as well as brought about unlawfully by 'force and fear'); her proctor also argues that the unlawful marriage with William de Hopton was preceded by two legal and consummated marriages, the second of which was still valid at the time of the forced union between William de Hopton and Constance. See J. B. Post, 'Ravishment of Women and the Statutes of Westminster', ed. J. H. Baker, *Legal Records and the Historian* (London, 1978), pp. 185–206, and Sue Sheridan Walker, 'Punishing Convicted Ravishers: Statutory Strictures and Actual Practice in Thirteenth and Fourteenth-Century England', *Journal of Medieval History* 13 (1987), pp. 237–50.

[35] See Richard Helmholz, *Canon Law and the Law of England* (London, 1987), especially ch. 12, 'The Roman Law of Guardianship in England, 1300–1600'

[36] See above note 5.

[37] Havelok, as a thrall, and not as the rightful King of Denmark, has no legal claim to the inheritance of his future wife as he is in service to his lord, and is not free.

'karf on two here þrotes' (471) of Havelok's sisters, leaving them 'Leyen and sprauleden in þe blod' (475). He then arranges Havelok's death and seizes the throne of Denmark for himself. We may say here however, that although Godard abuses recognised guardianship conventions, his actions have more to do with his fulfilling the role of a Herod figure, than that of a realistically identifiable guardian. He does not excite legal concern so much as repugnance at his awareness of the vulnerability of children as a means to his own ends. If this is the case then it is interesting, and pertinent, that it is the English guardian, Godrich, rather than the Danish villain, Godard, who is developed beyond the stereotypical villain to raise (English) legal issues of wardship and its abuse. It is also possible that as a Danish villain, the reviled Godard is a target for an understandable xenophobia which, after all, is not really so far removed from medieval English memories.

Inheritance and minority are themes found many times within the wardship romance genre, as is the theme of waste, which we find Gamelyn's eldest brother committing upon Gamelyn's property:

> Sone the elder brother . gyled the 30nge knaue;
> He took into his hond . his lond and his leede
> And Gamelyn himselfe . to clothen and to feede.
> He clothed him and fedde him . yuel and eek wrothe,
> And leet his londes for-fare . and his houses bothe,
> His parkes and his woodes . and dede nothing wel . . .

> (Gamelyn, 70–5)

If we compare this with the similar passages in Havelok the Dane, where Havelok and his sisters are imprisoned in a castle by their legal guardian and kept

> . . . for hunger and for kold,
>   Or he weren þre winter hold.
>   Feblelike he gaf him cloþes;
>   He ne yaf a note of hise oþes   (416–19)

and where Goldborough is imprisoned

> And þerehinne dede hire fede
> Povrelike, in feble wede   (322–3)

or with the apparent maltreatment of Bevis by his guardian uncle in Beues of Hamtoun, where Sabere

> Clothed the child in a pore wede,
> And he said: 'Beues, thou mvst kepe
> vppon the ffeld all my shepe . . .'   (274–6)

we are alerted to the fact that the legal duties of guardians, such as provision for the basic needs of their wards, adequate care and custody, protection for inheritance without unnecessary waste, and illegal profit from marriage, were easily open to abuse.[38]

We are first introduced to William of Palerne when he is four years old, and under threat of poisoning by his uncle (as is his father) who wishes to have the throne of Sicily, and presumably William's mother, for himself. He is thwarted, however, by the intervention of a mysterious werewolf, who carries William across the Strait of Messina on his back, and hides him in a cave in a forest in Rome. William is then found by a kindly cowherd, who kisses and cuddles him and 'ful cherli þat child tok in his armes . . . and bitok it to his wif tiȝtly to keep' (64–6), thus ensuring his welfare and introducing us to the first of William's four foster-parents (five, if you count the wolf), before he is finally reunited with with his mother and sister. William's sister is herself a ward who is under threat of a marriage brought about by 'force and fear'; the threat is carried out by the werewolf's real father.[39] The werewolf himself is a maltreated stepson who is turned into a werewolf by his wicked stepmother in an attempt to gain his inheritance for her own first-born. This echoes quite strongly the apparent concern medieval lawyers had with the safety of the custody of wards upon the remarriage of the surviving parent, for as we are told by the author of *Très ancien coutoumier*, a contemporary of Glanvill:

A fatherless heir must be in ward to someone. Who shall be his guardian? His mother? No. Why not? She will take another husband and have sons by him and they, greedy of the heritage, will slay their first born brother, or the step-father shall slay his step-son.[40]

---

38 Sabere's 'maltreatment' of Bevis is only for show: it is so that Bevis may escape with his life from the murderous designs of his mother. In fact Sabere is an excellent guardian, risking his own life to save that of his ward.

39 The King of Spain (father of the bewitched werewolf, Alphouns) tries to force William's sister into marriage with his second son, Braundinis. He thinks it will be possible to force the issue as William's mother is ruling her lands alone; she, however, following her daughter's wishes, vehemently opposes the union. In retaliation, Braundinis and his father lay waste her lands. Thus we have further wardship explorations concerning widowed mothers as guardians. Female guardians are apparently more vulnerable than male guardians; moreover this part of the plot of *William of Palerne* might be hinting that female guardians are more sympathetic to the potential plights of their wards than some of the legal literature might suggest, although it is important to note that William's mother remains unmarried. Unmarried widowed female guardians were often threatened by other potential (male) guardians, but were considered as no real threat within the wardship system, and were therefore held up as ideals. Widowed mothers who remarried were not, on the whole, favoured as guardians; Bevis's mother is vilified, and although this vilification is justified by her appalling behaviour, one cannot help but notice how well she fits the stereotype as presented in *Très ancien coutoumier*. See note 40 below.

40 *Très ancien coutoumier* is part of a composite text in two volumes, entitled *Coutoumiers de Normandie* and edited by Ernest-Joseph Tardif (Rouen, 1881, 1903). The quotation is taken from vol. 1, pp. 10–11. It is an important early-thirteenth-century Norman legal treatise, which is, I think, pertinent to this study of wardship romances given the Anglo-Norman origins of *Horn*, *Havelok* and *Beues*, and of much of early English law.

Or in this case, the stepmother will bewitch her stepson. The concern is still relevant though, and appears again in *Beues of Hamtoun*, when Bevis's mother has her husband killed, and then demands that her son's guardian take his life. Her wish to kill Bevis is voiced after her remarriage. The above legal passage is full of stereotypes, and these stereotypes are used time and again in the romances to illustrate points of contention and concern. As shown above, they may also be found in legal narratives:

> A fatherless heir must be in ward to someone [pathos]. Who shall be his guard-ian? His mother? No. Why not? She will take another husband and have sons by him [stereotype of female conduct – e.g. Bevis's mother] and they, greedy of the heritage [another stereotype – e.g. Alphouns's step-brother], will slay their first born brother [stereotypical outrage against primogeniture and patriarchy], or the step-father [wicked stepfather stereotype as can be found in *Beues of Hamtoun*] shall slay his stepson.

The stereotypes I have drawn attention to are not the only ones intended for censure within this passage; the passage itself is an overall and generalised diatribe against all types of guardians, all of which can be found within the wardship romances. The preferred guardian the passage is leading towards is actually (and not surprisingly) the lord; and yet statutes show that he was probably the worst type of guardian of them all (especially if he were the king) in terms of financial and guardianship abuse.[41] Thus we see that even legal material such as treatises are prone to their fair share of propaganda.

Another area where the wardship romances may help us with sociological and legal gaps is in the area of care and custody. We know through the legal records who had legal and formal responsibility for the guardianship of the average ward, but we often do not know how important was considered the task of day-to-day care and nurture. It is often only by accident that we find out who such *de facto* guardians were, yet in the romances there is ample evi-dence of them, and the importance they played in the physical and emotional well-being of the child is made clear. In the romances these *de facto* guardians often take the form of surrogate parents; we have already seen the cowherd and his kindly wife in *William of Palerne*, who take the abandoned William into their home and hearts. Then there is Grim the fisherman and his wife, who look after Havelok as one of their own:

> '. . . Y shal þe fete
> Bred an chese, butere and milk,
> Pastees and flaunes – al with suilk . . .'   (643–5)[42]

---

[41] See especially *Magna Carta*, c.6.

[42] This is not the case at first though. Until they realise that Havelok is the rightful heir to the throne of Denmark, they treat him appallingly. The care they show after this realisation redeems them; to begin with the ignorant Grim is only following the orders of his master; see Maldwyn Mills, 'Havelok and the Brutal Fisherman', *MÆ* 36 (1967), pp. 219–30.

In *William of Palerne* it is the Emperor of Rome who first acts as a formal guardian for William, although it is his daughter Melior to whom is entrusted the actual emotional and physical care:

> 'Dere douȝter, y do þe to wite,
> I have a pris presant to plese wiþ þe hert.
> Have here þis bold barn, and be til him meke,
> and do him kepe clenely
> . . . for me lof loke him wel'   (410–13; 430)

whilst in *Beues of Hamtoun* it is again the royal foster-father's daughter who is given the task of *de facto* guardianship. Josian carries out this task gladly, until Bevis reaches the age of fourteen (puberty); upon attainment of such age Bevis becomes a warrior, a man and no longer needing *de facto* care, falls in love with Josian, and she with him.[43] It is significant that these informal guardians are females, or couples, and that this *de facto* guardianship takes place, in each instance, before the ward reaches puberty. This may suggest that before a ward is able to marry he or she requires stable care of the kind a good mother, or family unit, will provide. By the same token it may also suggest that before a ward is able to have a 'normal' stable life (not necessarily to include marriage) he or she must have the same type of stable care. The wardship romances also tell us (as do some, but not many, of the legal records that we have) that emotional day-to-day care was considered to be important for the ward, especially before the age of puberty. The legal records, on the whole, do not tell us this specifically, yet the wardship romances do. This may be wish-fulfilment highlighting the lack of such care in the lives of wards; it may also be that the romances are pointing out that not only was such stable care necessary, but that it actually did occur. It does not seem unreasonable to suggest that both possibilities are probabilities given different sets of circumstances. Whatever the case may be, this representation and recognition of the need for care in the wardship romances is much more explicit than it ever is in the legal material.

These are only a few examples; there are many more, and they can all be read in conjunction with the relevant legislation, and more particularly court cases, in much greater detail. Even at this simple level though, they do show us that there was a definite connection between the legal and moral concerns about wards and guardians during this period, and the literature in which wards and guardians appeared. True, the wardship romances cannot be accepted as a representation of reality in the way that legislation can, but neither then can the legal cases. Both are subjective, both are suggestive, both are delivered and recorded in a certain way, to and for a certain audience, and to achieve a certain desired result; and yet both are valid forms of

---

[43] One might expect the text to bring into question the appropriate nature of male/female wardships/guardianships (and vice versa) in the light of this relationship; however, it does not appear to do so.

discourse within their own, and possibly borrowing from each other's, genre. Both legal disputes and romances can, after all, be said to be in some sense aiming at resolutions: legal settlements and the narrative closures typical of romances can both be seen as means of actually and symbolically resolving problematic issues. The distinction we may find between fiction and reality in the romances and the legal cases is perhaps illusory; the truths we find within the romances have a value, and a relevance, which transcend the specifics of time and space and fact. We may be certain that just as these truths were being told in the romances, so fictions were being woven in the cases. By breaking down these genre distinctions, and learning as much from the truths as we do from the facts, we can perhaps better understand, interpret and reconstruct the issues present within the lives of the fictional and the non-fictional medieval ward, both siblings of a similar discourse.

Middle English Romance and the *Gesta Romanorum*

DIANE SPEED

I Introduction

A MONGST scholarly efforts to locate both individual Middle English
romances and the amorphous entity 'Middle English Romance' in shifting generic discourses, one recurrent topic has been the parallels observable
between certain romances and the *Gesta Romanorum*, ultimately the most
extensive and widely disseminated of the medieval exemplum collections.
Given renewed interest in the generic boundaries of Middle English romance
in the post-modern situation, together with a surge of interest in exemplum
generally and the *Gesta Romanorum* in particular,[1] it may be opportune to
look further into the nature of the interrelationship. This paper is offered as a
point of departure.

The corpus of Middle English romance assumed here is that embraced by
standard modern surveys of the field such as the *Manual of Writings in Middle
English*, Rice's *Annotated Bibliography*, and Barron's critical survey *English
Medieval Romance*.[2] The corpus of the *Gesta Romanorum* requires more
comment.

Two branches of the *Gesta* are distinguished:[3] the continental Latin and
the Anglo-Latin, both with vernacular translations. It remains uncertain
whether the *Gesta* originated in Germany or England, which of the two exist-

---

[1] E.g. Claude Bremond, Jacques Le Goff and Jean-Claude Schmitt, *L''Exemplum'*, Typolo-
gie des sources du Moyen Age occidental 40 (Turnhout, 1982); Jacques Berlioz and Marie
Anne Polo de Beaulieu, eds, *Les 'Exempla' médiévaux: Introduction à la recherche* (Carcassonne, 1992); Brigitte Weiske, *Gesta Romanorum*, 2 vols (Tübingen, 1992); Nigel F. Palmer,
'Exempla', *Medieval Latin: An Introduction and Bibliographical Guide*, ed. F. A. C. Mantello
and A. G. Rigg (Washington, DC, 1996), pp. 582–8.
[2] *Manual*; Joanne A. Rice, *Middle English Romance: An Annotated Bibliography, 1955–1985*
(New York, 1986); W. R. J. Barron, *English Medieval Romance* (London, 1987).
[3] First by Francis Douce, *Illustrations of Shakspeare and of Ancient Manners*, 2 vols (London,
1807), II, p. 362.

ing branches developed first, and at what point before 1342, the date of the earliest manuscript, Innsbruck Universitätsbibliothek lat. 310, the first compilation was made. The two branches differ in terms of the exempla included, the order in which they are placed, and the treatment of many of the shared items. There is also considerable variation from one individual text to another, partly because each exemplum can be regarded as discrete within the whole. Every extant manuscript and incunabulum of the *Gesta* is effectively a distinct version of the work.

If a centre is missing from the *Gesta* configuration, so, too, is an outer circumference. Sometimes an exemplum does not appear in early texts or in many texts. Although a *Gesta* exemplum usually consists of a narrative plus an allegorical moralisation, not widespread in exemplum collections, the latter is sometimes absent or not allegorical. Again, although many open with the formula 'X (a supposed emperor) reigned in the city of Rome, who . . .' or recognisable variations, other openings also occur. Any or all of these grounds may be used to distinguish exempla that belong to the '*Gesta* proper' from others added to the 'original' collection, or the mere appearance of an exemplum under the *Gesta Romanorum* heading may be deemed to admit it to the corpus. It is ultimately an ideological decision whether definition of the collection determines which items 'belong' or whether the appearance of items under that heading participates in the definition of the collection. To date, the theoretical issue of boundaries has not been seriously confronted in *Gesta* scholarship, and in the absence of clear guidelines romance scholars have tended to take an inclusive view which admits over three hundred exempla. The generic implications of comparing romances and *Gesta* exempla will be affected by one's understanding of the status of a particular exemplum *vis à vis* the collection.

In the survey below, each romance I have found associated with the *Gesta* is listed along with the relevant exemplum, giving its chapter number in one or more of the following editions where possible (one might have expected comparisons only with the Anglo-Latin or Middle English, but because the discourse has been generally in terms of analogue both branches are involved). The continental Latin is cited, as is usual, from Hermann Oesterley's 1872 edition, in which chapters 1–152 are based on a printing of c.1472 and chapters 152–81 on additions in the expanded version printed c.1473; an appendix contains further items from German manuscripts as chapters 182–96 and items from other, unspecified manuscripts (apparently at least one Anglo-Latin) as chapters 197–283. This is supplemented by Wilhelm Dick's 1890 edition of the 1342 manuscript (he omits all moralisations, but they have in fact entered little into the discourse).[4] The Middle English is cited from Sidney J. H. Herrtage's 1879 edition of MSS BL Harley 7333 and Additional 9066, which contain different translations (with a partial edition

4 Hermann Oesterley, *Gesta Romanorum* (Berlin, 1872); Wilhelm Dick, *Die 'Gesta Romanorum'*, Erlanger Beiträge zur englischen Philologie 7 (Erlangen, 1890).

of Cambridge University Library Kk.1.6, similar to the latter); Additional 9066 contains forty-six chapters found in other *Gesta* texts, but forty are unique.[5] There is as yet no edition of the Anglo-Latin, but a useful account of a number of manuscripts may be found in J. A. Herbert's *Catalogue of Romances*;[6] the relevant chapter in MS BL Harley 2270 is cited, as the manuscript most frequently representing the Anglo-Latin in existing scholarship.

The parallels that have been noticed may be considered under headings according to the extent of the correspondence: (1) the same story; (2) full analogues, with some variation in detail; (3) partial analogues, where the analogue represents a whole-story unit within the romance; (4) correspondence in a significant motif, less than a whole-story unit. The list of scholars who have recognised the particular parallel includes the main founders of the discourse and significant modern contributors, but an exhaustive list is beyond the scope of this paper.

II Survey

1.1 *Apollonius of Tyre* (verse fragment and prose romance)[7]

Oesterley chapter 153, in the expanded print and without a moralisation; otherwise referred to only as chapter 57 in Cod. Colmar. Issenh. 10 (fourteenth century). It is a moot point whether these occurrences represent a developing tradition of including *Apollonius* in the *Gesta* or a random coincidence. The correspondence to one or other English romance is noted by Warton, Swan, Hibbard, the *Manual* and Archibald.[8]

---

5   Sidney J. H. Herrtage, *The Early English Versions of the Gesta Romanorum*, EETS ES 33 (London, 1879). The contents of a fourth manuscript edited by Karl Sandred are not pertinent here.

6   J. A. Herbert, *Catalogue of Romances in the Department of Manuscripts in the British Museum* (London, 1910), III, pp. 183–271. An edition of the Anglo-Latin by Philippa Bright and Diane Speed is in progress.

7   Verse: ed. Halliwell 1850, rptd Albert H. Smyth, *Shakespeare's Pericles and Apollonius of Tyre: A Study in Comparative Literature* (Philadelphia, PA, 1898), pp. 49–55; prose: *Kynge Apollyn of Thyre*, trans. R. Copland, ptd Wynkyn de Worde, 1510, facsimile by Edmund W. Ashbee, Roxburghe Club (privately printed, London, 1870).

8   Thomas Warton, *The History of English Poetry*, 4 vols, rev. edn (London, 1824), 1, pp. ccxxxv–ccxxxvii; Charles Swan, translating the continental Latin, *Gesta Romanorum: Entertaining Moral Stories*, rev. Wynnard Hooper, preface by E. A. Baker (London, 1905), pp. 451–3; Laura Hibbard, *Mediæval Romance in England: A Study of the Sources and Analogues of the Non-Cyclic Metrical Romances*, new edn (New York, 1963), pp. 164–5; *Manual*, p. 145; Elizabeth Archibald, *Apollonius of Tyre: Medieval and Renaissance Themes and Variations*, (Cambridge, 1991), pp. 190–3 *et passim*.

1.2 Guy of Warwick[9]

Oesterley chapter 172; Dick chapter 194; Harley 2270 chapter 70. Oesterley's *Gesta* text again belongs to the expanded print, but the exemplum is found in several continental manuscripts as well as the Innsbruck.[10] The story evidently came into the continental *Gesta* early on, and Oesterley's text has a full moralisation, which suggests a firm assimilation to the dominant pattern. It is common in the Anglo-Latin, albeit with the hero's name as Josias; the availability of the romance itself in English may account for the non-appearance of the story in the Middle English *Gesta*. The continental *Gesta* is actually rather closer to the romance than is the Anglo-Latin. In both branches the narrative is greatly abbreviated in relation to the romance: the first half, dealing with Guy's pursuit of his lady, is extremely compressed, leaving the focus on the hero's adventures with Thierry and his own end. The correspondence is noted by Warton, Swan, Herrtage, Herbert, Hibbard, the *Manual*, Klausner (1975) and Richmond.[11]

Klausner rightly points out that the romance and the *Gesta* share a focal concern with the two mutually exclusive loves in Guy's life, that of lady and Lord.[12] In the *Gesta*, however, the two loves are a device to initiate the main action of the tale, that of Guy's deeds as a crusading knight and penitent, whereas in the romance they are, rather, a theme informing the overall narrative. The different structural functions of the idea highlight different narrative principles in generically distinct works: in the *Gesta* the idea is proposed and then demonstrated in the subsequent action, whereas in the romance the idea emerges from within the action.

2.1 Le Bone Florence of Rome[13]

Oesterley chapter 249; Dick chapter 150; Herrtage chapter 69 (Harley); Harley 2270 chapter 101. Oesterley's text comes from an unspecified manuscript. Like the *Guy* exemplum, however, this appears in several continental

---

9 *The Romance of Guy of Warwick*, ed. Julius Zupitza, EETS ES 42, 49, 59 (London, 1883, 1887, 1891).

10 Listed by Oesterley: Marburg. D.20; Ratisbon. 47; Tubing. (Wilhelmstift.) X.14; Stuttgard. theol. et philos. 184; Fuldens. B.12; Wallerstein. II. lat. 23; Hannov. XIII.859; Monac. lat. 4691; Colmar. Issenh. 10; Turic. C.113; Berol. Grimm. 81. Listed by Herbert: BL Add. 21430 and Add. 10291.

11 Warton, *The History of English Poetry*, 1, pp. ccxliii–ccxlv; Swan, *Gesta Romanorum*, pp. 461–6; Herrtage, *The Early English Versions of the Gesta Romanorum*, p. 529; Herbert, *Catalogue of Romances*, p. 209; Hibbard, *Mediæval Romance in England*, pp. 130, 134–6; *Manual*, p. 30; David N. Klausner, 'Didacticism and Drama in *Guy of Warwick*', *Medievalia et Humanistica* ns 6 (1975), pp. 103–19 (114); Velma Bourgeois Richmond, *The Legend of Guy of Warwick* (New York, 1996), pp. 61–5.

12 Klausner suggests that the romance as it appears in the Auchinleck manuscript may actually have been influenced by the Anglo-Latin *Gesta*, but there is no evidence that the latter existed before the fifteenth century.

13 Ed. Carol Falvo Heffernan, Old and Middle English Texts (Manchester, 1976).

manuscripts as well as the Innsbruck,[14] and has a full moralisation. The central figure is unnamed in the *Gesta*. The correspondence is noted by Hibbard, Schelp, Mehl and Heffernan.[15]

2.2 *Sir Isumbras*[16]

Oesterley chapter 110; Dick chapter 192; Herrtage chapter 24 (Harley); Harley 2270 chapter 30. In the continental texts the central figure is the saint Placidus-Eustace, and after reinstatement and reunion he and his family are martyred, though triumphantly. In the Anglo-Latin and Middle English the central figure is unnamed and the story much like *Isumbras*. The correspondence is noted by Warton, Douce, Madden, Herrtage, Gerould, Herbert, Hibbard and Schelp.[17]

2.3 *Robert of Sicily*[18]

Oesterley chapter 59; Dick chapter 148; Herrtage chapter 23 (Harley, Additional, Cambridge); Harley 2270 chapter 29. The central figure in the *Gesta* is regularly named Jovinian. The correspondence is noted by Warton, Madden, Herrtage, Herbert, Hibbard, Hornstein and Schelp.[19]

The three stories may be said to offer variations on a theme. In each case the central figure, for different reasons, undergoes severe trials before eventual triumph, in a context of Providential testing and rescue. The Providential theme is one that is coincidentally congenial to forms and expectations in both romance and exemplum.

---

[14] The same manuscripts as for *Guy*, omitting Marburg. D.20 and Hannov. XIII.859, adding Monac. lat. 8497.

[15] Hibbard, *Mediæval Romance in England*, pp. 15–16, 21; Hanspeter Schelp, *Exemplarische Romanzen im Mittelenglischen*, Palaestra 246 (Göttingen, 1967), pp. 117–18; Dieter Mehl, *The Middle English Romances of the Thirteenth and Fourteenth Centuries* (London, 1967), p. 145; Heffernan, *Le Bone Florence of Rome*, p. 7.

[16] Ed. Maldwyn Mills, *Six Middle English Romances* (London, 1973), pp. 125–47.

[17] Warton, *The History of English Poetry*, 1, pp. ccxxiv–ccxxv; Douce, *Illustrations of Shakspeare*, II, p. 375; Frederic Madden, ed., *The Old English Versions of the Gesta Romanorum*, Roxburghe Club (London, 1838), p. 510; Herrtage, *The Early English Versions of the Gesta Romanorum*, p. 463; Gordon Hall Gerould, 'Fore-runners, Congeners, and Derivatives of the Eustace Legend', *PMLA* 19 (1904), pp. 335–448 (368–9 *et passim*); Herbert, *Catalogue of Romances*, pp. 203, 207; Hibbard, *Mediaeval Romance in England*, pp. 3, 7–9; Schelp, *Exemplarische Romanzen im Mittelenglischen*, pp. 55–6.

[18] Ed. Walter Hoyt French and Charles Brockman Hale, *Middle English Metrical Romances*, (New York, 1930, rptd 1964), pp. 931–46.

[19] Warton, *The History of English Poetry*, 1, p. cci; Madden, *The Old English Versions of the Gesta Romanorum*, pp. 509–10; Herrtage, *The Early English Versions of the Gesta Romanorum*, p. 462; Herbert, *Catalogue of Romances*, p. 202; Hibbard, *Mediæval Romance in England*, p. 58; Lillian Herlands Hornstein, 'King Robert of Sicily: Analogues and Origins', *PMLA* 79 (1964), pp. 13–21 (14); Schelp, *Exemplarische Romanzen im Mittelenglischen*, pp. 76, 79.

Diane Speed

3.1 *Syr Tryamowre*[20]

Herrtage chapter 78 (Additional). The relevant story is that of 'the dog of Montargis': a calumniated queen, sent into exile in the company of an old knight, is beset by her lecherous accuser; after the knight dies defending her and she escapes, his dog returns to court, the truth is realised, the villain killed, and the queen reinstated. The story was best known as attached to Sibyl, wife of the emperor Charlemagne, the form it has in the *Gesta*; in the romance she is Margaret, wife of Ardus of Aragon. The correspondence between the exemplum and the main story in *Syr Tryamowre* is noted by Madden, Herrtage, Hibbard, the *Manual* and Fellows.[21] The exemplum has a brief moral, not in allegorised form.

3.2 *The Awntyrs off Arthure*[22]

Herrtage chapter 81 (Additional). The relevant story concerns a dead woman who appears to her son in torment for her sins, and through the masses he says for her is released to heaven. A partial analogue is found also in Herrtage chapter 67 (Additional), where the mother explains why she is tormented, but cannot be saved. The correspondence between both exempla and the main story in *The Awntyrs* is noted by Herrtage, Klausner (1972) and Shepherd, and between chapter 67 and *The Awntyrs* by Madden.[23] Neither exemplum has a moralisation.

3.3 *Rauf Coilȝear*[24]

Oesterley chapter 20; Dick chapter 149; Herrtage chapter 48 (Harley, Additional, Cambridge); Harley 2270 chapter 56. The relevant story is that of 'the king incognito': a ruler accepts the hospitality of one of his subjects and only subsequently reveals his true identity. The correspondence between the initial episode of the exemplum and the main story in *Rauf Coilȝear* is noted by Smyser, Walsh, Harris and Speed.[25]

---

20 Ed. Jennifer Fellows, *Of Love and Chivalry: An Anthology of Middle English Romance*, (London, 1993), pp. 147–98.
21 Madden, *The Old English Versions of the Gesta Romanorum*, pp. 528–9; Herrtage, *The Early English Versions of the Gesta Romanorum*, p. 505; Hibbard, *Mediæval Romance in England*, p. 284; *Manual*, p. 130; Fellows, *Of Love and Chivalry*, p. xvii.
22 *The Awntyrs off Arthure at the Terne Wathelyne*, ed. Stephen Shepherd, *Middle English Romances: Authoritative Texts, Sources and Backgrounds, Criticism*, Norton Critical Edition (New York, 1995), pp. 219–43.
23 Herrtage, *The Early English Versions of the Gesta Romanorum*, pp. 503, 505; David Klausner, 'Exempla and *The Awntyrs of Arthure*', *Mediaeval Studies* 34 (1972), pp. 307–25; Shepherd, *Middle English Romances*, pp. 366–7; Madden, *The Old English Versions of the Gesta Romanorum*, p. 528.
24 Ed. Diane Speed, *Medieval English Romances*, Durham Medieval Texts 8 (Durham, 1993), pp. 196–235.
25 H. M. Smyser, 'The Taill of Rauf Coilyear and its Sources', *Harvard Studies and Notes in Philology and Literature* 14 (1932), pp. 135–50 (139); Elizabeth Walsh, 'The King in Disguise', *Folklore* 86 (1975), pp. 3–24 (17); Joseph Harris, 'The King in Disguise: An

3.4 *Sir Cleges*[26]

Herrtage chapter 90 (Additional). The relevant story is that of 'the strokes shared': a poor man brings something precious to the king, but in order to gain admittance has to promise shares in his reward to the king's servants; he requests twelve strokes, which are duly distributed to the servants, and he is himself given a real reward for his wit. The correspondence between the exemplum and the central episode in *Sir Cleges* is noted by Herrtage, McKnight, Reinhard, Hibbard, Schelp and Speed.[27] The exemplum has a full moralisation.

The story element concerned is the main one in *Syr Tryamowre*, *The Awntyrs*, and *Rauf Coilȝear*. In all three, this main story contains a subordinate one of a conventionally chivalric kind, at the end of which the main story is brought to a conclusion. The story of the calumniated queen in *Syr Tryamowre* is itself found elsewhere in Middle English romance, and as a general story of a persecuted woman has even more romance analogues. That of the apparition in torment, on the other hand, is essentially a pious legend without obvious romance potential, and its dominance in *The Awntyrs* is what gives that romance its acknowledged problematic quality. That of the king incognito dominates the chivalric story in *Rauf Coilȝear* in a way that makes this poem, too, somewhat problematic as a romance, in that it subordinates chivalry to the concerns of the common man and the comedy of human frailty.

In the case of *Sir Cleges*, the story element concerned is itself contained within and dominated by the chivalric story of the spendthrift knight. The romance as a whole thus comes across as one essentially concerned with chivalric loss and restitution through the working of Providence (not unlike *Sir Isumbras*), rather than of just deserts effected through human wit, the message of the strokes-shared story in isolation.

Of these four stories, only one, that of the king incognito, belongs to common *Gesta* tradition. Whereas the other exempla consist entirely of the story concerned, however, this is only one element in a longer exemplum. Unlike the situation in *Rauf Coilȝear*, the king incognito incident here generates not exchanges between king and subject that articulate social satire, but a serious narrative of prophecy, attempted murder, its thwarting and eventual fulfilment of prophecy. The satire in the romance narrative is overt, and

International Popular Tale in Two Old Icelandic Adaptations', *Arkiv för nordisk filologi* 94 (1979), pp. 57–81; Speed, *Medieval English Romances*, p. 199.

[26] Speed, *Medieval English Romances*, pp. 171–95.

[27] Herrtage, *The Early English Versions of the Gesta Romanorum*, p. 507; George H. McKnight, *Middle English Humorous Tales in Verse*, Belles-Lettres Series 2: Middle English Literature (Boston, MA, 1913), p. 71; John R. Reinhard, 'Strokes Shared', *Journal of American Folklore* 36 (1923), pp. 380–400 (383, 395–6); Hibbard, *Mediæval Romance in England*, p. 80; Schelp, *Exemplarische Romanzen im Mittelenglischen*, p. 95; Speed, *Medieval English Romances*, p. 171.

makes an explicit moral point that would probably inhibit further interpretation; the narrative developments in the exemplum, however, have their overt meaning only as story, leaving potential for moralisation through allegorisation. The range of the king incognito narratives located by Smyser confirms the natural home of this story in tale or anecdote; the pattern of concealment, discovery and outcome is, like the Providential theme of *Guy*, coincidentally congenial to forms and expectations in both romance and exemplum.

4.1 *King Horn*[28]

Oesterley 193; Dick chapter 151; Herrtage chapter 12 (Harley); Harley 2270 chapter 18. The relevant motif is actually a combination of two, 'the seven years' troth' and the riddling image of the intact fishing-net (meaning that the lady has waited for her lover). The correspondence is noted by Herbert and Hibbard.[29]

4.2 *The Squyr of Lowe Degre*[30]

Oesterley chapter 193; Dick chapter 151; Herrtage chapter 12 (Harley); Harley 2270 chapter 18. Here the relevant motif is 'the seven years' troth' by itself. The correspondence is noted in the *Manual*.[31]

4.3 *Sir Degarré*[32]

Oesterley chapter 81; Dick chapter 170; Herrtage chapter 61 (Harley); Harley 2270 chapter 69. The relevant motif is actually a combination of two, that of 'the unnatural union' and 'the exposure of the child'. The continental *Gesta* story is the legend of St Gregory, according to which he was the child of an incestuous union of a brother and sister, and himself unknowingly married his mother, the unnatural union occurring twice; in the Anglo-Latin and the Middle English the central figure bears a different name and dies without becoming pope. The combined motif is central to both romance and *Gesta*, but the circumstances are quite different. The correspondence is noted by Madden and Herrtage.[33]

---

28 Ed. Rosamund Allen, *King Horn: An Edition Based on Cambridge University Library MS. Gg. 4.27(2)*, Garland Medieval Texts (New York, 1984).
29 Herbert, *Catalogue of Romances*, p. 193; Hibbard, *Mediæval Romance in England*, pp. 93–4.
30 Ed. William Edward Mead, *The Squyr of Lowe Degre: A Middle English Metrical Romance*, Albion Series of Anglo-Saxon and Middle English Poetry (Boston, MA, 1904).
31 *Manual*, p. 157.
32 Ed. A. V. C. Schmidt and Nicholas Jacobs, *Medieval English Romances*, 2 vols (London, 1980), II, pp. 57–88.
33 Madden, *The Old English Versions of the Gesta Romanorum*, pp. 519–20; Herrtage, *The Early English Versions of the Gesta Romanorum*, p. 489.

4.4 *Sir Eglamour of Artois*[34]

Oesterley chapter 81; Dick chapter 170; Herrtage chapter 61 (Harley); Harley 2270 chapter 69. Here the relevant motif is the unnatural union by itself, but the circumstances are even more different from those of the romance: the parental union is unconventional (unmarried) rather than unnatural, and the mother-and-son union is not consummated. The correspondence is noted by Madden and Herrtage.[35]

4.5 *Ywain and Gawain*[36]

Oesterley chapter 216; Dick chapter 158; Herrtage chapter 60 (Harley); Harley 2270 chapter 68. The relevant motif is that of 'the grateful lion', essentially the stuff of fable; although the circumstances are different, there are some similarities in the associated action. The correspondence is noted by Madden and Herrtage.[37]

4.6 *Sir Gowther*[38]

Oesterley chapter 59; Dick chapter 148; Herrtage chapter 23 (Harley, Additional, Cambridge); Harley 2270 chapter 29. The relevant motif is that of 'the proud emperor', which is the basis of *Robert of Sicily*. Gowther's overbearing behaviour, however, is more berserk than arrogant, and results from the fact that his father is an incubus. The correspondence is noted by Madden, Herrtage and Bradstock.[39]

4.7 *William of Palerne*[40]

Herrtage chapter 26 (Harley); Harley 2270 chapter 30. The relevant motif is that of 'the defence of the child', in the exemplum by a dog that is mistakenly thought guilty of attacking the child and killed, in the romance by a werewolf, who is the central figure and lives on. A doubtful correspondence is noted by Hibbard.[41]

---

[34] Ed. Frances E. Richardson, EETS OS 256 (London, 1965).

[35] Madden, *The Old English Versions of the Gesta Romanorum*, pp. 519–20; Herrtage, *The Early English Versions of the Gesta Romanorum*, p. 489.

[36] Ed. Maldwyn Mills, *Ywain and Gawain, Sir Percyvell of Gales, The Anters of Arther* (London, 1992), pp. 1–102.

[37] Madden, *The Old English Versions of the Gesta Romanorum*, p. 519; Herrtage, *The Early English Versions of the Gesta Romanorum*, p. 487.

[38] Ed. Mills, *Six Middle English Romances*, pp. 148–68.

[39] Madden, *The Old English Versions of the Gesta Romanorum*, p. 510; Herrtage, *The Early English Versions of the Gesta Romanorum*, p. 462; E. M. Bradstock, '*Sir Gowther*: Secular Hagiography or Hagiographical Romance or Neither?', *Journal of the Australasian Universities Language and Literature Association* 59 (1983), pp. 26–47 (45).

[40] Ed. G. H. V. Bunt, *William of Palerne: an alliterative romance*, Mediaevalia Groningana 6 (Groningen, 1985).

[41] Hibbard, *Mediæval Romance in England*, p. 219.

4.8 *The Knight of Curtesy*[42]

Oesterley chapter 56. The relevant motif is that of 'the eaten heart', but the lady in the exemplum eats from her lover's skull instead of eating his actual heart. The correspondence is noted by Hibbard.[43]

4.9 *Amys and Amyloun* [44]

Oesterley chapter 116; Dick chapter 120; Herrtage chapter 55 (Harley); Harley 2270 chapter 63. Warton notes that the likeness of the two youths in the exemplum is a central motif also in *Amys and Amyloun*, but he actually refers only to the French version of the romance.[45] Without mentioning the romance, Herbert reports the presence of the actual *Amys and Amyloun* story in a continental Latin manuscript not known to Oesterley, MS BL Egerton 2258, chapter 65, though it does not seem to appear elsewhere in *Gesta* texts.[46]

A further number of minor parallels that have been observed between various of the romances and *Gesta* exempla are not discussed here. These concern the passing use of motifs whose function is basically decorative rather than essential to the narrative, or merely similar words and phrases, which occur also more widely. Warton, for instance, as an early writer of English literary history, refers to *Sir Launfal* and other texts to illustrate expressions he found in the *Gesta*.

III Conclusions

1.   Insofar as the story analogues and motifs shared by romances and *Gesta* tales are essentially folklore elements, it would undoubtedly be possible to discover many more through a methodical analysis of both corpora, and the ensuing comparisons would increase our understanding of the mass of story materials circulating in the Middle Ages available to fill a range of cultural functions. For a start, other versions of the romances cited might also be considered.

2.   Although the manner of the moralisations may help to identify an exemplum as belonging to the *Gesta*, they have themselves been of little significance in relating the exempla to the romances – only the narrative is usually

---

42 *The Knight of Curtesy and the Fair Lady of Faguell: A Study of the Date and Dialect of the Poem and its Folklore Origins*, ed. Elizabeth McCausland, Smith College Studies in Modern Languages 4.1 (Northampton, MA, 1922).
43 Hibbard, *Mediæval Romance in England*, p. 260.
44 Ed. Françoise Le Saux, Exeter Medieval English Texts and Studies (Exeter, 1993).
45 Warton, *The History of English Poetry*, 1, p. ccxxvii.
46 Herbert, *Catalogue of Romances*, p. 247.

referred to. It would seem that *Gesta* exempla have often been drawn into the discourse because they have been available in editions of the best known collection, rather than for any inherent specialness in the *Gesta* stories. Indeed, some of the parallels cited occur idiosyncratically in one *Gesta* text and might as well have been cited from another collection, had that been on the shelf. The *Gesta* provides a useful starting point for generic comparison, but ultimately the true field for such research is the whole mass of extant exempla.

3.   There was evidently a two-way traffic between romance and exemplum: not only is basically exemplum material found in romance (for example the apparition story in *The Awntyrs*), but basically romance material is found in exemplum (for example *Guy*). Exploring the nature of the appeal for the exemplum writer in the latter case would, of course, shed light on the medieval reception of the romance.

4.   One matter to be addressed concerns the term 'exemplary'. Klausner (1975), for instance, compares *Guy of Warwick* with the legend of St Alexis: the *Gesta* hero adopts an ascetic approach to living for God, whereas the romance hero confronts secular life, but both are 'exemplary' in their own way, constructing patterns which themselves mirror Christ's ways and hold out that mirror to the reader. Richmond, similarly, observes that the *Guy* story is inherently 'exemplary' and reads the *Gesta* hero as an imitation of Christ. The word 'exemplary' often enters discussions of romance, connoting 'imitation', and the main kind of literature to which it relates the romances is hagiography.[47] 'Exemplary' in that context refers to 'exemplum' in its rhetorical meaning of analogy, as opposed to its generic meaning as a kind of medieval text like the *Gesta*.[48] As it stands, some caution is needed in reading or using the word 'exemplary'.

5.   A question implicit in the foregoing discussion is whether, if some of the romances have so much in common with exempla, from the *Gesta* or elsewhere, there might be a case for identifying some of the exemplum narratives as romance. An immediate objection would be that the romances are essentially vernacular products and for the most part in verse, whereas the exempla are essentially Latin products and in prose, with further cultural implications in each case. It might also be added that the romances are, on the whole, longer, more explicatory in style, and packed with more circumstantial detail than the shorter, sparser and more compact exempla. But, true as this contrast is for much of the period, in the course of the fifteenth century a *rapprochement* between the two kinds of writing is evident within *Gesta* tradition specifically.

---

[47] E.g. Susan Crane Dannenbaum, 'Guy of Warwick and the Question of Exemplary Romance', *Genre* 17 (1984), pp. 351–74, with no reference to exempla. Schelp uses *exemplarische* of romances that contain material variously from hagiography and exemplum.
[48] See, for example, Palmer, 'Exempla', p. 582.

Beginning with Hoccleve's translation of two *Gesta* exempla into English verse in his *Series* of 1422,[49] English versions of the *Gesta* were being produced alongside the Latin texts. As time passed, moreover, the moralisations seem to have been regarded as expendable, indicating concern with the stories *per se*. MS BL Additional 9066 gives variously full moralisations, simple morals and no moral. Cambridge University Library Kk.6.1 omits the moralisations altogether, as does Oxford MS Balliol 354 (early sixteenth century), in its single *Gesta* story. Since prose romances were becoming popular, therefore, vernacular prose narratives from the two sources might lie side by side in the homes of well-to-do laity. Interestingly, just before Caxton set up his press in Westminster and began printing English prose romances, it seems that he was involved in the printing of the Latin *Gesta Romanorum* in Cologne;[50] and Wynkyn de Worde printed an English *Gesta* (c.1510)[51] as well as romance.

It is tempting to see mirrored in the relationship between medieval prose romances and exempla that between today's novel and short story, of which these medieval types are, arguably, the respective precursors.

---

[49] *Hoccleve's Works*, 1: *The Minor Poems*, ed. Frederick J. Furnivall, EETS ES 61 (London, 1892), pp. 140–78, 215–42.

[50] Norman Blake, 'William Caxton', *Middle English Prose: A Critical Guide to Major Authors and Genres*, ed. A. S. G. Edwards (New Brunswick, NJ, 1986), pp. 389–412 (394–5).

[51] Facsimile by Ronald Templin, Exeter Medieval English Texts (Exeter, 1974).

Sir Amadace and the Undisenchanted Bride: the relation of the Middle English romance to the folktale tradition of 'The Grateful Dead'

ELIZABETH WILLIAMS

THE first person to point out the connection of the Middle English romance of *Sir Amadace*[1] with the folktale tradition usually known as 'The Grateful Dead' seems to have been the antiquary George Stephens. His idiosyncratically titled edition, *Ghost-Thanks or The Grateful Unburied*, published in 'Cheapinghaven' (his name for Copenhagen) in 1860, added several fresh analogues, in addition to *Sir Amadace* itself, to the already considerable collection of variant versions. Others were later identified, and G. H. Gerould, by the time he produced his major monograph in 1908,[2] was able to summarise and compare over a hundred examples, ranging in time from the first century to the nineteenth, and in place from Spain to Siberia.

The list continued to grow, and with the appearance of Aarne's definitive classification of the folktale genre in 1910 (revised by Stith Thompson in 1928)[3] the study of the oral, though not, unfortunately, the literary versions, was set on an entirely new footing. Liljeblad's exhaustive study of 1927[4] carried the particular exploration of the 'Grateful Dead' theme even further, but he too was concerned far more with oral than literary traditions. Therefore Gerould's now somewhat outdated account is still the one that seems

---

[1]   Editions used: *Sir Amadace and the Avowing of Arthur*, ed. Christopher Brookhouse, *Anglistica*, vol. XV (Copenhagen, 1968); *Six Middle English Romances*, ed. Maldwyn Mills (London, 1973), pp. 169–92. Quotations are from Mills, *Six Middle English Romances*, and follow the Ireland MS.
[2]   Gordon Hall Gerould, *The Grateful Dead: the History of a Folk Story*, The Folk-Lore Society No. 60 (London, 1908; Kraus Reprint, 1967).
[3]   I refer throughout to the second revision: Antti Aarne, *The Types of the Folktale*, translated and enlarged by Stith Thompson, FF Communications No. 184 (Helsinki, 1961).
[4]   Sven Liljeblad, *Die Tobiasgeschichte und andere Märchen mit toten Helfern* (Lund, 1927).

most accessible to those who seek to explore the use of this folktale motif in literary contexts.[5] It does, however, need to be treated with some care.

Gerould prefaced his study with a summary of what he called 'the story reduced to its lowest terms', a summary which in fact begs most of the important questions that arise in discussions of literary uses of the theme:

> A man finds a corpse lying unburied, and out of pure philanthropy procures interment for it at great personal inconvenience. Later he is met by the ghost of the dead man, who in many cases promises him help on condition of receiving, in return, half of whatever he gets. The hero obtains a wife (or some other reward), and, when called upon, is ready to fulfil his bargain as to sharing his possessions.[6]

Gerould comments: 'Nowhere does a version appear in quite this form; but . . . the simple story must have proceeded along some such lines.' As it stands it is actually quite a good resumé of the plot of *Sir Amadace*. That phrase, 'the simple story', however, obscures the fact that what he summarises is really a complex story, and these are not its 'lowest terms'.

Its complex nature is indicated by the fact that the summary itself acknowledges two points where important plot-differences may occur: first, the bargain to share winnings, struck between the ghost and the hero, is found only 'in many cases'; and secondly, although those winnings may include a valuable wife, they may instead be 'some other reward'. These variants can be crucial, as the whole Divided Winnings theme, in which the wife is usually involved, can set the original motif of the Grateful Dead on quite a different, even a contradictory, course. The 'simple story' is 'simply' about gratitude: the corpse returns to reward the person who generously buried him. But of all the tales assembled by Gerould, only four stop there, with the straight payment of the debt. The vast majority develop this payment into a further plot, and Gerould in fact accepts that the story is multi-themed.[7] But in stories like *Sir Amadace*, where the second theme is the bargain to share winnings, the climax often takes the form of a test, even a very harrowing test, which seems to turn the 'simple story' on its head: such a test is hardly a good way to express gratitude. We end, in fact, with a Grateful Dead plot plus a Test plot – not a simple story at all, but a powerful indication that the 'Grateful Dead' label should in fact be regarded as signifying not a complete narrative but an initial motif only, which leads in to a wide variety of complex tales.

Although Gerould included the older, literary versions in his analysis,

---

5   It is, for instance, cited in the bibliography to *Sir Amadace* in *Manual*, p. 329; and by the poem's most recent editor, Edward E. Foster, *Amis and Amiloun, Robert of Cisyle, and Sir Amadace* (Michigan, 1997), p. 143. As a collection of texts and summaries, Gerould is, of course, still valuable; it is his categorisation and analysis that have been in some respects superseded.

6   Gerould, *The Grateful Dead*, p. x.

most of his texts are folktales, collected from oral tradition in modern times. Anything recorded in earlier periods is necessarily literary, and where a known folktale plot can be recognised in a medieval romance, it will, by the very nature of the case, never be possible to demonstrate conclusively that it derived from oral tradition. With *Sir Amadace*, however, the earlier history of the plot is peculiarly rich, and although no firm conclusions can be drawn about its sources, variations in treatment and material among the extant versions allow for some suggestive comparisons to be made.

Interestingly, the so-called 'Grateful Dead' plot survives in two versions which are very early indeed, one genuinely simple, the other a complex and sophisticated literary narrative. The simple one takes the form of a brief exemplum, cited by Cicero in *De Divinatione* (I.27) to demonstrate the validity of warning dreams. It concerns a certain Simonides

> who once saw the dead body of some unknown man lying exposed and buried it. Later, when he had it in mind to go on board a ship he was warned in a vision by the person to whom he had given burial not to do so and that if he did he would perish in a shipwreck. Therefore he turned back and all the others who sailed were lost.[8]

This is a clear example of the Grateful Dead motif uncompounded with anything else. It is indeed so bare that Gerould had grave doubts that it even belonged in the set, but Gerould, as we have seen, did not regard the simple debt-and-payment structure as constituting the whole story of the Grateful Dead. And this is all we have in *Simonides*: the pious act and the grateful response as straightforward cause and effect. Nothing else follows, there is no Divided Winnings agreement and the reward is not a marriage. This is, in fact, a classic exemplum – a rather limited narrative form with explicit moral function. It is also, incidentally typical of one line of transmission for the episode which continues to feature in exempla collections of the Middle Ages.[9] But this genuinely simple version suggests powerfully why it makes such limited appearances in this bare form: it may be conclusive as a moral demonstration, but it does rather lack punch as a story. The straight repayment is too tidy; it needs some twist, some additional development, if it is to grow into a full-blown narrative.

Now, as Gerould's summary and the vast majority of his examples imply, the motif nearly always is so developed, acting as the introduction to a

[7] The later terminology of 'motif' and 'tale-type' had yet to be established; Gerould conceived 'the simple motive of The Grateful Dead' as existing in fixed combinations with a limited number of other 'themes' (p. 26).

[8] Cicero, *De Senectute, De Amicitia, De Divinatione*, with an English translation by William Armistead Falconer, Loeb Classical Library (London, 1923), pp. 284–7.

[9] See, e.g., Danielle Regnier-Bohler, 'La largesse du mort et l'éthique chevaleresque: le motif du mort reconnaissant dans les fictions médiévales du XIIIe au XVe siècle', *Reception et identification du conte depuis le moyen age*, ed. Michel Zink and Xavier Ravier (Toulouse, 1987), pp. 52–63.

sequence of events that may dramatically alter, or conflict with, its apparently obvious moral implications. However, moral implications are far less obvious in the more complex emotional climate of a romance or a folktale than in an exemplum. Two key episodes, the hero's encounters first with the corpse, then with the revenant helper, indicate the difference between the clear-cut morality of the exemplum and the more ambiguous crosscurrents of the developed Divided Winnings plot.

As Gerould's summary indicates, the opening move in the tale, the burial of the corpse, is an act of pure, selfless charity, not easily performed. In almost all versions the corpse is a total stranger, and in many, the hero spends the very last of his money on the burial, reducing himself to complete penury. The moral implications of this seem obvious: 'To give and not to count the cost' is a traditional Christian virtue – hence the tale's adoption as a medieval exemplum. But generosity, even to the point of recklessness, is also an admired quality in chivalric romance – and often, indeed, in folktale too: the exceptions are those tales which stress the triumph of wise self-interest over blind idealism. But all three genres generally endorse the virtue of a generous act.

However, at the point where the second plot-strand takes over, when the Grateful Dead reappears and offers to share winnings, the actions of the characters are not quite so easy to assign to a single, clear moral or narrative convention. The Grateful Dead himself certainly seems to be attaching an unexpected condition to what ought to be an unqualified act of gratitude. The hero's reactions seem simpler, but that very simplicity is revealing. One thing that Gerould's summary does not stress is that when he meets the corpse for the second time, in the guise of his mysterious benefactor, the hero does not recognise him. Realistically, this is hardly surprising – on the previous occasion he had been extremely dead – but what is more important than mere realism is that here again the hero appears to be reacting with purely natural kindness to a total stranger: he does not know the man any more than he knew the corpse he buried, but in those versions where he makes a bargain to divide winnings with him, the agreement is as generous and spontaneous as the act of burial. This is a frank, not a calculated, response, and is the same on both occasions.

From a literary viewpoint this seems like good, consistent characterisation, and from a Christian, and indeed a chivalric, moral stance it also seems wholly commendable: the hero of a romance should practise what the Gawain-poet called fraunchyse.[10] But is not this impulsive candour also a little rash? Romance and folktale may both approve of a generous hero, but unconsidered bargains also have a way of turning against those who make them, particularly when they are struck with persons of not quite normal human status. The hero generally, and Sir Amadace certainly, accepts the stranger as

---

10 Sir Gawain and the Green Knight, ed. J. R. R. Tolkien and E. V. Gordon, 2nd edn revised by Norman Davis (Oxford, 1968), l. 652.

'normal': he does not recognise him. Nor did Sir Gawain when he met Sir Bertilak for the second time. Should they both have read the signs a little more carefully? The bargain the stranger offers is not the act of Christian love which ought to repay the charitable act of burial; but it is just the sort of act that might be performed by someone from the Otherworld, whose denizens frequent both medieval romance and international folktale. Should Snow White have recognised the old woman who offered her the apple? Is this one of those occasions when a touch of suspicion might be wiser than chivalric frankness? I will return to this question of the status of the stranger when I come to discuss *Sir Amadace* in more detail. But first it is useful to take a look at the second of these early versions of the tale, which is also one of the most complex.

The apocryphal book of Tobit may date back to the second century BC.[11] Its status as part of the Biblical canon has always been dubious, but its presence in the Vulgate means it was very well known throughout the Middle Ages. A highly sophisticated, literary rendering, it differs in a number of important details from later versions of 'The Grateful Dead'. If it represents an ancient Semitic version of the story, as scholars seem to think,[12] then it has already come a long way from its source.[13]

Working on different principles from Gerould, Aarne and Thompson divided the 'Grateful Dead' stories into four main groups, Nos. 505–508.[14] Tobit is covered by 507B, *The Monster in the Bridal Chamber*, which is analysed as a sequence of three stages:

I.   *The Grateful Dead Man*
II.   *The Monster in the Bridal Chamber*
III.   *The Dividing in Half*

The first of these shows the simple Grateful Dead motif already attached to the problematic Divided Winnings:

(a) The hero ransoms a corpse from creditors who refuse its burial. (b) The grateful dead man in the form of an old man, a servant, or a fox later helps the hero on condition that they are to divide all winnings.

---

[11] Carey A. Moore, in *The Oxford Companion to the Bible*, ed. Bruce M. Metzger and Michael D. Coogan (New York and Oxford, 1993), p. 747.

[12] In addition to the analyses of Aarne/Thompson and Liljeblad, see also G. Huet, 'Le conte du "Mort Reconnaissant" et le livre de Tobie', *Revue de l'histoire des religions* 71 (1915), pp. 1–29.

[13] 'This early redaction of the story is so thoroughly adapted to the Hebrew literature of which it forms a part that it would surely seem to represent the results of a long period of change and adjustment': Stith Thompson, *The Folktale* (Berkeley, rptd 1977), p. 52.

[14] *Types of the Folktale*, pp. 171–5. Liljeblad divides into six groups (*Die Tobiasgeschichte*, pp. 29ff) and rejects the title 'The Grateful Dead' for the whole set, preferring to see this as an introductory motif only.

The story told in Tobit shows obvious variations from this: in particular, many corpses are involved, not just one, and the burial is done not by the hero, Tobias, but by his father, Tobit, while it is Tobias who is rewarded. Further, the dead men are not debtors, though debts and payments are important elsewhere in the plot. But the corpses Tobit buries are not connected with him personally, apart from being fellow Jews, so his action has that air of selfless charity that gives the story point as a moral exemplum; it also leads to his fall from a position of respect into poverty, ostracism and even blindness.

Much more significant is the fact that the helper, though in the guise of a servant, is not one of the dead but the Archangel Raphael, travelling incognito. In other words, this oldest known version of the story that Gerould and Aarne/Thompson all refer to as 'The Grateful Dead', does not actually contain a Dead Helper.[15] The motif may reflect an ancient and widespread cultural respect for the duties of the living to the dead,[16] as suggested by the two ancient versions, Tobit and *Simonides*, but as the story develops, it seems clear that what matters is not the nature of the act of giving that the hero performs, but the generosity with which he performs it. It is true that in many of the extant stories, the burial of a corpse is what sets the action on its course, but in others the hero performs some other act of piety or generosity, perhaps towards the shrine of a saint, or an animal in distress, who later returns to repay him.[17] As we have seen, Aarne/Thompson include a fox in their list of possible helpers, and Liljeblad considered that the animal is the older motif in stories of this type, the revenant corpse a later substitution.[18] All of this lends support to the argument that 'The Grateful Dead' is not a complete tale at all but an initiating motif only, replaceable by something else, and the plot it leads into can go in several different directions.[19] One such direction is the Divided Winnings plot, and the resulting moral complication emphasises that the two motifs are in fact quite separate.

The problem does not arise in the carefully motivated narrative of Tobit, where the agreement to divide winnings is merely hinted at: before they set out Tobit meticulously settles with the hired stranger for wages of a drachma a day with the possibility of a bonus if things go well. When they do go supremely well, both father and son urge him to 'accept of half of all things that they had brought'[20] – an offer which Raphael graciously declines as he reveals his identity. So, although half was not agreed to beforehand, half is

---

15 Liljeblad throughout prefers this term, which does not carry the implications of gratitude which so many of the stories in fact undermine, but the sinisterly evocative title of 'The Grateful Dead', inaccurate or ironic as it often is, will probably remain in use.

16 See, e.g., Gerould, The Grateful Dead, pp. 162 ff; Laura A. Hibbard, *Medieval Romance in England* (New York, 1924), p. 76; Danielle Regnier-Bohler, 'La largesse du mort', pp. 54ff.

17 See e.g., Gerould, The Grateful Dead, pp. 82–3, 135ff.

18 Liljeblad, *Die Tobiasgeschichte*, pp. 21, 97; cf. Gerould, pp. 158–61.

19 Liljeblad, *Die Tobiasgeschichte*, pp. 12–14.

20 Tobit 12.5 (Douay/Rheims translation).

offered at the end, but crucially there is no test involved; this is just a good business arrangement, initiated not by the helper but by the helped.

The second stage of Aarne/Thompson's tale 507B, *The Monster in the Bridal Chamber*, is summarised thus:

> All bridegrooms of a princess have perished during the bridal night . . . The hero marries her on the advice of the grateful dead man who kills the dragon (or serpent) who comes into the chamber to kill the bridegroom.

For 'princess' read Sara, daughter of Raguel; for 'grateful dead man', Raphael; and for 'dragon (or serpent)', the demon Asmodeus, and the plot fits.

Stage three, *The Dividing in Half*, is rather spectacular in Aarne/Thompson's summary:

> The dead man cleanses the princess of enchantment by cutting her in two so that her serpent brood is driven from her body.

This makes Tobias's smelly fumigation with the fish-guts look rather tame, but it also suggests that the unfortunate bride is more than just in the monster's power: she is actually possessed by it, and therefore needs to be not merely freed of its presence but ritually cleansed or disenchanted. Texts of the book of Tobit are subject to enormous variation, and although none seems to mention cutting Sara in two, Huet refers to a Chaldean text in which Raphael instructs Tobias to ensure that the fumigating smoke penetrates under her garments.[21] The text that lies behind the Authorised Version does not suggest that the smoke has any other function than to disgust Asmodeus and drive him off. However, the medieval Vulgate seems to provide at least a hint of exorcism, or magical ritual, as Tobias has to observe three nights of sexual continence before he may 'take the virgin': only on the third night will he 'obtain a blessing that sound children may be born'.[22] So there may have been more involved in the original story than just smoking the demon off the premises. A need to disenchant the bride also, of course, provides justification for any suffering inflicted upon her, and the sophisticated, double-focussed plot of Tobit, its events overtly orchestrated by God, shows clearly that the needs of Sara are just as important as those of Tobit and Tobias; this is quite different from the single focus of the traditional folktale, where events and characters are all subsidiary to the progress of the hero.[23]

Old as it is, Tobit cannot be seen as the sole source of the later versions. Its distinctive features, with the angel in place of the Grateful Dead and the hero's role divided between father and son, are usually seen as mere local

---

[21] Huet, 'Le conte du "Mort Reconnaissant" ', p. 10, citing A. Neubauer, *The Book of Tobit* (Oxford, 1878).

[22] Tobit 6.22, 21 (Dovay/Rheims translation).

[23] See, e.g., Max Lüthi, *The European Folktale: Form and Nature*, trans. John D. Niles (Bloomington and Indianapolis, 1986), p. 64.

adaptations to the Jewish cultural context of a story which, in the course of many centuries, gave rise to a number of different forms. In the majority of cases the dead man is present and helps his benefactor to repair his fortunes via an advantageous marriage, but there is not always a monster in the bridal chamber, the helper does not have to be dead, or even human, and the story adapts readily to other cultural and literary conventions besides the Jewish.

Sir Amadace, written probably in the late fourteenth century, belongs to a small but distinct group of medieval tales in which the processes of fortune-repairing and bride-winning have been given a chivalric setting.[24] There are some half-dozen medieval narratives that treat this theme, in nearly as many languages, though none is close enough to *Sir Amadace* to be considered its immediate and only source.[25] All these narratives have chivalric features although not all are fully-developed romances. All include the agreement to divide winnings; in all the wife is won in a tournament, usually quite easily and certainly with no suggestion that she requires disenchantment; and finally, when the stranger returns to demand his share, the hero is not usually asked to divide his wife as well as his property.[26] With no disenchantment or demon lover to deal with, any justification for this division disappears. The demand for it in *Sir Amadace* thus startlingly highlights the moral discrepancy between the two plot-motifs of the so-called 'Grateful Dead' and the testing of the hero's readiness to stand by his bargain to divide winnings.

Not all these medieval texts are easily accessible, but it looks very much as if *Sir Amadace* is the first extant version in which the hero is asked actually to cut his wife in half, or to include his child in the sacrifice.[27] This climax does not occur in the two earlier French texts that are closest to it, *Richars li Biaus* and *Lion de Bourges*.[28] It does however get into the fifteenth-century prose romance of *Olivier de Castille et Artus d'Algarbe*, which was translated into

---

[24] See Gerould, *The Grateful Dead*, pp. 33ff; Liljeblad, *Die Tobiasgeschichte*, pp. 58ff; Aarne/Thompson No. 508, *The Bride won in a Tournament*.

[25] The following list of texts and editions updates the information in Gerould and Lilje-blad: *Richars li Biaus, roman du XIIIe siècle*, ed. Anthony J. Holden, CFMA (Paris, 1983); *Lion de Bourges, poème épique du XIVe siècle*, ed. William W. Kibler, Jean-Louis G. Picherit and Thelma S. Fenster, 2 vols (Geneva, 1980); *Die Rittertreue*, ed. M. Meier-Branecke (Hamburg, 1969); *La Novella di Messer Dianese e di Messer Gigliotto*, ed. A. d'Ancona and G. Sforza (Pisa, 1868); *Om Pippinus Franka Konung*, ed. G. Stephens in *Ghost Thanks*, pp. 73–4. For the romance of 'Oliver of Castille' see below, note 29.

[26] Aarne/Thompson's analysis of No. 508, *The Bride won in a Tournament*, seems to imply that the third section of the tale, *The Dividing in Half*, may include the dividing of the bride, but they cite only recently collected folktale versions, not the medieval literary texts. The same seems to apply to the twenty-five variants which include a demand to kill the child, cited by Gerould, *The Grateful Dead*, p. 156.

[27] This impression is confirmed by Brookhouse, *Anglistica*, p. 23. Laura Hibbard seems to be in error, however, in *Mediæval Romance in England*, p. 75. For summaries and discussion of the texts listed in note 25 see Gerould, *The Grateful Dead*, *passim*, and Brookhouse, *Anglistica*, pp. 16–24.

[28] For editions see above, note 25. That cited for *Lion de Bourges* is the version in alexandrines only: the version in octosyllables seems not yet to be in print.

English and printed by Wynkyn de Worde in 1518.[29] This is also the only other version in which the interval between the hero's marriage and the return of the helper is sufficiently long to have produced a child, in fact two children, one of whom has to be handed over while the lady, as in *Sir Amadace*, is to be cut in half. *Olivier*, however, is a compound tale in which the linked motifs of the Grateful Dead and the divided Winnings have been further intertwined with the romance of the Two Brothers,[30] where the sacrifice of a child to save the life of a beloved companion relates clearly to the tale's theme of sworn brotherhood. This theme is also apparent in the relationship of Amadace and his ghostly helper but it is quite unconnected with the death of the child, and Liljeblad showed that the sacrifice of wife and child, real or threatened, came from two separate traditions within the wider group of so-called 'Grateful Dead' stories. The dividing of the wife belonged with those in which she required disenchantment; the sacrifice of the child with another group in which the hero's helper was not a revenant corpse but a comrade who was killed during this violent process, the blood of the child being then required to heal him.[31] Before the fifteenth century it is only in *Sir Amadace* that the double threat is found, without any benevolent intent but solely, it seems, to emphasise the relentless nature of the supernatural helper.

Dramatically, the episode also provides an extremely powerful climax. In these chivalric texts the hero wins his bride conventionally enough in a tournament. Without an episode of rescue or enchantment, however, the plot, like that of the simple exemplum, is rather thin. This is made up for in the French texts (*Richars li Biaus*, *Lion de Bourges* and *Olivier et Artus*) by relegating the Grateful Dead material to the status of a mere episode in a lengthy network of heroic adventures. *Sir Amadace*, however, is far more compact, built around a single plot which gains depth and strength by developing themes and motifs that were either in it already or arise naturally from the chivalric setting.

One of these themes is referred to by Gerould as the Spendthrift Knight.[32] The notion of debits and credits is already present to some degree in Tobit, and in the French romances the corpse which the hero buries out of charity is that of a debtor who was also a knight. In *Sir Amadace* he was a merchant but,

---

[29] See Gerould, *The Grateful Dead*, pp. 15, 92–4; the French original of this text is not yet in print but an edition is being prepared by Danielle Regnier-Bohler. For the Wynkyn de Worde translation see *The History of Oliver of Castile*, ed. R. E. Graves, Roxburghe Club (London, 1898); and *The Hystorye of Olyuer of Castylle*, ed. Gail Orgelfinger (New York and London, 1988). I discuss this and some other post-*Amadace* treatments of the Grateful Dead material in a volume of essays in honour of Peter Meredith, edited by Catherine Batt, *Leeds Studies in English* 29 (1998), pp. 411–26.

[30] Aarne/Thompson No.303; unlike the medieval 'Amis and Amiloun' group, however, this folktale does not seem to include the child-sacrifice.

[31] See Liljeblad, *Die Tobiasgeschichte*, pp. 117–23; cf. Aarne/Thompson No. 516, *Faithful John*, and note 30.

[32] See especially Chapter 7.

as the embittered account of his widow makes clear, he was a merchant who behaved like a knight, until his *largesse* made a debtor of him. This brings to the fore the ambiguous nature of liberality.[33] From the Christian point of view charity is the prime virtue, and burial of the dead one of the works of mercy. Yet prodigality is a vice. But there is a social as well as a moral side to the problem. The dead merchant fed and clothed the poor 'for Goddus sake' (155) – another work of mercy:

> Yette he didde as a fole:
> He cladde mo men agaynus a Yole
> Thenne did a nobull knyghte. (156–8)

The implication of the widow's words seems to be that he had ideas above his station and would have done better to have had a more responsible, even a more mercantile, attitude to cash. Amadace, like his French counterparts, has also overspent his inheritance, but even though lavish expenditure is proper for a knight, he still recognises the ironic parallel. Bestowing his last ten pounds on the burial is an expression of kinship as well as a work of mercy:

> Yondur mon that lise yondur chapell withinne
> He myghte full wele be of my kynne. (208–9)

The knight and the merchant are equals in this, even companions. When the merchant returns from the dead in the guise of the White Knight, he seems actually to have achieved the status he aspired to in life, and his bargain with Amadace to share winnings strengthens the brotherly bond between them even more.

But it is a macabre and terrible kind of brotherhood when, at the climax of the story, the White Knight comes to demand his half-share in Amadace's wife and child. This is the point at which the conflicting demands of the Grateful Dead and the Divided Winnings motifs reach their final impasse. Any possible parallel with the Monster's Bride tradition, or with The Two Brothers, is outweighed by the sheer arbitrariness of the demand, for there is no enchantment to break here, no life to be saved, only the ruthless fulfilment of a given word. It is an outrageous act and critics have been much bothered by it.[34]

It also seems to have bothered the composers of some of the folktale versions adduced by Liljeblad, who offer various explanations for it. In one Scandinavian tale, for instance, the dead helper justifies the torment he inflicts on the hero, by first threatening to kill the child and then relenting, on the grounds that he wanted the father to share the agony and the joy he himself

---

33 See the discussions in Mills, *Six Middle English Romances*, pp. xix–xx; Brookhouse, *Anglistica*, p. 21.
34 E.g. Mills, *Six Middle English Romances*, pp. xxi, 223 (note to lines 769–71).

had felt when he first lay unburied and then was laid to rest. This may be a logical extension of the brotherhood theme but is hardly grateful. A Swedish tale which lies further from the central tradition is also of interest. In this there is no child involved and the helper is not a corpse but a whale which the hero had rescued earlier, but only after a delay; to make him share both the agony of doubt and the relief, the whale subjects him to a similar delay by plunging him under water three times before finally saving his life.[35]

At the risk of special pleading, it might be argued that the poet of *Sir Amadace* may have been working along similar lines when he included the harrowing scene in the chapel, another episode that is unique to this poem. By twice, fruitlessly, sending his squire to investigate before going himself, Amadace could be seen as subjecting the unburied corpse to just such an agonising delay, which the White Knight's double punishment makes him answer for when he first demands 'Half thi child and halfe thi wyve' (707), and then makes him choose the most beloved to kill first. The parallels are not very exact, but there is at least a hint of a traditional triadic structure, and when the White Knight finally stops the execution he does so in words that at least hint at the theme of shared agony and joy that is present in the Scandinavian folktale:

> I con notte wite the gif thou were woe,
> Suche a ladi forto slo,
>   Thi wurschip thus wold save.
> Yette I was largely as gladde
> Quen thou gafe all that evyr thou hade,
>   My bones forto grave.   (781–6)

The phrasing is highly elliptical, but both agony and joy are mentioned, and it would be logical for the shared experience of the two debtors to be extended even to this final threshold of pain.

The existence of such folktale analogues does not, of course, prove anything about the genesis of *Sir Amadace*. That its author worked at least in part from a literary source (or sources) seems clear: different as he is in character, the Dead Helper returns as a White Knight in the French analogues also, and it could further be argued that the articulate development of themes, such as chivalric brotherhood or the ambiguous nature of *largesse*, is a thoroughly literary process. There is, however, no literary precedent for the threat to kill the wife and child at the end, and the presence of an almost identical climax in the later *Olivier et Artus* raises some interesting questions.[36] We are not accustomed to look for sources of French romances in English ones but,

[35] Liljeblad, *Die Tobiasgeschichte*, pp. 100–101.
[36] For discussion of this text see Danielle Regnier-Bohler, 'Traditions et structures nouvelles chez Philippe Camus: la genèse de *l'Histoire d'Olivier de Castille et Artus d'Algarbe*', *Etudes littéraires sur le XVe siècle*, Actes du Ve colloque international sur le moyen français, Milan, 6–8 mai 1985, vol. III (Milan, 1986), pp. 53–72.

lacking as we do a direct source for *Sir Amadace*, it is not impossible that both authors found this dramatic climax independently, perhaps in a folktale. As we have seen, the physical division of a bride, and the equally bloody slaughter of a child, both have places, though admittedly separate places, in this vast web of interrelated stories. The situation in *Olivier et Artus* is complicated by the integration of the Two Brothers plot, but the author of *Sir Amadace* at least, in search of a strong conclusion for his story, could perhaps have drawn either on a folktale in which the wife-division was necessary to end an enchantment, or on one in which the blood of a child was needed to resuscitate a helper who was not a 'Grateful Dead' but a beloved companion. Both these serve in their different ways to explain the otherwise inexplicable violence of the story's climax, but the fact remains that the author of *Sir Amadace* does not explain it, unless we take another hint from folktale and read the White Knight's actions as a ruthless manifestation of brotherhood, pursued to its bitter end, with an enforced sharing of agony as well as joy.

There is however another way of approaching the problem. The discontinuity between the two halves of the plot in *Sir Amadace* is a real one and stems from an essential conflict between the logical demands of the two motifs of the Grateful Dead and the Divided Winnings. But it becomes far less obvious if we distance the enigmatic helper a little from the notorious 'Grateful Dead' and see him more in terms of the 'White Knight'. As explained in the plot he is of course a Dead Helper, but as actually portrayed in his later appearances in the action he is surely far closer to one of those mysterious Otherworld figures who, as noted above, draw unsuspecting heroes into tricky bargains in both romance and folktale.

He has, for instance, little of the divine aura that his analogue has in Tobit, or in the much closer *Lion de Bourges*, where he is assumed into heaven at the end with flights of angels.[37] As a white horseman he may seem angelic (638), but the porter's astonished description, as he arrives to claim his bargain: 'Milke quite is his stede,/ And so is all his other wede' (655–6), is far more evocative of the fairy troop in *Sir Orfeo*.[38] Indeed, dressed and mounted in this single uniform colour, his closest match seems to be with the Green Knight, whose sinister combination of comradeship and threat is echoed in no small way throughout *Sir Amadace*. Both the White Knight and the Green show the same lordly geniality in giving, with an apparently innocent condition tossed in at the close.[39] The bargain to divide winnings is not so very different from the bargain to exchange, and both land their respective heroes in similar tough dilemmas of 'trawthe'.

---

37 For his portrayal in this text see J.-L. Picherit, 'Le merveilleux chrétien et le motif du mort reconnaissant dans la chanson de *Lion de Bourges*', *Annuale Medievale* 16 (1975), pp. 41–51.

38 'Al on snowe-white stedes;/ As white as milke were her wedes': *Sir Orfeo*, ed. A. J. Bliss (Oxford, 1966), ll. 145–6.

39 *Sir Gawain and the Green Knight*, ll. 835ff, 1105; *Sir Amadace*, ll. 472ff, 490.

Something of the same aura of mystery also hangs about both. On his first appearance, it is true, the White Knight speaks much more overtly like an emissary of God (440–56), but when he arrives at the end to claim his due this sense of divine sanction seems almost completely submerged in personal ruthlessness. It is indeed this climactic scene of *Sir Amadace* that provides the most dramatic parallels, especially with the Green Knight's initial entry into Arthur's court. Both arrivals are completely unheralded and both shock by their deliberate overturning of social custom, threatening the start of a meal with an act of bloodshed. Both visitors, offered a generous welcome, decline all but their one outrageous request.[40] Both strike onlookers with a splendour or beauty that seems not quite human, and although both give an impression of chivalric stature each has something missing: the Green Knight puzzles by his lack of armour, the White by his lack of attendants.[41] Later, the confrontation between Gawain and the Green Knight at the end of the poem suggests further similarities, with its conclusion of mercy delivered after barely deserved pain and the threat of execution. Both knights, in short, seem to inhabit a mysterious hinterland where normal human standards do not apply, and both depart at the end to realms that are never quite identified.[42]

This portrayal of the White Knight as an Otherworld figure rather than a Christian revenant does not do away with the moral difficulty intrinsic to the plot, but it does put it in a different context by emphasising his function rather than his character. He may start out as the 'Grateful Dead', but as the poem progresses, he seems to loosen his connection with the God-ruled universe and align more with the arbitrary world of faerie, whose inhabitants are all too likely to indulge in bizarre bargains and to insist on their fulfilment to the letter. Moreover, the sense of duality in his presentation, that as the 'Grateful Dead' he is a divine emissary but as the White Knight something far less morally assignable, may be seen not as a dramatic flaw but a reflection of the different principles of folktale, where characters subsidiary to the hero have local functions only, as motifs, not as characters in their own right.

The story's status as folktale may also help to account for, though it does not remove, the moral hitch at the point where the Divided Winnings theme comes in, as this can be detached from literary and moral arguments about theme and consistency of character and be seen to be a genuine motif, with the sole purpose of producing a better ending. The disjunction may be smoothed over by thematic, literary development of the *largesse* idea, and by a subtle change of emphasis by which the White Knight carries an aura not of the grave but of faerie, which sets him apart from normal standards. The fact remains, however, that folktale motifs do not have to be consistent; they need have a local function only.

[40] *Sir Gawain and the Green Knight*, ll. 256–73; *Sir Amadace*, ll. 679–708.
[41] *Sir Gawain and the Green Knight*, ll. 203ff; *Sir Amadace*, ll. 673–5.
[42] *Sir Gawain and the Green Knight*, ll. 2478; *Sir Amadace*, ll. 794, 799–800: the variant reading of the Advocates MS here is 'Ther west no man wher he become'.

A key episode here, again unique to *Sir Amadace*, is the shipwreck which is the source of the hero's wealth. The fact that he gets rich by other means in other versions indicates its purely arbitrary nature, and helps explain what, in a purely literary narrative, would be an odd discrepancy. When he comes upon the wreck, the shore is covered not only with riches for the taking, but also with the corpses of the drowned. If Amadace had been a psychologically consistent character, scrupulous about the burial of the dead, he would surely have done something about these. But he does not. He is acting in folktale mode, passively following instructions, and the shipwreck is a pure motif, of local significance only: it is simply a source of wealth, and its other implications are irrelevant to the story.

So he takes the riches, as the White Knight had indicated that he should, and has no qualms about lying about them when accounting for them to the King. These are the local actions of a folktale hero, reacting only to a present situation, not the consistent acts of a psychological character. Amadace is in fact demonstrating his relationship to that other opportunist hero whose story is closely analogous to his, who made his fortune with the aid not of an old man, a servant, or even a fox, but a cat, who encouraged him, most successfully, to pass himself off as the Marquis of Carabas.[43]

---

43 Aarne/Thompson 545B. Liljeblad (*Die Tobiasgeschichte*, pp. 29, 37) seems to consider that Puss-in-Boots should be more closely related to the 'Grateful Dead' group of tales. See also Gerould, *The Grateful Dead*, pp. 42, 70.

The *Sege of Melayne*: a fifteenth-century reading

PHILLIPA HARDMAN

THE Middle English romance of the *Sege of Melayne* is something of a puzzle. Usually classed as one of the English romances of Charlemagne, it is almost unique among them in that no trace exists of a French original.[1] It survives in a single, incomplete manuscript copy of the mid-fifteenth century, in MS BL Additional 31042 (the London Thornton MS), lacking one or more leaves midway through the text and another one or more at the end.[2] It is thus missing the conclusion of the narrative: the story breaks off amid preparations for a battle. There is also considerable uncertainty about the genre of the poem. In a recent study Stephen Shepherd reviews and draws together the various different generic characteristics that have in the past been claimed for the *Sege of Melayne* – heroic (in the manner of a *chanson de geste*), homiletic, and hagiographic – to suggest that the romance is 'a kind of generic "hybrid" ' (a persuasive idea that would probably suit other Middle English romance narratives as well).[3]

In Shepherd's view, the *Sege* can best be understood as 'a true crusading poem', employing 'just the kind of images, incidents and attitudes that were

---

[1]   See Janet M. Cowen, 'The English Charlemagne Romances', *Roland and Charlemagne in Europe: Essays on the Reception and Transformation of a Legend*, ed. Karen Pratt (London, 1996), pp. 149–68; H. M. Smyser, 'Charlemagne Legends', *Manual*, pp. 80–100, 256–66; S. J. Herrtage, ed., *'The Sege off Melayne' and 'The Romance of Duke Rowland and Sir Otuell of Spayne' together with a fragment of 'The Song of Roland'*, EETS ES 35 (London, 1880); Maldwyn Mills, ed., *Six Middle English Romances*, 2nd edn (London, 1981); Stephen H. A. Shepherd, ed., *Middle English Romances* (New York, 1995). Quotations from the *Sege of Melayne* are taken from Shepherd's edition; those from *Sir Otuell* are taken from Herrtage's edition.
[2]   For discussion of the London Thornton MS, see John J. Thompson, *Robert Thornton and the London Thornton Manuscript, British Library, MS Additional 31042*, Manuscript Studies II (Cambridge, 1987) .
[3]   Stephen H. A. Shepherd, ' "This grete journee": The Sege of Melayne', *Romance in Medieval England*, eds Maldwyn Mills, Jennifer Fellows and Carol M. Meale (Cambridge, 1991), pp. 113–31.

71

the mainstay of medieval crusading propaganda'.[4] Among the features of the *Sege of Melayne* that persuade him of its active crusading spirit are certain similarities to *Capystranus*, a later Middle English tail-rhyme romance printed by de Worde in 1515, based on the crusade against the Turks culminating in the siege of Belgrade in 1456. As Shepherd remarks, comparison with *Capystranus* indicates that 'actual events on the Continent' could inspire 'a romance which, in Britain, then sustained a topical interest (and purpose) long after the original events were over'; but were the interest and purpose solely to do with 'a propagandistic crusading theme' (p. 122)? Douglas Gray, on the contrary, suggests a hagiographic impetus for the concentration on the part played by the eponymous friar, St John Capistrano, and for the intensification of the miraculous elements of the story; he remarks in this connection that 'the popular Charlemagne romances seem to have been in the author's mind'.[5] Indeed, some similarities between *Capystranus* and the *Sege of Melayne* are very marked and it may be that *Capystranus* can be of significant use in an attempt to understand the incomplete text of the *Sege of Melayne*.

I should like to propose a different perspective, starting from the evidence of readership shown in the unique copy of the poem in its context in the London Thornton MS. Stephen Shepherd distinguishes the *Sege of Melayne* from

> the other Charlemagne romances – or indeed other 'crusading' romances such as *Richard Coeur de Lion* or *The Siege of Jerusalem* [which] by comparison seem concerned less with persuading their readers to defend Christianity against its enemies than . . . with reaffirming Christian belief through . . . stories of past victories for the Faith (p. 117).

However, the manuscript evidence seems to go against this distinction; there are three romances in the London Thornton MS besides the *Sege of Melayne*: *Duke Rowlande and Sir Otuell* (another Charlemagne romance), *Richard Coeur de Lion* and the *Siege of Jerusalem*. It seems that the compiler of this collection saw no serious conflict of interest between the four romances – in fact, quite the reverse.

As has often been observed, the first four or five texts in this manuscript form a coherent historical and thematic sequence.[6] These are: an abbreviated text of the *Cursor Mundi* that stops at the end of Jesus's ministry, the *Northern Passion*, the *Siege of Jerusalem*, the *Sege of Melayne* and *Sir Otuell*. It is clear

---

4 Shepherd citing Dieter Mehl, *The Middle English Romances of the Thirteenth and Fourteenth Centuries* (London, 1968), pp. 153–4.
5 Douglas Gray, ed., *The Oxford Book of Late Medieval Verse and Prose* (Oxford, 1985), p. 459.
6 For discussion of this sequence, see Phillipa Hardman, 'Reading the Spaces: Pictorial Intentions in the Thornton Manuscripts, Lincoln Cathedral 91 and BL MS Add. 31042', *MÆ* 63 (1994), pp. 250–74.

from the ordering of the texts that the sequence takes its meaning from the centrally placed narrative of the Passion. The transitions from the *Cursor Mundi* to the *Northern Passion*, and from the *Northern Passion* to the *Siege of Jerusalem*, are marked by precise linking inscriptions in Latin which stress the centrality of the death of Christ: the *Siege of Jerusalem* is given the alternative title, 'Quomodo Titus et vaspasianus Obsederunt et distruxerunt Ierusalem et vi[n]dicarunt mortem domini Ihesu Christi'. There is no link from this text to the *Sege of Melayne*, although a space that might conceivably have been intended for one has been left at the appropriate place in the manuscript (fol. 66r). However, the *Sege of Melayne* does extend the sequence of biblical and historical material in an apt though different way, and the continuity of the texts is suggested by the narratives themselves. At the end of the *Siege of Jerusalem* Titus returns in triumph to Rome, having punished the Jews 'that torment trewe god'. This leads into what reads like the next episode in the sequence, despite the lapse in time, as the *Sege of Melayne* opens with the heathens in their turn overrunning Rome and offering every possible insult to God by laying waste the cities of Christendom, dispossessing the pope, destroying the images of Christ crucified and the Virgin in churches and abbeys and replacing them with heathen idols and torturing Christian people. Clearly, retribution is required again. Similar motivation also colours the opening of *Sir Otuell*: as the action begins, Charlemagne's intention is described as 'to kepe þe heythyn here/& struye there goddes Enymys' (47–8).

Any differences in form or style between these texts are obviously of no concern to the compiler: the governing consideration is their compatibility as episodes in Christian history. The *Northern Passion* ends with a scene which seems to point towards the following romances of revenge, in which 'Sir Pilate' instructs the four knights who guarded the tomb to conceal the fact that Jesus has risen and they swear to do so 'by þaire god Mahowne', thus conflating Jewish and Muslim enemies and identifying them both as idolatrous infidels.[7] The miracles performed by Jesus in His infancy and during His ministry in the gospel narrative are continued in the *Siege of Jerusalem* with the miraculous cure of Vespasian by the power of the vernicle, the relic of Christ's Holy Face imprinted on Veronica's veil. This theme links with the spectacular miracle of the crucifix in the *Sege of Melayne*, the crucifix functioning in this incident as a sort of memorial relic.

The last narrative in the sequence, the *Romance of Duke Rowlande and of Sir Otuell of Spayne*, appears as a sequel or companion romance to the *Sege of Melayne*, perhaps added by Thornton when it fortuitously became available.[8] Each of these romances is followed by a devotional lyric: the *Sege of Melayne*

---

7 See Matthew 28.11–15; the author assumes Pilate to be a Jewish leader, a not uncommon misconception (see, for example, the ballad 'Judas'). A similar conflation of Jews and Muslims may be seen in use of the term 'synagoge' in *Firumbras* for the place in which the Saracens keep their idols (246, 1388).

8 Hardman, 'Reading the Spaces', p. 264.

by a highly wrought poem to the Virgin, and *Sir Otuell* by another lyric of identical form, Lydgate's 'Cristes Passioun'. Both lyrics have a practical application, as becomes clear in the last stanza of each. The first concludes with a prayer to the Virgin to plead for us with her crucified son; the second ends with an envoy recommending that the poem be read once a day before the crucifix: 'No bettir socour, nor support in your neede/Than offte thynkyng on Crystys passioun.'[9]

This collection of texts in the London Thornton MS can thus be seen to constitute a complete history of Christian salvation from the creation through the redemption to the acts of Christ's heroes in the world, defending the Faith and overcoming God's enemies. The lyrics are carefully placed to encourage the reader's personal, devotional response to the Passion-centred narratives. In ordering the texts in this way, Thornton was not violently forcing the *Sege of Melayne* into an unnatural context but was responding to signals in the text that make this an entirely natural way to understand the poem.

It is precisely the interest in Charlemagne as champion of the Faith which motivated Caxton, in 1485, to print his *Lyf of the Noble and Crysten Prynce Charles the Grete*. After translating the preface from his source, the French prose *Fierabras*, in which the book is presented as 'made to thonour of the frenssh men', Caxton felt it necessary to add another preface emphasising the importance of the text as Christian history, presenting Charlemagne as one of the three Christian Worthies.[10] The stress Caxton lays on the function of his 'Life of Charlemagne' as Christian history is mirrored in the *Sege of Melayne*, and also in *Capystranus*, by a feature which is somewhat unusual in English versions of Continental sources, as noted by many commentators: the frequent reference to Charles's French forces as 'our men', 'our Cristyns', and so on. The same device appears in *Sir Otuell* in descriptions of encounters between the Saracens and 'oure folkes' (1528), 'oure batell(s)' (1124, 1454, 1464). Indeed, throughout both Charlemagne romances in the Thornton MS 'our' men are normally identified as 'the Cristynde', 'the Cristen oste', 'the Cristen folke', 'oure Cristen knyghtis', not as the French, and the territory which they defend is not only France but the whole realm of 'Cristyante' or 'Crystyndome'.[11] A clear example of this deliberate construction of the

---

9   H. N. McCracken, ed., *Lydgate's Minor Poems I: Religious Poems*, EETS ES 107 (London, 1910), pp. 216–21 (ll. 119–20).

10   S. J. Herrtage, ed., *Caxton's Lyf of Charles the Grete*, EETS ES 36–7 (London, 1880–1).

11   There are just four references to men 'of Fraunce' in the *Sege of Melayne* (281, 880, 1061, 1294) and none at all in *Sir Otuell*, and in the *Sege* it is the treacherous Ganelon who repeatedly refers to France. *Sir Otuell* can be compared with the other two English versions of the French *Otinel*, *Otuel* and *Otuel and Roland*: in both there is frequent reference to Charles's men as the French and the source is cited as 'in frensche' (*Otuel and Roland*, 717), 'in romaunse' (*Otuel*, 716), whereas *Sir Otuell* has no mention of a French source and no reference to the Christian side as the French. See Mary Isabelle O'Sullivan, ed., *'Firumbras' and 'Otuel and Roland'*, EETS OS 198 (London, 1935); Sidney J. H. Herrtage, ed., *'The Taill of*

Christian reader's response in the *Sege of Melayne* can be seen in a narratorial aside during a mêlée in which there was 'many a Sarazene slayne':

> We may thank Gode that is in heven
> That lent us myghte and mayne;
> Thay sloughe tham downn with swerdis bright;
> The Cristynnd faughte in Goddis righte.   (1098–1101)

Maldwyn Mills follows Smyser in surmising that these first-person phrases in the *Sege of Melayne* derive from a lost French source ('nos gens' being a common collocation in *chansons de geste*) and suggests that the density of such phrases in the English poem must be deliberate, 'an attempt to naturalise a foreign mode of poetry so that its new audience might be totally involved in it' (p. xii).[12] It is not as odd as it may seem, however, that an English readership at the time of the Hundred Years War should have been able to identify with the forces of a King of France as Christian Emperor in the romances of Charlemagne: Edward III implicitly declared himself the rightful heir of Charlemagne when in 1340 at Ghent he solemnly assumed the arms and title of King of France by right of inheritance through his mother, Isabella of France, and his great-great-grandson Henry VI was indeed crowned King of France at Saint-Denis in 1431. The claim of the English monarch to the French throne was not in principle given up despite the loss of almost all possessions in France by 1453.[13] The idea of the King of England as a Christian Emperor is one that fifteenth-century English kings actively sought to encourage. Henry V revived Richard II's title 'Most Christian King' (a title bestowed by the pope on Philip IV of France, grandfather of Edward III, in 1311), and it was used by Henry VI, Edward IV and Henry VII.[14] The claim

---

Rauf Coilyear' with the Fragments of 'Roland and Vernagu' and 'Otuel', EETS ES 39 (London, 1882).

[12] See Smyser, *Manual*, p. 93; W. R. J. Barron, *English Medieval Romance* (London, 1987), p. 96; Cowen, 'English Charlemagne Romances', pp. 157–8. Shepherd elaborates Mills's suggestion to support his view of the poem as a crusading romance: 'The reader is repeatedly invited to feel at one with the cause espoused and to join in the action which supports the cause' (p. 131). However, the density of first-person references in the *Sege of Melayne* is not unique (*pace* Shepherd, pp. 130–1); *Firumbras* has an elaborate system of narratorial comments punctuating the action with appeals to the audience on behalf of 'oure cristyn knyhtys' (53, 98, 205, etc.).

[13] Henry V gained the throne of France for himself and his heirs in the treaty of Troyes in 1420; Edward IV was recognised by Charles of Burgundy as the rightful King of France in a treaty of 1474. Henry VI had Great Seals as King of France with the legend 'Henricvs Dei Gracia Francorvm et Anglie Rex' (see A. B. Wyon, 'The Seals of Henry VI as King of France', *Journal of the British Archaeological Association* 40 (1884), pp. 275–89). The title 'Rex Franciae' was still in use on Georgian coinage.

[14] Edward IV is described by Caxton in the colophon to *Charles the Grete* as 'the noble and most Christian king', echoing the title he attributes to Charlemagne himself. Caxton ends two other major chivalric texts with reference to Richard III and Henry VII as 'kyng of Englond & of Fraunce', and styles Henry VII 'the hiest & most cristen kyng & prince of the

to be a Christian Emperor is symbolised by the adoption of a new imperial crown of state, a closed crown surmounted by a cross, probably first worn by Henry V, which figures significantly in royal iconography.[15] The part of France that features most prominently in the romances of Charlemagne (apart from Paris) is of course that adjacent to Spain, and it was over this very area, ancient Gascony, that the English had the longest actual dominion.

For all these reasons, translators, writers and copyists of Charlemagne romances in English in the fourteenth and fifteenth centuries may well have considered the material as much the inheritance of their English readers as it was of the French, both in terms of their general Christian heritage and more specifically in respect of their French connections. During the Hundred Years War it could even have been thought a patriotic act to appropriate the texts, claiming them for England by means of translation or imitation just as the claim to France itself was pursued by means of war.

Both *Capystranus* and Caxton's *Charles the Grete* contain accounts of Charles's recovery of the relics of the Passion. The connection with the cult of the relics is of course a major feature of French Charlemagne texts and the importance of the relics is not diminished in the Middle English romances. It seems very likely that it is the knowledge of their presence in the abbey of St Denis that lies behind the remarkable cluster of references in the *Sege of Melayne* to processions and pilgrimages made to the abbey by Bishop Turpin and King Charles, and to the miraculous provision of white horses and the miraculous bell-ringing that mark Rowlande's visit to the abbey on his return to Paris. There may also be an oblique reference to the most important relic won by Charles, the crown of thorns (which Charles himself wears in *Roland and Vernagu* and *Firumbras*), in Turpin's rebuke to the king for his decision to stay at home:

> Criste for the sufferde mare dere,
> Sore wondede with a spere,
> And werede a crown of thorne.'   (701–3)[16]

world'. See Alfred T. P. Byles, ed., *The Book of the Ordre of Chyualry* (1484), EETS OS 168 (London, 1926) and *The Book of Fayttes of Armes and of Chyualrye* (1489), EETS OS 189 (London, 1932).

[15] The imperial crown was an important element in royal iconography from the mid-fifteenth century. Henry V is frequently represented as wearing it (see three portraits in Kathleen L. Scott, *Later Gothic Manuscripts 1390–1490*, Survey of Manuscripts Illuminated in the British Isles VI, 2 vols (London, 1996), ills 304, 363, 498); it appears on the foundation charter of King's College, Cambridge (MS Mun, KC-18-N1, 1446) surmounting the arms of Henry VI, greatly enlarged and supported by angels; Edward IV is portrayed wearing it on a genealogy roll that also contains a striking frieze of seven kings and dukes representing Edward's titles, in which *Rex Anglie* stands between *Rex Francie* and *Rex Castellie* and wears an imperial crown (Philadelphia, Free Library, MS European 201). The crown appears on the Great Seal of England from 1471 and on coinage from 1489.

[16] The spear of the Passion, not one of the relics given to Charles in the French sources, was added to the relics in English romances of Charlemagne (see Barron, pp. 99–100). Turpin's allusion may then be doubly significant.

While there is no explicit reference to the cult of relics in the *Sege of Melayne*, it does show strong signs of interest in images of, and devotion to, the crucified Christ and the Virgin Mary. The first part of the *Sege of Melayne* tells how the heathen forces of the Sultan Arabas overrun Italy, make war upon Christendom and torture and kill the Christians, making martyrs of men, women and children. Throughout the land, in a symbolic crowning act of destruction, the heathens burn 'the emagery that ther solde bee/Bothe the Rode and the Marie free' (25–6) and set up their idols in place of the holy images. The choice of these particular images is of course highly significant. Not only were they prominently displayed in parish churches (where the Sultan's men no doubt found them), but the crucifix and the Madonna were also the two most frequent images in devotional art, often paired in diptych representations. The awareness of Christ crucified and His Virgin mother as twin recipients of prayer and devotion is shown throughout the *Sege of Melayne* in the forms of intercession used by the Christians, but the Saracens' destruction of the crucifixes and images of the Virgin informs the romance in a more fundamental way than these simple and commonplace verbal formulae.

This unequivocal act of sacrilege has a structural function in the narrative, for it demands answering acts of divine intervention by which the undiminished power of Christ crucified and of Mary may be demonstrated. One such act is spectacularly provided at the climax of the first, disastrous encounter between the Christian knights and the Saracens. The Sultan insists that Rowlande and his three companions, the sole survivors of the 40,000-strong Christian army, renounce their faith, to which Rowlande answers with a summary of the Creed: [17]

> 'For sothe, thou Sowdane, trowe thou moste
> One the Fader and the Sone and the Holy Goste:
> Thire thre are alle in one
> That borne was of Marye fre,
> Sythen for us dyede one a tree –
> In other trowe we none.' (409–14)

The Sultan seizes on the mention of the cross to pour scorn on gods that he can burn by the hundred like any 'rotyn tree', and sends for a crucifix to prove his point. An image of the suffering Christ is brought, 'Fourmede ewenn als He gane blede' (428) – a typically realistic late-medieval representation; the Christian knights immediately 'bygane thaire Crede', signalling their faith, and Rowlande prays for a miracle:

---

[17] There is a parallel for this detailed exposition of the Christian faith in *Otuel and Roland*, where the episode of Otuel's claiming the fight with Clarel on the strength of Clarel's having insulted his Christian beliefs is extended by Otuel's twelve-line approximate recitation of the Creed (1331–42). A further parallel exists in the elaborate catechising between Roland and Vernagu taken from the *Pseudo-Turpin* (*Roland and Vernagu*, 665–784).

> . . . 'Thou that was borne of a may,
> Schewe thou, Lorde, thi meracle this day,
> That with thi blode us boghte.'   (431–3)

The crucifix miraculously withstands all attempts to burn it but instead strikes the Saracens insensate as if with lightning, allowing the four Christian knights to throw them all into their own fire.[18] Rowlande acknowledges that 'this meracle es schewede thorowe Goddis grace' (479).

The whole episode is constructed with an underlying parallel between the experience of the four knights and the story of Christ's Passion: the knights pray 'To Criste that Judas solde' (466), establishing a link to their own situation, betrayed by the advice of the treacherous Ganelon; the Sultan taunts them when at first nothing happens in an echo of the chief priests and scribes at Calvary: 'How solde he than helpe another man/That for hymselfe no gyn ne kan?' (443–4); the cross finally splits asunder with a crack that seems to burst the whole building, recalling the rending of the Temple veil at the moment of Christ's death (467–9).[19] This parallel has a double effect: first, the miracle becomes a representation of the Crucifixion itself, as well as a supernatural defeat of the infidels, a dramatic reminder of Christ's redemptive suffering, like the enactments of the Passion in the mystery cycles or the vivid meditations in which late-medieval devotees imagined themselves present at the scene of Christ's death. It recalls Charlemagne's prayer in *Charles the Grete* (and its French and Latin antecedents) when he sees the relics of the Passion, that Our Lord 'for the glorye of hys name presently wold renewe the myracles of hys holy passyon' (pp. 35–6). Secondly, the ordeal of the knights is seen as an imitation of Christ's Passion, like the sufferings of the martyrs, in line with the martyrdom claimed for the 40,000 slaughtered knights who, spared by their wounds from the pains of hell, will 'hy to heven one heghe' (360).

Although the miracle allows the four knights to escape after killing the Sultan, the narrative informs us immediately that the Saracens crowned Garcy instead, and Rowlande has to tell Bishop Turpin that all 40,000 men are dead. The story clearly requires further miraculous intervention to complete the Christian victory and, as a parallel to the miracle of the crucifix, to reassert the power of the Virgin after the desecration of her images. As the conclusion of this unique text is lacking, there is no way of knowing precisely how the story might have brought this about, but a peculiarly striking episode seems to have been designed to lead up to just such an action. When Rowlande reveals the extent of the defeat, Turpin responds with fierce grief and roundly rebukes Mary for failing to protect the Christian knights, even though they were fighting as her own champions:

---

18 There may be influence here from the incident in *Firumbras* when Naymes blinds the Saracens by showing them the relics of the Passion (1413–18).
19 See Matthew 27.41–42, 51.

'A! Mary mylde, whare was thi myght
That thou lete thi men thus to dede be dighte
That wighte and worthy were?
Art thou noghte halden of myghtis moste,
Full conceyvede of the Holy Goste?
Me ferlys of thy fare.

Had thou noghte, Marye, yitt bene borne,
Ne had noghte oure gud men thus bene lorne –
The wyte is all in the!
Thay faughte holly in thy ryghte,
That thus with dole to dede es dyghte –
A! Marie, how may this bee?' (548–59)

As in Rowlande's reply to the Sultan, the language of Turpin's outburst has
doctrinal overtones. Mary is addressed by the phrase 'of myghtis moste', often
appropriately used of Almighty God and here suggesting a belief in Mary's
pre-eminent power, as shown in popular contemporary devotions such as the
Madonna of Mercy, that is close to heterodox Mariolatry.[20] In the following
line, the reference to her conception without original sin is expressed in the
words used in the Apostles' Creed for the Incarnation of Christ: 'full conceyvede of the Holy Goste' ('conceptus est de Spiritu Sancto'). It makes an
exceptionally strong statement of faith which is interestingly similar to the
phrase used in a fourteenth-century Carmelite sermon on the Virgin Mary:
'concepta spiritus sancti gratia pura et immaculata ab originali culpa'.[21] The
Immaculate Conception of the Virgin was a highly controversial issue in the
fourteenth and fifteenth centuries, the Carmelites and Franciscans being
zealous promoters of the doctrine in opposition to the stringent theology of
the Dominicans.[22] The formulae used in Turpin's speech thus indicate a
strong devotion to the Virgin, drawing on both popular and learned
traditions.

But Turpin's rebuke to this powerful figure scarcely fits the idea of Marian
piety. Mills comments on 'the extreme oddness of this passage' and on Turpin's 'astonishing' behaviour, suggesting that it may be based on a scene such as
that in the *King of Tars* (646–57) where a defeated sultan destroys the images
of his gods.[23] A similar motif occurs in a number of Charlemagne romances:
in *Otuel and Roland*, for example, an episode closer to the *Sege of Melayne*

---

[20] For discussion of the cult of the Madonna of Mercy, see P. Perdrizet, *La Vierge de Miséri-
corde* (Paris, 1908); see also *The New Catholic Encyclopedia*, 17 vols (New York, 1967), IX,
pp. 359–69; Georg Söll, *Mariologie, Handbuch der Dogmengeschichte*, ed. Michael Schmaus et
al., III, 4 (Freiburg, 1978); Hilda Graef, *Mary: A History of Doctrine and Devotion*, 2nd edn
(London, 1985).
[21] See Valerie Edden, 'Marian Devotion in a Carmelite Sermon Collection of the Late
Middle Ages', *Mediaeval Studies* 57 (1995), pp. 101–29 (p. 107).
[22] See Edden, 'Marian Devotion', p. 107, n. 14.
[23] Mills, *Six Middle English Romances*, pp. xiii, 194.

shows Garcy and his knights rebuking their gods at length for allowing Clarel to be killed (1529–58).[24] It is surely problematic, however, that such an echo creates an effect in which it seems that, in Mills's words, Turpin 'is being presented as pagan rather than Christian' (p. xiii). A striking instance of the same effect occurs in *Firumbras*, where parallel episodes show first Charlemagne and then the Saracen Balam offering violence to the sacred images of their two religions before being restrained by the good counsel of a knight and repenting (1113–32; 1385–1402). Charles threatens: 'The vygours and þe autar, þat in holy chyrche be3th found,/I schal hem adoun falle and bete to þe grounde', concluding: 'Ne schal I neuer worschyp god, whyles þat y leue' (1119–22).

Shepherd sees Turpin's rhetoric in the context of crusading literature, by comparison with which he finds it 'is not altogether extraordinary', and draws an analogy with a similar outburst in *Capystranus* (p. 125). Gray points out that the basis of this motif in *Capystranus* is to be found in a chronicle account of the siege, where the friar appeals to God, saying 'Come, lest the Turks and unbelievers say, Where is God?' (p. 460). This is precisely the tenor of the first part of Capystranus's complaint, as he asks God 'Why hast thou forgoten us?' and begs Him to 'Loke on thy people that do thus dye; . . . And helpe thy men to save' (469–73).[25] The language here has clear echoes of the Psalms:

> I will say to God: Why hast thou forgotten me? and why go I mourning whilst my enemy afflicteth me? Whilst they say to me day by day: Where is thy God?
> (Ps. 41. 10–11; Douai version)

> Help us O God our saviour: and for the glory of thy name O Lord deliver us . . . Lest they should say among the Gentiles: Where is their God? And let him be made known among the nations before our eyes, by the revenging the blood of thy servants which hath been shed. (Ps. 78. 9–10)

Indeed, the friar reproaches God by reminding Him how often he says the Psalms, among his other service, and threatens that if God lets His men die, he is determined 'Forever to forsake thy laye' (486–8), much like Charlemagne in *Firumbras*. The Virgin Mary is similarly reproached and threatened (489–500). The climax of Capystranus's prayer is a plea for a miracle by which God may show that He is still as powerful as when He stopped the sun for Charlemagne, or parted the Red Sea for the Israelites (501–12). It is this second element of his complaint, echoing the Psalmist's demand that God show His strength in vengeance, that may provide the clue to understanding

---

24 'Firumbras' and 'Otuel and Roland', pp. 45, 106–7. The parallel passage in *Sir Otuell* gives a comparison for Turpin's vow not to eat or drink until Milan be taken (1190, 1349) in Garcy's swearing 'by appolyne,/Þat mete ne drynke scholde done hym gude/are he struyed hade Cristen blode' (1347–9).

25 For a modern edition of *Capystranus*, see Shepherd, *Middle English Romances*, pp. 391–408.

the point of Turpin's parallel outburst towards the Virgin Mary in the *Sege of Melayne*.

This strange incident can best be explained in the context of the popular story cycles of the 'Miracles of the Virgin'. As Peter Whiteford points out, the devotional attitude of the miracle stories centres on the position of Mary as Queen of Heaven and intercessory mediatrix between God and sinful men.[26] Although theologians carefully defined this doctrine in relation to Christ's redemptive mediation, it was all too easily interpreted in popular devotion as attributing miraculous saving power directly to the Virgin. For example, in a story printed by Wynkyn de Worde, a monk judged to hell for negligence in saying the divine office is saved by calling on the Virgin: 'And as the deuyll began to take power of hym, he cryed and sayd, "Holy Mary, helpe me!" And anone our blessyd Lady delyuered hym from the fende.'[27] In the well-known story of the pregnant Abbess, the Virgin not only saves the penitent Abbess from disgrace but also pardons her sin.[28] Other miracles show Mary's power over the elements as she commands storms to cease, saves her favourites from the sea, or protects them from fire.[29] This is precisely how Turpin views the Virgin in his tirade, seeing her chief characteristic as her 'myght', and appealing to her reputation for surpassing power ('halden of myghtis moste') and her notorious favouritism towards those who honour her ('Thay faughte holly in thy ryghte') in his disappointed expectation of victory.

Turpin's truculent attitude to Mary resembles that shown in a range of miracle stories where a devotee of the Virgin rebukes her for failing to prevent some catastrophe, after which Mary miraculously reverses the disaster. For example, several stories concern mothers who have lost their children despite relying on the protection of the Virgin, and they complain vehemently at her negligence, even seeking to coerce her into restoring the lost child by taking the image of the child Jesus as hostage.[30] Turpin's intemperate casting away of his crozier and mitre and his avowed intention to take to the wars instead (542–7) is perhaps a similarly coercive stratagem. A close parallel to the tone of Turpin's outburst is found in the story told of St John Damascene (a noted proponent of Mariological doctrine), where the saint upbraids the Virgin for not preventing the loss of his hand in a false prosecution:

26 Peter Whiteford, ed., *The Myracles of Oure Lady from Wynkyn de Worde's edition*, Middle English Texts 23 (Heidelberg, 1990), pp. 11–17.
27 *The Myracles of Oure Lady*, no. 20, p. 57.
28 For lists and titles of tales, see H. D. L. Ward, *Catalogue of Romances in the Department of Manuscripts in the British Museum*, 3 vols (London, 1883–1910), II, pp. 586–740; also Whiteford's index of miracles in Middle English (pp. 134–8).
29 Ward, 'Light on the Masthead', 'Pilgrim in the Sea', 'Childbirth in the Sea', 'Child Saved from Drowning', 'Ave Maris Stella', 'Jew of Bourges'.
30 Ward, 'Child-Christ Seized as a Pledge', 'Child Rescued from Wolf', 'Boy Unhurt in Fire'.

'Is this, my Lady, the reward of my services? . . . For this hand oft in writing prepared hymns in thy praise, . . . Where were you when I suffered my injuries?
Behold, to my shame, ay and to yours also, the severed hand of your follower
hangs in the church.'[31]

Turpin also expresses a sense of injustice at Mary's failure to act on behalf of
those who espoused her cause and he accuses her of culpable negligence in
letting them be killed. A similar reproach is levelled against her in a version
of the widely known story of the monk with an ulcerated mouth cured by
Mary's milk, when the monk's guardian angel bewails the sufferings of the
devout man: 'O Lady of Mercy, is this the reward, this the honour given to the
faithful?'[32] Mary responds immediately by curing the monk, 'as if to make
amends for the neglect of her servant with which she was charged' (p. 54),
just as she restores St John Damascene's hand and returns the children
unharmed to their mothers. However, the *Sege of Melayne*, unlike these
simple miracle narratives, defers the satisfaction until later, in characteristic
romance fashion.[33]

In the next section of the romance, the Christians and Saracens encounter
again at Milan. Charles, in single combat with the self-styled 'chefe of hethyn
thede', is invited to abandon the fight, give up his Christian faith and be
rewarded with two kingdoms. Turpin bursts out: 'A, Charles, thynk appon
Marie brighte/To whayme our lufe es lentt!' (1041–2), then addresses himself
to the Virgin, as if giving her a second chance:

> 'And if ever that thou hade any myghte,
> Latt it now be sene in syghte
> What pousté that thou hase:
> Latte never oure kynge with dynt of brande
> Be slayne with yone Sarazene hande,
> Ne ende, Lady, in this place.' (1043–8)

Again, the focus is on Mary's 'myghte' and 'pousté' in her role as patroness
with power over life and death. Like Capystranus, Turpin sounds an echo of
Psalm 78 with its challenge to God to save His people in the sight of the heathens, and as in the Miracles of the Virgin, the challenge is based on utter
confidence in Mary's power to grant whatever is asked, despite the conten-
tious tone.

It is likely, then, that the end of the romance involved a miracle of some
kind in which Mary intervened in the course of events on behalf of her

---

31 Johannes Herolt, *Miracles Of the Blessed Virgin Mary*, trans. C. C. Swinton Bland
(London, 1928), no. XXXIII, pp. 55–7; see Ward, 'John of Damascus'.
32 Herolt, no. XXXII, pp. 53–5; see Ward, 'Milk: Tongue and Lips'.
33 It is interesting that in the version of 'The Lost Foot Restored' found in the Vernon MS
(Bodleian Library, MS Eng. poet. a.1), the miracle is told as evidence that the Virgin always
answers the prayers of the sick and sorrowful in the end, though she may delay her answer for
a long time to encourage perseverance in prayer.

knights, perhaps, as is the case in numerous miracle stories, acting through a statue or painted image in a way that would parallel the miracle of the crucifix and avenge the insult inflicted by the Saracens' destruction of her images. A number of tales tell how an image of the Virgin miraculously assisted her faithful in battle or saved a city;[34] others show her jealous concern for the reverence due to her image, often punishing blasphemers with death.[35]

The 550 lines remaining of the romance consist of a suspenseful series of incidents, seeming on the whole to promise a Christian victory but interspersed with setbacks such as Turpin's being wounded twice and the arrival of Saracen reinforcements. The state of play at the point where the text breaks off suggests that the Christians have only to make a final assault on the walls to win Milan. They have already killed 60,000 Saracens, given God the glory for the victory, and Charles has distributed honours to his men. If the ending of the story was to afford an example of the power of the Virgin Mary by a conclusive miracle then two possibilities suggest themselves. There is an analogue for a miraculous end to a siege in another Charlemagne romance, *Roland and Vernagu*, where Charles twice takes a city when its walls fall down in response to his prayers – and in Charles's prophetic dream near the beginning of the *Sege of Melayne* an angel did indeed 'dange' down the city walls (127–9).

Alternatively, and perhaps more appropriately, the Virgin might be expected to perform a miracle to save the life of the wounded Turpin, whose plight in the last complete stanza of the text moves Charles to lament his seemingly inevitable death with tears and a generous eulogy. The relation of the *Sege of Melayne* to the rest of the Charlemagne cycle appears to be that of a 'prequel', dealing with events prior to the stories of Otinel and Roncesvalles, in both of which Turpin has a part to play. Turpin's vow to go without food, drink, sleep or medical attention until Milan be taken has brought him to this death-like state, causing the whole army to mourn for him – but it also, as a narrative device, requires both the successful conclusion of the siege and the miraculous return to life of the Bishop. Who better to show her power in this way than the Virgin, the almighty Lady of the miracle stories whom Turpin challenged?

In following the *Sege of Melayne* with the Marian lyric, 'O florum flos', Thornton seems to have recognised this Marian emphasis in the romance. The poem elaborately praises Mary's beauty, feature by feature, and the artificiality of its form and descriptive language coupled with references to her skin 'Moste merueylously depaynttede 3ongly & white' (fol. 80r) and to the angels kneeling before her 'shryne' and 'Image' (fol. 81r) strongly suggest the model of a contemporary statue or devotional painting of the Virgin and

---

34 Ward, 'Arrow Intercepted', 'Parmese Army aided by the Virgin'; 'Purification' (Whiteford, 'How the Virgin's Image ended the Plague'), 'Plague at Rome'.
35 Ward, 'The Virgin's Image Insulted', 'The Bleeding Child-Christ', 'Scoffer at Mary-Image Beaten', 'Saracens cannot Deface Mary-Image'.

Child.[36] The prayer with which the lyric concludes asks Mary to display her breast to Christ, that He might show His wounds to His Father on our behalf – a traditional chain of intercession exactly in the spirit of the miracles of the Virgin (one of which is known as 'The Virgin Bares Her Breast').[37] It sets Turpin's devotion to Mary in a wider context of affective prayer to the Mother of God.

Turpin's glad acceptance of his suffering, which has been read as part of a specifically crusade-oriented heroic piety, also has a wider application when seen in context in the Thornton MS. He explains his refusal to let his wounds be tended in a way that represents his behaviour as an imitation of Christ:

> 'What! wenys thou, Charls,' he said, 'that I faynte bee,
> For a spere was in my thee,
> A glace thorowte my syde?
> Criste for me sufferde mare;
>
> He askede no salve to His sare,
> Ne no more sall I this tyde.'   (1343–8)

Lydgate's lyric 'Cristes Passioun' which is grouped with the romance in the Thornton MS provides a gloss on this passage. Each stanza exhorts the reader constantly to remember Christ's Passion; in one stanza Turpin's action is precisely echoed as Christ says: 'To ffynde thy salve my flessh was al to-rent,/Whan thou art woundid, thynk on my passioun'. The earlier description of the spear wound in Turpin's side (1301–5), a laceration measuring 'a schaftemonde of his flesche', recalls the popular devotional images of the wound in Christ's side and the much copied 'mensura vulneris'.[38] Turpin's is a particularly literal imitation of Christ, but the point stressed in Lydgate's poem is that any affliction, any 'worldly dystresse' and especially the 'hour whan þu shalt die' (31, 111), is an opportunity for everyone to remember and imitate Christ in His Passion. Read in the devotional context provided in the Thornton MS, Turpin's extreme behaviour and extravagant language can in part be seen as a highly coloured narrative example of the abandonment of

---

36 The angels are described as kneeling in homage to Mary's 'pure Image/Chefe chosen chaste trone of þe Trynite'. This strongly suggests a devotional image of the *Vierge ouvrante* type, in which the hollow model of the Virgin opens to reveal within a further devotional image of the Trinity known as the Throne of Grace or the Mercy Seat Trinity. See, for example, Henk van Os, ed., *The Art of Devotion in the Late Middle Ages in Europe, 1300–1500*, trans. Michael Hoyle (London, 1994), pp. 50–7, plate 16.

37 See Ward, p. 635.

38 See Eamon Duffy, *The Stripping of the Altars: Traditional Religion in England 1400–1580* (New Haven, 1992), p. 245. The *mensura vulneris* has a particular relevance in this romance context, for in one variant of the popular so-called Letter to Charlemagne the legend asserts that Charlemagne was instructed to carry into battle 'a representation or measure of the side Wound of Christ' (Duffy, pp. 273–5). There is an interesting parallel to Turpin's Christ-like wound in *Firumbras* where Charlemagne, fighting to free his men and to regain the relics of the Passion, is wounded 'in fyue places of hys body' (1620), an allusion pointed up shortly afterwards by Firumbras's appealing to 'goddys wowndys fyue' (1698).

self and identification with the sufferings of Christ traditionally recommended in spiritual writings but with a new fervour in late-medieval piety.

Sir Otuell, the companion romance that Thornton apparently decided to append to the *Sege of Melayne*, shares its explicit appeal to Christian readers to identify with Charlemagne and the douzepers as historic defenders of their Faith against 'goddes Enemy'. Both poems are remotely based on Charlemagne's campaign in Lombardy and confine their action to the two locations of Paris and Lombardy. One possible reason why writers and readers in the fourteenth and fifteenth centuries were interested in romances dealing with tyrannical despots ruling in Lombardy lies in the notoriety of the Signori, the 'tyrants of Lombardy' taken by Chaucer and Gower as stereotypes of wicked rulers known for their cruelty and debauchery.[39] The reputation of the most famous of the Signori, the Visconti of Milan, may well have had something to do with the choice of Milan as the 'riche cité' occupied by a tyrant given over to lechery (*Sege*, 866–74).[40] The fall and death of Bernabò Visconti in 1385 was widely reported as a cause for general satisfaction.[41] In both poems, then, Charlemagne's defeat of a Lombard tyrant might have been taken to represent the triumph of good and virtuous rule over the vicious and corrupt.

Sir Otuell also shares the prominence given in the *Sege of Melayne* to the Virgin Mary; for example, Charles urges Rowlande to fight 'In þe name of Marie of Heuen' (447) and Otuell, once converted, declares: 'I make avowe to mylde Marie,/that I hafe now chosen to my lady' (643–4). As in the *Sege of Melayne*, the action in *Sir Otuell* turns upon a miracle, but here it is the appearance of the dove of the Holy Spirit precipitating Otuell's conversion and baptism (577–85) rather than any direct divine intervention in the action on behalf of beleaguered Christians, in keeping with the central motif of conversion in the Otuel story. However, the abbreviated conclusion in this version, which disposes of Garcy in three brief lines (1573–5) in order to emphasise Otuell's happy ending with his wedding and a feast to celebrate his newly established status: 'A gud Cristyn man was hee' (1593), suggests that here too, an effort is being made to relate the romance to the experience of the ordinary Christian reader.

Caxton's output indicates that there was a ready market in the late fifteenth century for stories of the three Christian Worthies, Charlemagne, Arthur and Godfrey of Boloyne.[42] It is perhaps not surprising therefore, es-

---

[39] See Phillipa Hardman, 'Chaucer's Tyrants of Lombardy', *Review of English Studies* 31 (1980), pp. 172–8.

[40] Shepherd, ' "This grete journee" ', notes that Pope John XXII preached a crusade against the Visconti in 1321–24; while I think it unlikely that this was the impetus behind a lost propagandist French romance (p. 118), it may have contributed to the choice of Milan as the setting for what was perhaps, as Barron suggests, a 'carbon-copy' sequel to translated Charlemagne romances, 'imitating a proven formula' (p. 96).

[41] See Hardman, 'Chaucer's Tyrants of Lombardy', pp. 173–4.

[42] See Carol M. Meale, 'Caxton, de Worde, and the Publication of Romance in Late Medieval England', *The Library*, sixth series, 14 (1992), pp. 283–98 (pp. 294–5).

pecially in view of the English claim to France, that writers earlier in the century, and copyists such as Robert Thornton, should choose romances of Charlemagne as well as Arthur for their compositions and compilations. Thornton's interest in the lives of world conquerors and his selective reading of the texts he copied are evident in his treatment of the alliterative *Morte Arthure* and the *Prose Life of Alexander*, where he seems to have been impressed by his heroes' progressive accumulation of empire above all, and in his title for *Richard Coeur de Lion*: 'The Romance of Kyng Richerd þe Conqueroure'.[43] It is therefore all the more striking that Thornton made no attempt to incorporate either of his Charlemagne romances into this pattern of what could be seen as a nostalgic harking-back to some former age of glorious imperial might, whether imaged as the British Arthurian past or the lost power of Christendom, as seen from the fragmented and uncertain world of mid-fifteenth-century England. He must have had an overriding sense of these texts as primarily contributing to the Christian edification of the reader.

In view of the unusually central and positive role in the *Sege of Melayne* given to the ecclesiastical hero, Turpin, it is perhaps not unlikely that the poem is the work of a clerical author. Certainly, the learned character of Turpin's allusion to the doctrine of the Immaculate Conception suggests as much. The English romances of Charlemagne that derive from French sources are marked by a strain of religious didacticism as seen in the passages cited above from *Roland and Vernagu* and *Otuel and Roland*. Indeed, the motif of the converted Saracen, which as Cowen points out is a predominant theme in the English Charlemagne romances (p. 153), provides a natural opportunity for catechesis as Christian knights seek to convey the essential truths of the Christian faith to unbelievers. No doubt one aim of such passages was to remind the reader or listener of these same truths. The author of the *Sege of Melayne* perhaps saw the potential of a romance of Christian chivalry of this kind as a vehicle for reinforcing some basic religious instruction and for expressing sentiments of fervour and devotion to the Christian faith that were equally appropriate to fictional heroes and to real-life listeners and readers.

Thus the *Sege of Melayne*, uniting themes of Christian instruction, religious revenge, miraculous power and affective devotion, fits very appropriately into its mid-fifteenth-century context in the London Thornton MS. If we accept the date usually proposed for the composition of the romance, 1400 or soon after, then Thornton's reading and contextualising of the *Sege of Melayne* gives us near-contemporary evidence for an understanding of the poem as primarily affirmative of the reader's Christian faith in terms both of orthodox doctrine and of popular devotion.

---

43 Hardman, 'Reading the Spaces', pp. 255–6.

Identity, Narrative and Participation: defining a context for the Middle English Charlemagne romances

ROBERT WARM

BEHIND the production of the Middle English Charlemagne romances there resides a paradox, a paradox which this paper seeks to explain. The mystery is simply this. Why was it that during a period of prolonged Anglo-French hostility, in a conflict which many commentators have identified as being instrumental in establishing a sense of English national identity,[1] romances which dealt with French heroes, and French military successes, were being composed, copied, circulated and read throughout England?[2] The answer to this question proves to be surprisingly simple. The Middle English Charlemagne romances are celebrating Christian heroes who happen to be French, rather than French heroes who happen to be Christian. They are deliberately ignoring the deadly rivalry between the two countries, and constructing an idealised vision of the past, within which true Christian knights fought the infidel rather than one another. That this is the case has, to some extent, already been suggested by Stephen Shepherd, who has opened up the debate about the contextual situation of *The Sege of Melayne*. His suggestion that this poem could best be understood in the context of crusade propaganda clearly recognises the status of the participants as Christian rather than French knights.[3] However, the idea that these poems were propaganda for a crusade misunderstands the development of the crusading ideal in the late

---

[1] The role of the Hundred Years War in establishing a sense of 'Englishness' has been noted by a number of commentators. See J. Barnie, *War in Medieval Society: Social Values and the Hundred Years War, 1337–99* (London, 1974), especially ch. 4, 'Patriots and Patriotism', pp. 97–116. Also, C. Allmand, *The Hundred Years War: England and France at War. c.1300–1450* (Cambridge, 1988), pp. 136–50.

[2] In terms of date, all of the texts I discuss here were produced in the late fourteenth and early fifteenth centuries. Indeed, of all the Middle English Charlemagne romances, it is only the two contained in the Auchinleck manuscript (c.1330–40) which cannot be dated to this period.

[3] S. Shepherd, ' "This grete journee": *The Sege of Melayne*', *Romance in Medieval England*, eds M. Mills, J. Fellows, C. Meale (Cambridge, 1991), pp. 113–32.

fourteenth and early fifteenth centuries. The crusade is not the terminus of these narratives, instead it is the means to an end.

What is really at stake in these Middle English poems is the concept of identity. There existed a very real feeling towards the end of the fourteenth century that, especially in the wake of the Schism of the papacy, Christendom as an effective and coherent body, bound together beneath the leadership of the pope, was in terminal decline. The emergence of nation-states and the increasing unwillingness of secular princes to submit themselves to any external authority constituted a grave threat to the unified Christian world. The Charlemagne romances must be located within this debate about authority. The world that they portray always seeks to emphasise the importance of Christian, as opposed to national, or secular, action. Those who act properly always act in accordance with the will of God.

In a sense, then, what these romances are providing is a narrative vision of the way the world should operate, as an antidote to the reality of an increasingly fragmented Christian meta-state. They are not reflecting the world as it was, but providing a model for how the world ought to be. For instance, despite being composed, copied and read throughout the time of the papal Schism, Christendom is represented as being unified rather than fragmentary. Prominence is given to figures of religious authority, the potency of relics and the role of sacramental power. The Church is represented as having an important role to play, not just in the world of personal spirituality, but in the world of political organisation as well.

In a fifteenth-century text such as *The Sowdone of Babylone*, for instance, the pope has a pivotal role to play.[4] After all, it is Rome which is initially under attack. When tidings reach the pope that the Saracens are slaying Christians and burning abbeys and churches, he immediately calls together a council (153), an act which he repeats following the death of Savaris (363–64). Soon afterwards, the pope holds yet another council, this time for the people of Rome rather than for their senators (451–54). It is at this final assembly that the pope organises a military campaign against Ferumbras and his father who are besieging Rome, a campaign which he intends to lead personally. One can see that here the pope's function transcends the purely religious. Not only does he operate as the supreme spiritual head of the Christian world, he is both a political leader and a warrior too. These three roles do not exclude one another. However, the function of the pope in *The Sowdone of Babylone* is problematised when he encounters Ferumbras on the battlefield. Ferumbras, seeing the pomp that surrounds him, confuses the pontiff for a secular sovereign and almost kills him by mistake.

The Saracen is clearly disappointed with his enemy's status, claiming that he would bring shame upon himself if he were to kill a priest (559–69). One

---

4   All references to this poem are taken from, *The Romaunce of the Sowdone of Babylone, and of Ferumbras his Son who Conquerede Rome*, ed. E. Hausknecht, EETS, ES 38 (London, 1881).

should ask, therefore, that if the poet is indeed demonstrating the validity of religious incursions into secular life, then why, in his role as a religious warrior, is the pope such an abject failure? Indeed, Ferumbras's assumption that the battlefield is no place for a priest is supported by Christian characters in the same poem. By this point we have already heard one of the papal advisers recommend that assistance should be sought from Charlemagne:

> 'That he come with his Dosyperys
> To reskue Cristiante fro this heþen.'   (373–74)

Charlemagne will come to the rescue, not just of the city of Rome, but of the community of Christendom itself. This point is reiterated later on, when, hearing news of the attack on the Christian centre, the king vows to expel Ferumbras and the Sowdone from the entirety of the Christian community:

> 'The Sowdon and Ferumbras?
> I nyl lette for no thinge,
> Till I him oute of Cristendome chace.'   (584–86)

Charlemagne's intervention is vital. The pope requires assistance, and he receives that assistance from a secular king who is aware of the responsibilities and obligations that he owes to the wider Christian community. The pope is not a successful warrior because, in a properly functioning world, he does not need to be. *The Sowdone of Babylone* proposes a partnership, where the religious authority of the pope is augmented by the military power of a willing secular king. The spheres of the religious and the secular are represented as being reconcilable. A religious war, which is a response to a papal request, mutates into a war which enables French expansionism. The regaining of the relics, a religious duty, is coupled with the winning of land and the continued safety of French borders. The message appears to be, if you are a secular ruler, look after God's interests and He will ensure that your secular affairs are taken care of. By the end of the poem the community of Christendom is represented as being stronger and healthier than ever. One can see then, that this poem acts to unify religious and secular interests. As in all properly functioning feudal relationships, there is a reciprocity between lord and vassal. God facilitates the achievement of worldly success, power and security, if the recipient serves him properly.[5]

The dangers which arise when a Christian ruler mistakenly refuses to fulfil his obligations to the divine are investigated in *The Sege of Melayne*.[6] It is sig-

---

[5] Shepherd has also recognised the reciprocity of the feudal relationship between God and man. Following D. H. Green, he notes that a distinctive feature of crusade literature is a feudalisation of this relationship, where God has an obligation to reward and protect those who pledge themselves to fight on his behalf: ' "This grete journee" ', p. 124.

[6] All references to this poem are taken from *The Sege of Melayne and The Romance of Duke Rowland and Sir Otuell of Spayne*, ed. S. J. Herrtage, EETS, ES 35 (London, 1880).

nificant that in this poem, Charlemagne becomes only a marginal actor in relation to the true hero of the piece, Bishop Turpin. Turpin's major function in the world of the poem is to re-establish the primacy of religious authority, and forcefully reassert the importance of religion in a world increasingly guided by secular powers. The rampant secularism that the Bishop opposes is most apparent in the figure of Ganelon, that arch-traitor of the Charlemagne corpus. In this poem, in his role as false counsellor, Ganelon persuades Charles from the outset that he should not personally respond to the Lord of Milan's request for assistance:

> 'Sir,' he sayde, 'þat ware a Synfull chaunce,
> Whatt sole worthe of vs in Fraunce
> And þou in þe felde were slayne?' (181–3)

This argument is repeated later, when the first force that is sent to relieve the city has failed and the pressure upon Charles to take decisive action increases. It would be much more sensible, recommends Ganelon, for Charles to remain in Paris and send somebody else instead of putting himself personally at risk:

> 'And byde thi selfe in this Citee.
> Slayne in þe felde gife þat þou bee
> Alle Fraunce may like it full ill.' (655–7)

Ganelon's first concern is for the fate of France. He is anxious, not so much for Charles's safety, as to what would happen to the nation should the king fall in battle. To our late nationalist perspective such concern is almost admirable, but within the context of the poem it is as treasonable as anything that Ganelon does in any other Charlemagne narrative. We must also note that Ganelon is not the only figure at the court who regards such secular concerns as paramount. To decide what action to take in the first instance, Charles calls a council, consisting of 'grette lordes bothe ferre and nere' (194). This assembly, of the most powerful lords in France, agrees with Ganelon, that Charles should remain at home for the sake of the country. It is important to remember that in *The Sege of Melayne* Ganelon is not the outsider that we find elsewhere. His is merely one voice among many. The assembled members of the political community urge Charlemagne to desist from holy war:

> þay prayede þe kynge on þat tyde
> þat he hym selfe at home walde byde,
> To kepe þat land riȝt thare. (199–201)

After the initial force sent to relieve Milan is all but wiped out, the secularist Ganelon is again prepared to ignore religious obligations in the interests of maintaining France's security. He even advises the king to submit to the Sultan:

> 'Or ells with In thies monethes three
> Als qwhitte of Fraunce sall ȝhe bee
>   Als ȝhe it neuer ne knewe.'   (598–600)

Ganelon's advice consistently subordinates the security of Christendom to the security of the nation. Heeding such counsel, the king informs Turpin that despite the disastrous first foray, he again intends to remain in Paris while the Bishop leads an army on his behalf:

> Bot take his nobill Cheualrye
> And wende forthe in to lumbardy,
>   'For I will kepe my Ryke.'   (664–6)

Charles explicitly tells Turpin why he is not going to crusade. Following Ganelon's advice, the king will 'kepe' his 'Ryke', that is guard his kingdom. The king, persuaded by the treacherous Ganelon, gives his secular position as national leader precedence over his role and responsibilities as a Christian ruler. Turpin's response is understandable outrage. Charles is not merely refusing to respond to the entreaties of a Christian lord who needs his assistance, or failing to fulfil a feudal obligation to avenge the men who died in the first expedition. He is acting in direct opposition to the instructions of God himself. Throughout these crusading poems, divine interventions furnish the Christian cause with the ultimate authority, and such authority cannot be easily ignored. Christian action is dehistoricised, placed beyond the whims and uncertain motivations of men. We may recall the miracle of the burning cross earlier in *The Sege of Melayne* (421–80), or the portents which preceded the destruction of the Jews in *The Siege of Jerusalem*.[7] Similarly, Charles has no choice about whether or not he should crusade, although he mistakenly believes that he has. The sword which the angel brings to Charles in his dream constitutes an unambiguous instruction for action (109–32). By disregarding God's specific commands, Charlemagne is neglecting his religious duties. Moreover, by refusing to recognise the obligation that he has, the king transgresses the boundaries of acceptable behaviour for a Christian ruler. Turpin brands Charles an 'Eretyke' (672), and repeats this accusation when he excommunicates him:

> 'And here I curse the, þou kynge!
> Be cause þou lyffes in Eresye,
> Thou ne dare noghte fyghte one goddes Enemy.'   (687–9)

What is heretical about Charles's behaviour, is not so much the refusal to crusade personally, but the belief that he has the power to decide what actions he may or may not perform. Like the Saracen sultans seen in this and

---

7   *The Siege of Jerusalem*, eds E. Kölbing and M. Day, EETS, OS 188 (London, 1932), ll. 1219–20.

other poems, he displays a belief in the autonomy of his actions. He does not recognise that he must answer to a higher authority. Turpin tells him the error of his ways, and twice makes him aware of the possible consequences:

> 'If Cristyndome loste bee
> þe wyte bese casten one the.' (697–8)

> 'Goddes byddynge hast þou broken,
> Thurghe þe traytour speche spoken
>   Alle Christendom walde þou schende.' (746–9)

Again, what is at stake, if Charles chooses to follow Ganelon's advice and ensure the continued safety of France, is 'Christendom'. The choice between nation and religion is represented as starkly as that. By neglecting Christian duties, the king places himself outside the community of Christendom, a position that is confirmed with his excommunication. As Turpin tells him:

> 'Nowe arte þou werre   þan any Saraȝene,
> Goddes awenn wedirwyne,
>   Of sorowe now may þou synge!' (694–6)

Charles has now become God's enemy ('wedirwyne'), a fact repeated a few lines later when Turpin declares, 'I calle the goddes foo' (738). Morally, religiously and legally, Charles now occupies the same position as the Saracens. Soon he also occupies the same physical position. The poem may be 'about' the siege of Milan, but the first siege that we really encounter is that of Paris itself, with Charles within, hard-pressed by Bishop Turpin and his clerical army (757–89). The point about this first siege is that Charles's position is legally identical to that of the Saracens later. The clerical army that is mobilised by Bishop Turpin draws its authority directly from the pope, as is made clear at the time of its composition. Turpin tells Charles that he will assemble the clergy:

> 'Of þe pope I haue pouste,
> Atte my byddynge sall þay bee
>   Bothe with schelde and spere.' (616–18)

Turpin claims papal authority for his assumption of military command. He has been given permission to fight against non-believers, and his authority supersedes that of a secular king like Charles. Thus, when Turpin excommunicates Charles, the authority already vested in him by the pope to fight against the enemies of God allows him to declare war on his king:

> 'For we are halden with þe righte
> Clerkes appon cursede men to fighte,
>   I calle the goddes foo.' (736–8)

Turpin, by excluding Charles from the Christian community and branding him an enemy of God, is sanctioned to crusade against him. The implication is clear. Kings, despite claiming autonomy from religious authority, remain subject to it. We witness Charles besieged in his own capital city, along with the advisors who have encouraged him to negate his religious duties, confronted by an army consisting of 'monke, Chanoun, Preste and frere' (620). We can be left in little doubt as to where this poem wants to locate the centre of political authority within the Christian world.

This representation of a division between Church and state would have had a certain resonance for a contemporary audience. Throughout the period of the Hundred Years War, initially a secular feudal, and later a national, conflict, Christian kings were often accused of putting their own interests ahead of the interests of Christendom as a whole.[8] As the Anglo-French wars rolled endlessly onwards, Christendom was actually contracting. The moral and religious concept of the Christian world was slowly being eroded and replaced by the purely geographical concept of Europe.[9] Whilst the military superpowers of England and France fought one another to a standstill, a highly efficient army of Ottoman Turks threatened from the east, growing stronger and bolder, while Egyptian forces massed in Asia Minor. In the east, Sofia fell to the Ottomans in 1385, followed by Nish a year later.[10] All of this occurred against the backdrop of a divided papacy, split by the Schism of 1378, an event from which the office could never truly recover. The idea that the pope was a divinely ordained vicar of Christ was no longer tenable. It is hardly surprising that many medieval Christians felt that the world as they knew it was on the wane.

A clue to the envisaged solution of the problems that ailed Christendom can be found in these romances, with their representation of the effectiveness and coherence of a properly organised Christian crusade. The idea that a crusade was the glue which could bind the Christian world into a whole found its most enthusiastic advocate in Philippe de Mézières, a courtier who had high-level contacts within the courts of both England and France.[11] Mézières desperately attempted to establish an accord between the two countries, arguing that all that was required to solve Christendom's problems was

---

8 As we will see, this was the accusation that Philippe de Mézières levelled against Richard II and Charles VI throughout his *Letter*. See Philippe de Mézières, *Letter to King Richard II: A Plea Made in 1395 for Peace Between England and France*, trans. G. W. Coopland (Liverpool, 1975). As is also clear from the influence of De Mézières, this debate regarding the conflict between secularism and religion, was carried on at the very highest level. Such debates persisted well beyond the Reformation. It is worth recalling that Sir Thomas More was martyred because of his refusal to accept that his king had more authority than the pope. On the way in which the initial feudal conflict was increasingly perceived to be a national contest, see Barnie, *War in Medieval Society*, pp. 97–116.

9 D. Hay, *Europe: The Emergence of an Idea* (Edinburgh, 1957), pp. 61, 83.

10 On the relationship between the perceived disintegration of Christendom and the resurgence of the crusading ideal, see J. J. N. Palmer, *England, France and Christendom: 1377–99* (London, 1972). For details of the Ottoman expansion, see pp. 180–3.

11 For a brief summary of the life and works of Philippe de Mézières, see Coopland's introduction to the *Letter*, pp. ix–xiv.

peace, unity and a crusade. The theory behind his *Letter to Richard II* was that a peace between England and France would rob the competing pontiffs of their major military and financial supporters, thereby precipitating the end of the Schism. The unoccupied soldiery could then be kept out of mischief by being sent to fight the Turks. De Mézières suggested that unless the course that he advocated was adopted, then Charles VI and Richard II would be neglecting their Christian duty and exacerbating the Schism by privileging secular over religious concerns. Instead of spilling the blood of fellow Christians, and thus damaging the Church, De Mézières writes, Christian 'brothers' are duty-bound to unite against the Saracens:

> And by the command of God and the two kings turn their weapons against the enemies of the Faith, to make recompense in the sight of God for the great evils which they have wrought.[12]

De Mézières is no pacifist. He does not call for a cessation of violence; rather he demands its redirection. This is clearly a strategy through which the illusion that Christendom exists as a coherent body is encouraged. In seeking to discover a model for such coherence it is unsurprising that writers turned to narratives of past crusading endeavours. The use of the past in romance narratives invariably has much more to do with remedying the perceived inadequacies of the present and future than with accurately representing a temporally distant world. The Middle English Charlemagne romances, by constructing an idealised narrative of Christian success unequivocally enabled by the will of God, sought to establish continuity between the crusading endeavours of the past and the proposed crusading endeavours of the future. Again, this is reminiscent of Philippe de Mézières's strategy. Like the romances, his *Letter* implores the potential heroes of the present to seek to emulate the heroes of the past. He mentions Godfrey de Bouillon, along with the other Christian Worthies. In matters of arms, De Mézières asks of the two kings:

> Let one of you be the noble Roland and the other the very perfect Oliver; and in matters of royal and imperial splendour, one of you imitate the very valiant and knightly Charlemagne and the other that very bold and excellent King Arthur, when you fight against the enemies of the Faith, against schismatics and heretics.[13]

Within this historiographic scheme, the heroes of the past exist both synchronically and diachronically, in that their actions transcend the specificity of the historical moment and continue to impinge upon the present. De Mézières's *Letter* implicitly invites Charles VI and Richard II to achieve a similar immortality, not merely by *imitating* their long dead predecessors, but

---

12 De Mézières, *Letter*, p. 15.
13 De Mézières, *Letter*, p. 70.

by *reanimating* them. It does not matter that Arthur and Charlemagne did not, and could not, exist simultaneously. Within the figures of the fourteenth-century kings such a union is possible.

In all of these poems, then, the crusade is represented as being the evidence for Christian solidarity, and the means by which such solidarity was achieved. However, this does not mean that we should simply categorise these romances as 'crusade propaganda', although as Stephen Shepherd has demonstrated, *The Sege of Melayne* owes much to this tradition.[14] Likewise, Mary Hamel has identified a similar role for *The Siege of Jerusalem*, a poem which is also present in the London Thornton manuscript.[15] Both Shepherd and Hamel are correct in relating these poems to the crusades, but the notion of their being 'propaganda' is far too rigid. After all, what is being 'sold' to the reading public is the idea of the crusade rather than the crusade itself. The days of popular crusading were well and truly over, so these poems were clearly not designed in order to whip readers up into a crusading frenzy.[16] In fact, the crusade is best regarded as a means rather than an end. If we wish to regard these narratives as 'propaganda', then they are propaganda for an effective centralised Christian Church, a concept that was becoming increasingly threatened by the end of the fourteenth century. This is not to say that the crusading dream had died. In fact, as Norman Housely's excellent study of the later crusades demonstrates, the model which has traditionally been posited, of a rapid decline in crusading, has proved to be unreliable. Instead, what did occur from around the start of the fourteenth century was a decline in actual physical crusade participation, as taxation was used and indulgences collected in order to finance increasingly professional armies.[17] What these romances offer, like crusade indulgences, is involvement in crusading without leaving the comfort of one's home. However, what these romances provide is not a substitute for involvement, nor a springboard for 'real' military service. Rather, they act as a means by which the reading public were able to 'participate' in a crusade, and thereby identify with the community of Christendom.

That such conduits of participation were necessary is due to the changing nature of the crusade in the later Middle Ages. For those pious maniacs who actually wished to go on a crusade, there was a very real narrowing of opportunities. The nature of European crusading had changed a great deal since the eleventh and twelfth centuries. It had grown increasingly defensive rather than expansionist, and the recapture of Jerusalem, the dream for generations of crusaders, was no longer seen as a feasible aim.[18] Furthermore, the growing

---

14 Shepherd, ' "This grete journee" '.
15 M. Hamel, 'The Siege of Jerusalem as a Crusading Poem', *Journeys Toward God: Pilgrimage and Crusade*, ed. B. N. Sargent-Baur (Kalamazoo, 1992), pp. 177–94.
16 On the decline of the popular crusades, see N. Housely, *The Later Crusades: From Lyons to Alcazar* (Oxford, 1992), pp. 55, 403, 408.
17 Housely, *The Later Crusades*, pp. 403–13.
18 On the increasingly defensive nature of the crusades, see A. Luttrell, 'The Crusade in the

professionalisation of the military, a process which occurred over a good length of time, led to the acceptance that a popular peoples' crusade could not remain a viable option. By the time that these Charlemagne narratives were appearing, there had been a recognition that a mass taking of the cross was likely to create more problems than it would solve. Any army raised in this way would inevitably be ill-trained, ill-disciplined and ill-equipped, especially at a time when the financial cost of warfare was spiralling. So what we witness as the popular crusade declines is a channelling of enthusiasm into other modes of participation, for instance, the sale of indulgences. However, the crucial point to be made here is that such modes of participation nourished the crusade spiritually as well as financially. Paying money to support the crusade was not a substitute for action, it was equated with action itself. The benefits and remissions from sin that were promised to those who donated money were identical to the spiritual rewards which awaited members of the community who physically fought for Christendom.[19] Similarly, the idea that one could honour a vow to crusade by sending a substitute to fight on one's behalf was already well established by the time that these narratives emerged.[20] There is no hierarchy of participation in evidence here, nor is there one regarding the reading of these romances. Narrative is not an inadequate substitute for action. It is equated with action itself.

What these romances encourage is a sense of active involvement in a crusading exercise, an involvement which fosters an identification with the community of Christendom. This sense of communal involvement is especially apparent in the Fillingham *Firumbras*, where we frequently find exhortations to pray in order that the resolution of the romance will be satisfactory.[21] Early on we are told:

> Nowe praye whe to ihesu cryst for hys holy name
> to saue oure knyhtys and schelde hem from schame! (52–3)

Several points must be made here. First, we notice the situation of narratorial interventions in the present tense. The word 'nowe' is frequently used to signal such interventions throughout the poem, creating a bridge between

Fourteenth Century', *Europe in the Late Middle Ages*, eds J. R. Hale, J. Highfield, and B. Smalley (London, 1965), pp. 122–55.

19 On the sale of indulgences, see M. Purcell, *Papal Crusading Policy: The Chief Instruments of Papal Crusading Policy and Crusade to the Holy Land from the final loss of Jerusalem to the fall of Acre: 1244–1291*, Studies in the History of Christian Thought II (Leiden, 1975), pp. 36–54. For a detailed consideration of the sale of indulgences in England on a crusade-by-crusade basis, see W. E. Lunt, *Studies in Anglo-Papal Relations During the Middle Ages II: Financial Relations of the Papacy with England: 1327–1534* (Cambridge, MA, 1962). Purcell points out that the idea that material contributions were equated to crusading action emerged post-1215 (p. 54).

20 Purcell, *Papal Crusading Policy*, p. 54; Lunt, *Studies in Anglo-Papal Relations*, p. 531.

21 References to this poem are taken from *Firumbras and Otuel and Roland*, ed. M. I. O'Sullivan, EETS, OS, 198 (London, 1935).

the reader and the historical distance of the events the poem contains. One might note that this technique recalls conventional crusading literature. As Mary Campbell has noted, crusade chronicles contain a number of novelistic features, such as the creation of suspense, and the location of action in real time.[22] Both of these features are apparent in the Fillingham *Firumbras*. Suspense is certainly in evidence in this poem, in that part of the fiction involves the narrator's alleged lack of foresight. He creates the pretence that even he is unaware of how the poem will be resolved. But this technique achieves far more than suspense. By situating the narratorial perspective within the linearity of his poem, the author is actually inviting the audience to participate in the narrative. We find a similar demand for our participation following the death of Maupyn:

> Now pray we for þe kny3tes þat beth in þe tour
> That god of hys grace bryng hem out of dolour!   (177–8)

As with a pantomime audience, there is the illusion that, as readers, our interventions actually matter. Our prayers and devotion, it is claimed, are able to affect the course of narrative events that are, in reality, already fixed. Christian superiority becomes a self-confirmed truth as our 'prayers' are answered favourably time after time, reading after reading. The importance of such exhortations becomes yet more relevant when we consider that communal prayers were almost certainly the most common form of crusade participation throughout this period. From the early thirteenth century onwards, Christian reverses often prompted the institution of special prayers, masses and processions in order to offer reparation for the sins to which such defeats had been attributed.[23] Furthermore, the preaching of a crusade, an important element of which was the securing of financial backing, was often accompanied by specific orders for prayers to be said throughout the Christian world, in order to encourage contributors. For instance, when pope John XXII proclaimed a crusade in July 1333, he issued a bull which ordered every cathedral, collegiate and parochial church to celebrate masses and offer prayers at least once a week for the recovery of the Holy Land.[24] The Church was clearly involved in the manufacture and dissemination of propaganda, not merely for a crusade, but to encourage a sense of collective identity with

---

[22] M. Campbell, *The Witness and the Other World: Exotic European Travel Writing, 400–1600* (Ithaca and London, 1988), p. 136.

[23] C. Tyerman, *England and the Crusade: 1095–1588* (London, 1988), pp. 95–6.

[24] Lunt, *Studies in Anglo-Papal Relations*, p. 528. In the later period by far the most successful preaching campaign was that which accompanied the Despenser crusade of 1383. This project merged national and religious interests, yet it is still worth considering the role of the Church in the dissemination of propaganda for it: see A. K. McHardy, 'Liturgy and Propaganda in the Diocese of Lincoln During the Hundred Years War', *Studies in Church History 18: Religion and National Identity*, ed. S. Mews (Oxford, 1982), pp. 215–27, p. 218, and Lunt, *Studies in Anglo-Papal Relations*, pp. 535–46.

fellow Christians, and with the community of Christendom. This collective identity was encouraged through prayers designed to assist both crusaders fighting abroad, and hard-pressed and isolated Christian 'brothers' in other lands.[25] The prayers that the narrator demands of his audience in the Fillingham *Firumbras* perform much the same function as those offered for crusaders throughout Christendom.

The audience must not then be regarded as passive observers, situated outside the text. Indeed, features such as the implication of a performance situation actually position the reader *within* the text. Of course, such stylised features of orality are present in a great many romances, but here, given the need to involve the audience in the action, they carry an extra resonance. The audience is regarded as possessing a set of values identical to those held by the narrative actors themselves. As readers, we are constructed as members of an all-male Christian group, actively involved in the narrative subordination of the Saracen other. We pray to assist the Christian knights, and our involvement results in our receiving rewards similar to those of the crusaders themselves. The act of listening to a battle as recounted in a romance becomes equated with the act of participating in the battle which that romance describes. If we consider the closing lines of some romances, we discover that the distinction between romance consumer and narrative actor becomes increasingly uncertain. *The Sowdone of Babylone* ends by asking for grace for those Christian heroes described:

> God lete hem never wete of wod.
> But brynge here soules to goode reste!
> That were so worthy in dede.
> And gyf vs ioye of the beste,
> That of here gestes rede!   (3270–4)

It is not just the participants who are commended to God, it is also the audience of readers.

'Rede' has displaced 'dede'. Action has been superseded by narrative.[26] In these Charlemagne romances we need only witness the deeds of military valour performed by the knights; actual participation has given way to a second-hand consumption of past deeds. This movement is even more pronounced at the close of *Firumbras*:

---

[25] On the representation of Christian brothers under threat from Saracens in far away lands, see J. Riley-Smith, 'Crusading as an Act of Love', *History* 65 (1980), pp. 177–92, p. 190.

[26] One might make a connection with Stephen Knight's argument that the Arthurian Grail quest evolved in order to provide a substitute target once the recapture of Jerusalem became unlikely. See S. Knight, 'From Jerusalem to Camelot: King Arthur and the Crusades', *Medieval Codicology, Iconography, Literature, and Translation: Studies for Keith Val Sinclair*, eds P. R. Monks and D. D. R. Owen (Leiden, New York and Köln, 1994), pp. 223–32.

> God for the Rode loue ȝeue hym hys benysoun,
> That hauen herd thys gest with gode deuocyon
> Of the spere & the naylys and of the crovn!
> Schullen [thay] have an .C. dayes vnto pardoun!
> Our lord graunt that it so be,
> Seyth all amen pur Charite!   (1835–40)

It is reading or listening which has led to this indulgence and it is the narrator who is ostensibly granting it. Once again, we find the differentiation between narrative and action becoming increasingly indistinct, just as the need to participate personally in crusades waned. Moreover, the idea that rewards could be enjoyed merely by listening finds an echo in the organisation of real crusades. For example, as well as offering remission to those participating financially and physically in the enterprise, the bull *Ad comemorandum recentis*, issued by pope John XXII in 1333, also offered a relaxation of forty days' penance to those who merely *listened* to the preaching of the crusade.[27] The closing lines of this version of *Firumbras* have obvious similarities. Furthermore, we find in this extract a condition attached to the granting of the pardon. It is not just what one listens to, it is also the manner in which one listens to it. The audience will only be rewarded if they have listened piously, that is with 'gode deuocyon'. Therefore, failure to be forgiven is a personal failure, not a failure of the giver. We see a similar emphasis upon the personal responsibility of the sinner regarding the granting of papal indulgences. According to the conditions laid down by St Bonaventure in the thirteenth century, the pope could grant indulgences, but divine forgiveness could only be guaranteed if the sinner had fully confessed and was genuinely contrite.[28]

In conclusion, then, these Middle English Charlemagne romances were produced in order to counter the increasing obsolescence of unitary Christendom by fostering a sense of metanational identity. What is primarily revealed, to adopt a far more contemporary phrase, is a two-track, two-speed Europe within which nationalists and metanationalists existed alongside one another, and competed for the same hearts and minds. These narratives are a part of this conflict, and they are immensely conscious of the need to try to construct a sense of cohesion within the Christian world. Moreover, the break-down of Christendom was not an issue which only preyed upon the minds of political 'high-rollers' such as De Mézières. Robert Thornton clearly had access to a variety of romance texts which were informed by the perceived fragmentation of the Christian world. Within Thornton's two manuscripts, we find that these issues are being investigated again and again across a variety of texts: *The Siege of Jerusalem*, *The Alliterative Morte Arthure* and *Richard Couer de Lion*, for example.[29] As such, the world which the Charle-

---

27 Lunt, *Studies in Anglo-Papal Relations*, p. 529.
28 Purcell, *Papal Crusading Policy*, p. 48.
29 I argue that the Alliterative *Morte Arthure* can best be understood as contributing to a debate about the relative distribution of power between religious and secular authorities: in

magne romances represent must be viewed much more as a model than as a reflection. This model is of a unified, strong and expanding Christendom. French and English become one, as De Mézières anticipated, fighting the infidel together as a union between audience and narrative actor occurs.

'Arthur and the Giant of Mont St Michel: The Politics of Empire Building in the Later Middle Ages', *Nottingham Medieval Studies* 41 (1997), pp. 57–71.

Caxton's Concept of 'Historical Romance' within the Context of the Crusades: conviction, rhetoric and sales strategy.

JOERG FICHTE

L ET me begin by pointing out that the title of this essay contains an error. Caxton never speaks of 'historical romance'. On the contrary, he repeatedly emphasises that some works to which we would clearly assign at least a semi-fictional status are histories. That holds true for *Charles the Grete*, which Caxton claims to be a conglomeration of various Latin and French histories including the *Speculum Historiale* by Vincent of Beauvais, and for *Kyng Arthur*, the historical reality of whose protagonist Caxton feels obliged to prove and affirm against some doubting Thomases. He is helped in this enterprise by 'hard' evidence: the presence of a number of visibilia that testify to Arthur's actual existence and a tradition of historiographical writings.[1] This line of argument is surprisingly scientific for Caxton because he is normally not concerned with establishing the truthfulness of the accounts he publishes. He just proclaims them to be histories, a term referring not primarily to their ontological status but to their utility. At second glance, of course, all the evidence adduced for Arthur's existence serves a different purpose: it justifies the publication of a work dealing with Britain's foremost, though greatly underrated hero, that is, England's contribution to the Nine Worthies. What looks like an argument foreshadowing the analytical methods of modern scholarship is basically a way of promoting a product, albeit a product that conforms to the contemporary notion of the nature and function of history. The nature of history is truthfulness or at least verisimilitude; its function is to furnish political and moral or religious instruction. The second objective is the primary one, since all history has an exemplary function. As William A. Kretzschmar has recently pointed out, 'Caxton's primary means of classification of works was to divide books of contemplation, with their prohibitions and precepts, from books of exemplary material in which the teaching

---

[1] *The Works of Sir Thomas Malory*, ed. Eugène Vinaver, 2nd edn (London, 1973), I, pp. cxliv–cxlv.

occurred in a different mode.'[2] Histories belong to the second category. Whatever their actual status as true accounts or verisimilar narratives, their function was to impart lessons to Caxton's audience.

With the term 'historical romance', I am trying to account for the imprecise ontological status of Caxton's histories, which partake of both historiography and romance. They conform to the definition found in the Prologue to *Polycronicon*:

> historye representynge the thynges lyke vnto the wordes enbraceth al vtylyte & prouffite. It sheweth honeste and maketh vyces detestable. It enhaunceth noble men and depresseth wicked men and fooles.[3]

As long as history served this purpose it could contain 'merueylles & wondres' or be 'wonderful', something we would associate with romance.[4] As a matter of fact, these qualifications, rather than detracting from history's veracity, were meant to be an inducement to the reader to discover truth even where the story was presented in a strange guise. Moreover, by postulating and emphasising the didactic function of history, Caxton could easily assemble narratives drawn from widely differing sources and pass them off as 'historical' accounts. Thus, *Godeffroy of Boloyne*, *Kyng Arthur* and *Charles the Grete*, originating as respectively a 'chronicle', a prose romance and a *chanson de geste*, are all subsumed under the nomenclature of 'Christian history', which in turn represents the continuation of Jewish and Ancient History. In short, we witness the divinely ordained historical process unfolding before our eyes. Caxton can maintain in good faith that the history of *Godeffroy of Boloyne* 'is no fable ne fayned thynge, But alle that is therin trewe'.[5] And he can stress the exemplary nature of this history, using it for instructive and hortatory purposes. In this respect, *Godeffroy of Boloyne* differs little from the other two works of this series chronicling the history of the three Christian Worthies. They too purport to offer moral guidelines to modern men as we read in the Prologue to *Charles the Grete*:

> For the werkes of the auncient and olde peple ben for to gyue to vs ensaumple to lyue in good & vertuous operacions digne & worthy of helth, in folowyng the good and eschewyng the euyl.[6]

Addressing himself more specifically to a group of 'noble men', Caxton states in the Prologue to *Kyng Arthur*:

---

2 William A. Kretzschmar, Jr, 'Caxton's Sense of History', *JEGP* 91 (1992), p. 526.

3 *The Prologues and Epilogues of William Caxton*, ed. W. J. B. Crotch, EETS OS 176 (London, 1928), p. 66.

4 *Ibid.*, p. 67.

5 William Caxton, *Godeffroy of Boloyne, or The Siege and Conqueste of Jerusalem*, ed. Mary Noyes Colvin, EETS ES 64 (London, 1893), p. 4.

6 William Caxton, *The Lyf of the Noble and Crysten Prince, Charles the Grete*, ed. Sidney J. H. Herrtage, EETS ES 36 (London, 1880), part I, p. 1.

I, accordyng to my copye, have doon sette it in enprynte to the entente that noble men may see and lerne the noble actes of chyvalrye, the jentyl and ver-tuous dedes that somme knyghtes used in tho dayes, by whyche they came to honour, and how they that were vycious were punysshed and ofte put to shame and rebuke.[7]

Although the didactic intent is also stressed in the preface to *Godeffroy of Boloyne*, Caxton seems to have been motivated by another purpose as well, when he chose to publish this particular work at this particular time. In con-trast to the two sequels completing the history of the other two Christian Worthies, this work is characterised by a sense of urgency: the realisation that it was high time for the princes of Christian Europe to make a concerted effort to fight the Turks. As Caxton states in the epilogue, he began translat-ing the work on 12 March 1481 and finished the translation on 7 June 1481,[8] at a time when crusading efforts were gathering momentum. His source is the *Roman de Eracles*, or *Livre d'Eracles* as it is also called,[9] a French work in prose based in part on the *Historia Rerum in Partibus Transmarinis Gestarum* by William of Tyre.[10] The Latin original, an account of the first crusade, which has been transmitted in only nine copies and one fragment, was little known in the late Middle Ages. As a matter of fact, only some Italian humanists like Biondo Flavio and Benedetto Accolti made use of it and did so in a way that would have appealed to Caxton: they incorporated portions of it in their exhortations to the Italian states to join the pope in his crusading efforts. Thus, in 1454 Biondo Flavio presented to Francesco Foscari, the Doge of Venice, a history called *De origine et gestis Venetorum* (Basel, 1531), which had the following subtitle: *Consultatio an bellum vel pax Turcis magis expediat rei publicae Venetorum*. Needless to say, Biondo Flavio opted for war. Ten years later Benedetto Accolti dedicated his work *De bello a Christianis contra barba-ros gesto pro Christi sepulcro et Iudaea recuperandis libri IV* (Venice, 1532) to Piero di Medici. This work, almost exclusively based on William's *Historia*, is an eloquent attempt to convince the Florentine leader to join the crusade started by pope Pius II in the summer of 1464.[11]

It is certainly no coincidence that the two Italian Humanists made use of the Latin original. It was appealing to them not only because of its well-presented documentation and its cogent argumentation but also because of its Latinity. Benedetto Accolti in particular was attracted to William's work

---

7 *The Works of Sir Thomas Malory*, ed. Eugène Vinaver, I, p. cxlv.
8 *Godeffroy of Boloyne*, ed. Mary Noyes Colvin, p. 312.
9 *Guillaume de Tyr et ses continuateurs: texte français du XIIIe siècle* (Histoire général des croisades), ed. Paulin Paris (Paris, 1879–80). This portion of the *Roman* or *Livre d'Eracles* recounts the history of the crusades, based on William of Tyre's chronicle, up to the year 1183.
10 Willelmus Tyrensis Archiepiscopus, *Chronicon*, ed. R. B. C. Huygens, Corpus Christi-anorum Continuatio Mediaevalis LXIII (Turnhout, 1986).
11 Ludwig Schmugge, 'Die Kreuzzüge aus der Sicht humanistischer Geschichtsschreiber', *Vorträge der Aeneas-Silvius-Stiftung an der Universität Basel* 21 (1987), pp. 8–13.

because of its fine rhetoric which caused him to write what Sybel has called 'die gebildetste Bearbeitung derselben [der Erzählung Wilhelms]' (the most erudite rendition [of William's narrative]).[12]

Needless to say, it was neither the erudition of William's work nor its style that attracted Caxton to it (he was aware that there existed a Latin original of the French version he chose to translate), but the subject and its treatment as he found it in the *Livre d'Eracles*. However, William's learned and well-documented historical record of the First Crusade had not only been translated into French, but had also been turned into a *chanson de geste*-like narrative. Instead of being a low-key, objective account of the various stages of this first Christian campaign to regain the Holy Land and its capital Jerusalem, the *Livre d'Eracles* treats these events in the form of a historical romance centered in the first nine books mostly on the life of Godfrey of Bouillon. We witness the conquest of the Holy Land by a dwindling army of Christian soldiers under the determined leadership of their courageous commander-in-chief Godfrey of Bouillon. Against overwhelming odds, hunger, thirst and a seemingly invincible enemy whose forces greatly outnumber the small band of Christian warriors, divided among themselves, Godfrey with the help of God defeats his enemy and conquers the Holy City of Jerusalem. In typical *chanson de geste*-fashion the lines are clearly drawn: on the one side the pagan infidels and on the other the Christian crusaders, who face one another in numerous encounters. The high points are the sieges of Antioch and Jerusalem, in which Godfrey rises to the position of a Christian hero, whose courageous deeds inspire his famished and exhausted men to super-human acts of valour. In heroic fashion he cuts a pagan adversary in half, thus giving a shining example of his prowess to his troops. In spite of the fact that they are hopelessly outnumbered, the Christians continue their siege of Antioch and are finally rewarded: the city falls through treason. Once inside, the crusaders put most of the unfortunate inhabitants to the sword, before they are themselves besieged by an enormous army. In vivid terms all the deprivations and sufferings of the Christian contingent are described. They finally decide to take on the enemy in the open field. Strengthened by their faith, the sick and desperate men win a splendid victory over the vastly superior forces of their pagan enemy, a feat which encourages them to march on Jerusalem. The battle for Jerusalem as it is described in the *Livre d'Eracles* is basically a repetition of events at Antioch recounted in the fashion of incremental narrative patterns. Under the leadership of Godfrey of Bouillon, who is the first to scale the walls, the Christian soldiers, tormented by hunger and thirst, finally succeed in taking the well-provisioned and ably defended town. As a terrible slaughter ensues, the streets are running with blood. More than ten thousand Turks are slaughtered within the enclosure of the temple. After the city is taken, the unwilling Godfrey of Bouillon is crowned King of Jerusalem and is

---

12 Heinrich von Sybel, *Geschichte des ersten Kreuzzugs* (Düsseldorf, 1841), p. 161.

immediately faced with a new enemy, the Emir of Egypt, who has come to reconquer the city. There is one more great battle against a haughty and proud enemy, who is likewise laid low. After some more successful skirmishes which help him to consolidate his power, Godfrey dies on 13 July 1100.

So much for the contents of the first nine books of the *Livre d'Eracles* which Caxton translates into English. The French source, as I have indicated before, continues with a narration of events after Geoffrey's death chronicling the history of the Kingdom of Jerusalem even beyond the time of William of Tyre's death in September of 1186. It is typical of Caxton that he finishes his account with the death of Godfrey of Bouillon, the true hero and protagonist of his version of the First Crusade. Like Roland or Charlemagne, Godfrey is an epic hero who distinguishes himself through his battles against the infidels. In the *Livre d'Eracles* and Caxton's translation he is a shining example of Christian valour, a virtue that Caxton believes to be particularly needed in his own days. Godfrey's exploits, accomplished almost four hundred years before, are a testimony of Christian commitment to a worthy cause, the liberation of the Holy Land that has now been languishing under pagan rule for more than three centuries. Thus the work is at once a chronicle of past Christian greatness and a forceful reminder of what the Christian princes should do at this very moment. The warnings, instructions and exhortations, which are so characteristic of this historical romance, point beyond its narrow time-frame to the present, when a concerted effort against the Turks was badly needed. Although Caxton does not insert any specific references to the contemporary situation, the frequent naming of the 'Turks' as the major pagan enemy and of the 'pilgrims' to designate the crusaders is very topical at his own time. The Turks, after all, posed the major threat to Europe in the fifteenth century. Thus, any reference to Turks, even within a historical context remote from the present, would surely arouse the interest of a contemporary audience. The term 'pilgrim', on the other hand, describes what was once regarded to be the true character of a peregrination to the Holy Land: an active penitential journey of the armed members of the *ecclesia militans*. Needless to say, no such 'pilgrimage' had been undertaken in the fifteenth century, the last crusade of 1395 only having reached Nicopolis in the Balkans. Still, the notion persevered, especially among the members of the nobility, that a military campaign was the only proper pilgrimage to Jerusalem. Two of Caxton's patrons, for instance, Anthony Woodville, Earl Rivers, and John Tiptoft, Earl of Worcester, were known for their crusading enthusiasm and their interest in pilgrimages – both went to the Holy Land, an enterprise commended by Caxton in the Epilogue to his translation of Cicero's *Of Nobility*, which appeared in 1481 shortly before the publication of *Godeffroy of Boloyne*.[13]

---

[13] *The Prologues and Epilogues of William Caxton*, ed. W. J. B. Crotch, p. 47.

The French *Livre d'Eracles* was a very popular work. It has been transmit-ted in more than seventy copies, several of which were owned by the Dukes of Burgundy.[14] According to the inventory of 1467 the ducal library featured a special collection of works on the subject of 'Oultre-Mer'.[15] Such interest in literature dealing with the crusades and the Holy Land at the court of Bur-gundy is not surprising in view of the fact that the dukes were great crusading enthusiasts. Philip the Bold had participated in the ill-fated crusade of Nico-polis in 1395 that had resulted in a disastrous defeat, and still rankled with his grandson Philip the Good, who, together with his courtiers, took the famous vow on the pheasant to go on a crusade upon the fall of Constantinople in 1453. In the years after the failure at Nicopolis, the dukes not only collected histories of the crusades and proposals of how to reconquer the lost Kingdom of Jerusalem but also commissioned such plans, as the treatises written by Bertrandon de la Broquière, Geoffroy de Thoisy and Waleran de Wavrin prove.[16]

The holdings of the ducal library and the crusading fervor of the Burgun-dian court are of some interest for our study of Caxton's *Godeffroy of Boloyne*, since Caxton had access to this library. As is well known, some of the books Caxton translated and published were either part of this library or associated with it. Many of the romances from the library that were translated by Caxton featured an idealised portrayal of the chivalric world. Thus they were meant to serve as courtesy books and chivalric manuals, a fact emphasised in Caxton's prologues and epilogues. The didactic value of the deeds of the heroes of the past is emphasised and their praiseworthy conduct held up as model exemplar for the present generation.

Godeffroy of Boloyne follows this general pattern of instruction and exhor-tation, but also goes beyond it. After making the general point that the histo-ries of the past have been written down by historiographers 'to thentente that gloryous Prynces and hye men of noble and vertuouse courage, shold take ensample tempryse werkys leeful and honneste',[17] Caxton singles out the noble deeds of the Nine Worthies. Quickly he introduces the three represen-tatives of Biblical history, Joshua, David and Judas Maccabaeus, who are fol-lowed by the three figures from ancient history, Hector, Alexander and Julius Cæsar. Then he turns to Christian history and lists, likewise in chronological order, Arthur, Charlemagne and Godfrey of Bouillon. The presentation of the lives and accomplishments of the three Christian Worthies was to become a programme. Whether Caxton envisioned the publication of a series of three books in 1481, though, is hard to say. It seems more likely that the successful sale of *Godeffroy of Boloyne* encouraged him to publish the other

---

14 Diane Bornstein, 'William Caxton's Chivalric Romances and the Burgundian Renais-sance in England', *English Studies* 57 (1976), p. 5.
15 N. F. Blake, *Caxton and His World* (London, 1969), p. 70.
16 George Doutrepont, *La littérature française à la cour des ducs de Bourgogne* (Paris, 1909), pp. 236–65.
17 *Godeffroy of Boloyne*, ed. Mary Noyes Colvin, p. 1.

two works in 1485, a time when Caxton – in view of the uncertain political situation – had to look for new literary patrons and a wider audience. In any case, it is worthwhile noting that he started his publishing enterprise on the three Christian Worthies not with the first figure, King Arthur, but with the last, Godfrey of Bouillon.

We do not need to look far for the reason for this decision. Caxton is motivated primarily by contemporary political events. In the prologue he points out the similarity between the present historical situation and that at the time of Godfrey of Bouillon. Then and now the 'mescreauntes and turkes' conspired against the Christians.[18] Although the conditions are similar, there is one decisive difference: while four hundred years earlier Godfrey had started his crusade from Constantinople and succeeded in liberating the Holy Land and Jerusalem, now Constantinople has been conquered by the Turks, Rhodes is being besieged and even the town of Otranto in Italy has been sacked. All of Italy up to Rome seems about to fall prey to the assailants, unless the Christian princes cease their internecine quarrels, unite against the common enemy and undertake the reconquest of the Holy Land and the Holy City of Jerusalem:

> Thenne for thexhortacion of alle Cristen prynces/ Lordes/ Barons/ Knyghtes/ Gentilmen/ Marchanntes/ and all the comyn peple of this noble Royamme, walys & yrlond, I haue emprysed to translate this book of the conquest of Iherusalem out of ffrenssh in to our maternal tongue, to thentente tencourage them by the redyng and heeryng of the merueyllous historyes herin comprysed, and of the holy myracles shewyd that euery man in his partye endeuoyre theym vnto the resistence afore sayd, And recuperacion of the sayd holy londe.[19]

The leader of such an enterprise could only be King Edward, to whom the book is dedicated. This dedication is followed by a prayer to God,

> that this sayd book may encourage, moeue, and enflamme the hertes of somme noble men, that by the same the mescreauntes maye be resisted and putte to rebuke, Cristen fayth encreaced and enhaunced, and the holy lande, with the blessyd cyte of Iherusalem, recouerd, and may come agayn in to cristen mens hondes.[20]

All noble men of high courage should read this book because in so doing they will know which way to take and what glorious and great feats of arms were performed by Godfrey of Bouillon. In the Epilogue the book is once more dedicated to King Edward.

Let us remember that Caxton translated the work between March and June 1481, that is, at a time when the events referred to in the Prologue were

---

18 *Ibid.*, p. 3.
19 *Ibid.*, p. 4.
20 *Ibid.*, p. 5.

still very topical. Even though the fall of Constantinople had occurred thirty years before, that event had left a lasting impression in Continental and English works of historiography and had redefined the image of the Turk, as we shall see.[21]

The first great siege of Rhodes had been lifted only nine months earlier in August 1480. After some minor attacks on the city's fortifications, followed by a heavy bombardment, the Turks under the leadership of Mesih Pasha launched what was to be the final assault on 28 July. The defenders, commanded by the Grand Master Pierre d'Aubusson, succeeded in stopping the attackers and throwing them back. Some 3,500 Turkish soldiers are reported to have been killed in a pitched battle that was to postpone the fall of the city for another forty years. The victory over the Turks was a cause of great rejoicing in the West, since it showed that Mehmed's armies were not invincible. The news of the Hospitalers' success spread like wildfire, that is, fast by late medieval standards, but not too fast. In France memorial services were celebrated by the order of King Louis XI, when it was learned in November that the Turkish assault had been turned back. In the same year three eye-witness reports appeared in print by Guillaume Caoursin, Giacomo de Curti and Mary Dupuis.[22] Of these the *Obsidionis Rhodiae urbis descriptio* by Guillaume Caoursin, the vice-chancellor of the order of St John, was the most popular. It went through a number of editions and was immediately translated into Italian, German and English. The English version, also dedicated to King Edward, was translated by John Kaye and published under the title *The Siege of Rhodes* in either 1481 or 1482.[23] Unfortunately, we know neither the precise date of publication (it must have been published after Mehmed's death on 3 May 1481) nor the publisher. The little volume (some fifty pages) occupies a unique position among early English prints: it is the only eye-witness report of contemporary events printed in England, and proves by its very existence the great interest in campaigns against the Turks at a time when Caxton was translating *Godeffroy of Boloyne* and preparing the work for publication.

The second contemporary event alluded to by Caxton is the fall of Otranto in August 1480, which was a matter of great concern to the ruler of Naples, Duke Alfonso, and pope Sixtus IV. In the *Diarium Romanum*, which gives 11 August as the date of the Turkish capture of Otranto, we read that the city was sacked, the older inhabitants killed, the younger reduced to slavery. Stefano Pendinelli, the aged archbishop, was slain with all his priests.

---

[21] Cf. Erich Meuthen, 'Der Fall von Konstantinopel und der lateinische Westen', *Mitteilungen und Forschungsbeiträge der Cusanus-Gesellschaft* 15 (1982), pp. 35–60.

[22] Guillaume Caoursin, *Obsidionis Rhodiae urbis descriptio*; Giacomo de Curti, *De urbis Collosensis obsidione anno 1480 a Turcis tentata*; Mary Dupuis, *Le Siège de Rhodus*. Cf. Robert Schwoebel, *The Shadow of the Crescent: The Renaissance Image of the Turk 1453–1517* (Nieuwkoop, 1967), p. 122.

[23] Guillaume Caoursin, *The Siege of Rhodes* (1482), trans. John Kaye, facsimile reproduction with an introduction by Douglas Gray (New York, 1975).

The churches were destroyed or converted into stables and quarters for the troops. Sacred relics were thrown to the dogs. Virgins were raped on the altars.[24] Reports of these outrages and the threat to Rhodes (the news of the great victory had not yet reached Rome) caused Sixtus IV to issue a bull in late summer of 1480 calling on all the leaders of the Italian states to stop their internal quarrels and exhorting the princes of Christian Europe, especially the German emperor and the kings of France and England, to unite against the common enemy.[25] A crusade against the Turks was proclaimed on 8 April 1481 and all European rulers were asked to join and assist in this enterprise. Otranto was recaptured on 10 September of the same year, mainly by Neapolitan and papal troops. However, the great joint effort the pope had hoped for, a crusade against the Turks, for which the time seemed to be so favourable, came to nought. It shared the same fate as the last great endeavour which had ended miserably with the death of Pius II on 15 August 1464 in Ancona, a failure that enabled Mehmed II to conquer large parts of the Balkan peninsula.[26]

Caxton's decision to publish an English version of the old crusading epic *Le Livre d'Eracles* has to be seen within this historical context. The time for such an enterprise appeared to be right, since many potential buyers were interested in the subject, having been alerted either by oral reports or by campaigns initiated by the Church to aid the beleaguered Christian outposts with money raised by the sale of indulgences. As the twelve sales drives in England between 1444 and 1502 testify, some awareness of the threat the Turks posed to Christian Europe existed even in England, although there was no immediate danger to this remote part of the world.[27] Thus mass printing, besides being a profitable business for the printers, had the effect of sharpening public awareness and concern, and helped to shape the opinions of contemporaries towards the Turks. Indulgences played a considerable role because they were widely distributed and had an immediate influence on the ordinary Christian. The indulgence of pope Sixtus, sold on 13 December 1476 to Henry Langley and his wife Catherine, the first surviving piece of print in England, was printed by Caxton in Westminster.[28] In 1480 Caxton printed two more issues of indulgences which were sold by John Kendale, a papal commissary and honorary infantry commander of the order of the Knights of St John. Kendale had received the support of his own king, Edward IV, who in a document of 29 April 1480 commanded all persons in Ireland to assist him in raising

---

[24] Cf. Kenneth M. Setton, *The Papacy and the Levant (1204–1571)* (Philadelphia, 1978), II, p. 345.
[25] *Ibid.*, p. 370.
[26] Cf. Norman Housley, *The Later Crusades, 1274–1580: From Lyons to Alcazar* (Oxford, 1992), pp. 109–111.
[27] Christopher Tyerman, *England and the Crusades, 1095–1588* (Chicago and London, 1988), p. 315.
[28] Paul Needham, *The Printer and the Pardoner: An Unrecorded Indulgence Printed by William Caxton for the Hospital of St. Mary Rounceval, Charing Cross* (Washington, 1986), p. 32.

money and men to fight the Turks. With the money raised Kendale was able to provision a ship in which he sailed for Rhodes. He never arrived there, though, his ship being seized by the Venetians.[29] In 1481 Caxton printed two more indulgences, both for the defence of Rhodes and the reconquest of Otranto, which were sold in England by Giovanni de Gigliis, a papal nuncio, who in 1476 had been appointed collector of the apostolic *camera* in England.[30]

To repeat then, the crusading spirit was very much alive at the beginning of the eighties, not only on the Continent but also in England. I do not want to speculate as to what extent crusading enthusiasts were actually committed to this idea. There must have been a considerable number of armchair crusaders who preferred reading about Christian campaigns against the Turks to being involved in them. Let us not forget that even a great supporter of the idea, like Philip the Good, died in 1467 without ever having realised the elaborate plans for a crusade drawn up in 1456, or having kept the promise made to pope Pius to take a leading part in the conquest of the Holy Land.[31] Edward IV, who favoured such an endeavour and assisted the papal attempts at raising money in his kingdom, withdrew his active support at the decisive moment, when his personal involvement was requested. When asked by Sixtus to participate in the campaign to reconquer Otranto, he pleaded urgent business at home that needed his attention. In a letter to the pope he excused his absence, though assuring him that he would have 'preferred being associated with the other sovereigns of Christendom in an expedition against the Turk' to making war upon Christians as he was forced to do to maintain his throne.[32] This is the same Edward who is praised by Caxton in the Prologue to *Godeffroy of Boloyne* as Godfrey's successor and for being the prince in Europe best suited to lead a crusade against the Turks, 'for to deserue the tenthe place' among the Worthies.[33] One is at first inclined to dismiss Caxton's lavish praise of Edward as an exercise in rhetoric, if it were not for a similar passage in MS BL Additional 10099. This manuscript contains a version of the *Chronicles of England* that is very close to Caxton's edition of 1480. After the concluding prayer for the welfare of the king, many phrases of which echo or parallel those in other prayers or dedicatory epilogues by Caxton, we encounter the following wish:

that ther may be a verray finall pees in all cristen reames, that the infidelis & mysscreauntes may be withstanden & destroied & our faith enhannced, which

29 Schwoebel, *The Shadow of the Crescent*, p. 137.

30 George D. Painter, *William Caxton: A Quincentenary Biography of England's First Printer* (London, 1976), pp. 104–05.

31 Richard Vaughan, *Philip the Good* (London, 1970), pp. 334–72.

32 Schwoebel, *The Shadow of the Crescent*, p. 134.

33 *Godeffroy of Boloyne*, ed. Mary Noyes Colvin, p. 5.

in thise dayes is sore mynusshed by the puissaunce of the turkes & hethen men.[34]

In this epilogue, too, the welfare not only of England but also of Europe is associated with Edward, who is seen as the defender of the Christian faith.

What are we to make of all this? Is there any way to ascertain or measure Caxton's sincerity? Is he just riding the tide of anti-Turkish sentiment, drawing on the repertoire of crusading rhetoric? Looking at the Prologue to *Godeffroy of Boloyne* again, there seem to be a number of phrases and concepts associated with the traditional 'exhortatio ad bellum contra barbaros'. Caxton refers to the power, the arrogance and the cruelty of the Turk, 'grete enemye of oure Cristen fayth, destroyar of Cristen blood, and vsurpar of certayn Empyres, and many Cristen Royammes and countrees'.[35] The text reverberates with phrases designed to produce a negative response in his envisioned readership. They paint a picture of the Turk that had become stereotypical after the conquest of Constantinople. Let us recall for a moment Pero Tafur's description of the Turks in his widely disseminated *Travels and Adventures 1435–1439*:

> The Turks are a noble people, much given to truth. They live in their country like nobles, as well in their expenditure as in their actions and food and sports, in which latter there is much gambling. They are very merry and benevolent, and of good conversation, so much so that in those parts [the countries around the Black Sea], when one speaks of virtue, it is sufficient to say that anyone is like a Turk.[36]

This account is followed by a favourable description of the Grand Turk himself and his household. Pero Tafur, a widely travelled gentleman from Spain, is an astute observer, usually not prone to making snap judgments or to reproducing stereotypes. He is a fairly reliable source of information, if one compares his accounts with others. Greek Constantinople, incidentally, is described by him as a sparsely populated city that in spite of all of its splendor makes a negative impression on him:

> the inhabitants are not well clad, but sad and poor, showing the hardship of their lot which is, however, not so bad as they deserve, for they are a vicious people, steeped in sin.[37]

The last part of the statement reflects some bias. There was little love in the West for the schismatic Greeks.

---

[34] Lister M. Matheson, 'Printer and Scribe: Caxton, the *Polychronicon*, and the *Brut*', *Spec* 60 (1985), p. 600.
[35] *Godeffroy of Boloyne*, ed. Mary Noyes Colvin, p. 4.
[36] Pero Tafur, *Travels and Adventures 1435–1439*, ed. and trans. Malcolm Letts (London, 1926), p. 128.
[37] *Ibid.*, p. 146.

Once Constantinople had fallen, the image of Turks and Greeks was reversed largely through the 'eye-witness' descriptions of the outrages and horrors committed by the conquerors and the propaganda produced by clerics in the employ of the Roman curia, who flooded the Western Church and the courts of Europe with letters, edicts and bulls, detailing the cruelty of the Turk and calling for a crusade against this enemy of Christianity. By Caxton's time, that is, thirty years after the fall of Constantinople, everyone knew what a bloodthirsty and cruel creature a Turk was, oppressing the Christians, defiling their sanctuaries and practising unspeakable perversions. Had not Mehmed the Conqueror himself raped the emperor's daughter and decapitated her in the Hagia Sophia on the statue of the Virgin turned into an executioner's block, after she had steadfastly refused to abjure her Christian faith and accept the teachings of Islam?[38]

There is no doubt that Caxton turned this negative image to his advantage. But the question still remains, if and to what extent he believed in the possibility of reconquering the Holy Land, an enterprise he vociferously advocates in the Prologue to *Godeffroy of Boloyne* and adduces as reason for his translation of the *Livre d'Eracles*. The book, after all, presents itself as serving a specific purpose: by reading of the glorious deeds accomplished by the leader of the first crusade, Godfrey of Bouillon, the reader, gentleman or commoner, should be incited to emulate this shining example. We may be inclined to dismiss Caxton's appeal to as wide as possible an audience, advocating something everyone would approve of and support, as a well-calculated sales pitch. On the other hand, it would be too simple to credit Caxton only with crass mercantile motives. *Godeffroy of Boloyne* for all of its topicality is not a massive erratic in Caxton's publishing programme. It too reflects his sense of the value of history and of works of historiography for the present. Whatever we may label these works, history, chronicle, *chanson de geste* or, as I have done, historical romance, for Caxton they were true historical records or verisimilar accounts. And as such they served an exemplary purpose: they were to inculcate lessons of noble behaviour and cause men to pattern their conduct on that of the great figures of the past. *Godeffroy of Boloyne* fits this general pattern because the protagonist is not only an exemplary figure but the incarnation of the Christian hero. As the exemplary Christian hero, moreover, he occupies a different status than the noble knights from antiquity populating Caxton's earlier historical romances, the *Recuyell of the Histories of Troy* and the *Histoire de Jason*. His accomplishments are living proof of the fact that the Holy Land and the city of Jerusalem, 'in whiche our blessyd sauyour, Ihesu Crist, redemed vs with his precious blood',[39] can be regained, if today's Christians (Caxton's readers) 'doo as this noble prynce Godeffroy of boloyne dyde, with other noble and hye prynces in

---

[38] Meuthen, 'Der Fall von Konstantinopel', pp. 38–9.
[39] *Godeffroy of Boloyne*, ed. Mary Noyes Colvin, p. 4.

his companye'.[40] Thus, Caxton outlines a common goal, the liberation of the holy places, that all Christians, at least in theory, could agree on. If his appeal was not heeded, Caxton had the consolation of having supported a good cause and having made good money in the process.

[40] *Ibid.*, p. 4.

Chaucerian Minstrelsy: *Sir Thopas, Troilus and Criseyde* and English metrical romance

NANCY MASON BRADBURY

SINCE Charles Muscatine long ago characterised the poem's interplay of forms as 'a genre unto itself', Chaucer's *Troilus and Criseyde* has frequently been described as incorporating, juxtaposing and critiquing the major genres of classical and medieval literature. Thus Monica McAlpine sees the poem played out along the axis from comedy to tragedy, and Paul Strohm writes of 'a narrative whole that constantly shifts its own coordinates, from tragedy to history to romance and back to tragedy again'.[1] Without denying the importance of the others, I wish to read the poem against just one of its constituent genres: English metrical romance. I argue that Chaucer's reception of native romance in *Troilus* is more positive, and more artistically significant, than one would assume from the almost exclusive emphasis on continental models in current criticism of the poem.[2] Chaucer's deep stylistic debt to English romance has been well documented,[3] but has

[1] Charles Muscatine, *Chaucer and the French Tradition*(Berkeley, 1957), p. 132; Monica McAlpine, *The Genre of Troilus and Criseyde* (Ithaca, 1978); Paul Strohm, *Social Chaucer* (Cambridge, MA, and London, 1989), p. 118.

[2] Chaucer's engagement with classical and continental authors is richly demonstrated in John Fyler, *Chaucer and Ovid* (New Haven, 1979); Winthrop Wetherbee, *Chaucer and the Poets* (Ithaca, 1984); John V. Fleming, *Classical Imitation and Interpretation in Chaucer's Troilus* (Lincoln, NE, 1990); and Thomas C. Stillinger, *The Song of Troilus* (Philadelphia, 1992). All include ample bibliographies of further work in this vein. I make this argument for metrical romance as a significant influence on Chaucer at greater length in the final chapter of my book, *Writing Aloud: Storytelling in Late Medieval England* (Urbana & Chicago, 1998).

[3] Derek Brewer argues that Chaucer's early poetry 'shows the romances to be the source of his first poetic nourishment' in 'The Relationship of Chaucer to the English and European Traditions', *Chaucer and Chaucerians*, ed. D. S. Brewer (London, 1966), p. 4. J. A. Burrow calls the style of the metrical romances 'the vigorous wild stock upon which were grafted Chaucer's other more literary and sophisticated styles' in *Ricardian Poetry* (London, 1971), p. 21; and Barry Windeatt observes that 'the whole of *Troilus* is full of echoes from the stock diction and gestures with which the English popular romances convey the sorrows of their characters' in *Troilus and Criseyde* (Oxford, 1992), p. 148. See also Ruth Crosby, 'Chaucer and the Custom of Oral Delivery', *Spec* 13 (1938), pp. 413–32; P. M. Kean, *Chaucer and the*

115

had surprisingly little impact on contemporary readings of *Troilus*. The influence on Chaucer of English romance is pervasive and undeniable: his poetry
frequently apostrophises a listening audience; it makes ample use of heavily
marked narrative transitions and of exclamations, oaths and asseverations; it
employs a large number of formulaic phrases and of rhyme-pairs familiar from
English romance. Yet it is interesting how rarely we have asked why the language of English metrical romance is there in Chaucer and what it means.
Chaucer's works show deep concern with issues of literary authority and
authorial self-definition. Why then does he sustain this connection to a tradition that could offer him little help in attaining the status of *auctor* or *poeta*?
Even if we imagine Chaucer writing primarily for an audience of social and
cultural peers like that posited by Strohm, there can be little question that he
expected his audience to be able to recognise the conventions of English
romance. How else could he have expected them to make anything more
than the Host of the Canterbury pilgrimage does out of *Sir Thopas*? John
Burrow has observed that anyone familiar with the romances can complete
Sir Thopas's fragmentary last line:

> Hymself drank water of the well,
> As dide the knyght sire Percyvell
>   So worly under wede,
> Til on a day . . .

'it so bifel', we can easily add because the rhyming phrase is so formulaic.[4]
Surely a contemporary audience could be expected to do the same. And yet
Chaucer uses versions of this highly conventional narrative transition
throughout his work: Ruth Crosby counted eleven examples of the whole
expression, along with innumerable variants on its two parts.[5] The knowledge that an audience will mentally anticipate the completion of a phrase
provides a poet with a powerful tool for variation, emphasis and surprise. In
fact, it offers just what we are sometimes told that medieval English poets
lacked: a set of previous linguistic experiences that the poet can draw upon
and put to new purposes.

The familiar opening lines of *Troilus* contain a number of genre-markers
that a fourteenth-century audience could associate with the performative
aspects of English romance:

Making of English Poetry (London, 1972), vol. 1, ch. 1; Laura Hibbard Loomis, *Sir Thopas*, in
Sources and Analogues of Chaucer's Canterbury Tales, eds W. F. Bryan and Germaine Dempster (Chicago, 1941), pp. 486–559; and Windeatt, '*Troilus* and the Disenchantment of
Romance', *Studies in Medieval English Romances*, ed. Derek Brewer (Cambridge, 1988), pp.
129–47. (Although Crosby cites minstrel-style language in Chaucer as evidence of oral
delivery, what her abundant evidence really shows is the extent of Chaucer's use of the language of metrical romance.)
4   J. A. Burrow, *Ricardian Poetry*, p. 20.
5   CT III, 1375, 1713; IV, 2225; VI, 160; VII, 748, 2423; LGW 1162, 1907. Crosby reports
about 53 occurrences of the first phrase alone and about 30 of the second.

> The double sorwe of Troilus to tellen,
> That was the kyng Priamus sone of Troye,
> In lovynge, how his aventures fellen
> Fro wo to wele, and after out of joie,
> My purpos is, er that I parte fro ye.   (I, 1–5)

In just five lines, we have a hero, son of a named heroic father, promises of 'aventures', the movement from 'wo to wele' (though this narrative unfortunately will not rest there) and the speaker's evoked presence: the imagined model for oral performance is the same one built into *Havelok* or *Guy of Warwick*. Chaucer's 'er that I parte fro ye' is the same 'ore I hense pase' (10) of the teller of *Torrent of Portyngale*. Although we know that *Troilus* will end with authorial self-presentation of a very different sort, it seems an intriguing choice to begin with this stance so familiar from English romance.

In fact, a careful read through the sources and analogues of *Sir Thopas* in the Bryan and Dempster volume shows how much the metrical romances there cited are also the stylistic sources and analogues of the *Book of the Duchess*, the *Parliament* and *Troilus*. If the easily-finished last line of *Sir Thopas* is parody, it must be in part self-parody because so many of the same stylistic features occur in *Troilus* and elsewhere in Chaucer's verse. Among the minstrel-style features parodied in *Sir Thopas*, one would have to include the six or seven lines padded by such asseverations as 'I telle it yow' (758) and 'it is no nay' (766). But asseveration is also well represented in nonparodic contexts: the formula 'the soth to seyne/ telle' occurs at least twenty-three times in *Troilus and Criseyde* alone; all but two instances occur in rhyme.[6] One whole line in *Sir Thopas* is pure asseveration:

> For sothe, as I yow telle may   (749),

but so is a line from *Troilus*:

> And shortly, al the sothe for to seye   (IV, 953).

Also prominent among *Sir Thopas*'s minstrel-style features are the romance doublets: 'game and glee', 'wele and wo', 'joy and bliss'. Three such pairings grace *Thopas*'s opening stanza, and they are interspersed throughout the poem. Yet Crosby's compilations show their profusion in Chaucer's most serious verse as well.[7]

An alliterative doublet, conspicuous for its irrelevance, accompanies Sir Thopas's impetuous choice of a love object:

---

[6]   TC I, 12, 591, 712; II, 520, 621, 684, 986, 1356, 1516, 1559; III, 355, 430, 1530, 1598, 1793; IV, 47, 503, 797, 953; V, 1012, 1028, 1035, 1349. See Crosby, 'Chaucer and the Custom of Oral Delivery', pp. 424–5, for many other conventional asseverations in Chaucer.

[7]   See Crosby, 'Chaucer and the Custom of Oral Delivery', pp. 421–3.

> And to an elf-queene I me take
>> *By dale and eek by downe!* (795–6)

Although the bouncing rhythm of the second line and its verbosity are here perceived as comic, we can find the identical rhythm and the same use of a universalising doublet in a passage from *Troilus and Criseyde*:

> And on the morwe unto the yate he wente,
> And up and doun, *by west and ek by este,*
> Upon the walles made he many a wente. (V, 1192–4)

The doublet makes up only part of the more leisurely five-stress line of *Troilus*, but this line's dignity is hardly saved by its opening feet, another minstrel-style doublet, 'up and doun'. Yet the context is Troilus's hopeless vigil at the gates of Troy, where the intent can be neither comedy nor derisive allusion to minstrelsy.

Another seemingly parodic use of doublets in *Sir Thopas* is the repetition within one elaborately tail-rhymed stanza of the formulaic pair 'ride and go':

> Til he so longe hath *riden and goon*
> That he foond, in a pryve woon,
>> The contree of Fairye
>> So wilde;
> For in that contree was ther noon
> That to him durste *ride or goon,*
>> Neither wyf ne childe. (799–806)

Although we might assume that only in parody would Chaucer set two minstrel-style doublets to rhyme with one another in a single stanza, in fact he had already done so in *Troilus*:

> 'Soon after that bigonne we to lepe,
> And casten with oure dartes *to and fro,*
> Tyl at the laste he seyde he wolde slepe,
> And on the gres adoun he leyde hym tho;
> And I afer gan romen *to and fro,*
> Til that I herde, as that I welk alone,
> How he bigan ful wofully to grone.' (II, 512–18)

In *Thopas*, the highly conventional phrase 'lady free' is rhymed with a tag: 'Now hold youre mouth, *par charitee,* / Bothe knyght and *lady free,* . . .' (891–2); so it is in *Troilus*, '. . . Han many a day ben, alwey yet, *parde,* . . . And for the love of God, my *lady fre,* . . .' (V, 142, 144). In *Troilus*, 'lady fre' or 'lady bright' occurs in rhyme nine times in Book V alone.[8] The *Thopas* narrator may sound inept when he brings his stanza to rest on a platitude:

8 *Fre*: V, 144, 669, 1362, 1390, 1405; *bright*: V, 162, 465, 516, 922. See Windeatt 'Disenchantment', for many more such phrases shared by *Troilus* and the anonymous metrical romances.

And there he swoor on ale and breed
How that the geaunt shal be deed,
   Bityde what bityde! (872–4)

Yet Chaucer gives the same commonplace to Criseyde at a crucial moment:

'But natheles, *bityde what bityde*,
I shal to-morwe at nyght, by est or west,
Out of this oost stele . . .' (V, 750–52)

Despite a long history of interpreting Chaucer's parody in just this way, we simply cannot take *Sir Thopas* as Chaucer's definitive dismissal of the minstrel style as an element of serious poetic compositions.[9]

The traditional interpretation of *Sir Thopas* has made it difficult for us to look dispassionately at the presence of the minstrel style in Chaucer's non-parodic verse. For centuries, the pilgrim-narrator's first tale has been regarded as a 'criticism of fourteenth-century minstrelsy'; more specifically, in the words of the eighteenth-century Chaucer editor Thomas Tyrwhitt, it was 'clearly intended to ridicule the "palpable, gross" fictions of the common rhymers of that age, and still more, perhaps, the meanness of their language and versification'.[10] The classic statement on the target of Chaucer's parody is that of Loomis in the Bryan and Dempster volume that has served for over half a century as the standard work on Chaucer's sources and analogues. As well as a valuable array of parallels between *Thopas* and the romances, she offers her view of the particular artistic failings of English romance parodied by Chaucer in *Thopas* including their 'long-winded and inconsequent stories', their 'want of plan and method and meaning', their 'excessive use of insignificant detail', their 'bourgeois absurdities in setting forth knight-errantry' and, above all, their use of the 'worn devices of minstrel style', with its 'reiterated commonplace rhymes and phrases'.[11]

It is difficult to say which has posed a greater impediment to assessing the role of English-romance style in Chaucer: the traditional reading of *Sir Thopas* as a simple rejection of that style or a modern embarrassment over formulaic language. Modern readers are understandably reluctant to dwell on

---

[9] In her compilation of the *Thopas* analogues, Loomis points out that Chaucer at times echoed his own poems (*Sir Thopas*, pp. 493, 550). Dieter Mehl, in *The Middle English Romances of the Thirteenth and Fourteenth Centuries* (London, 1969), observes that *Thopas* 'often makes fun of conventions which Chaucer himself used at other times in all seriousness' (p. 256). Kean also argues for a profound link between Chaucer's language and metrical romance: for example, 'some of the characteristics which are usually singled out as most original – and as most "Chaucerian" – in his dialogue are in fact those of earlier romances in English' (*Chaucer and the Making of English Poetry*, I.14).

[10] The first quotation is from the title of Arthur K. Moore's article, '*Sir Thopas* as Criticism of Fourteenth-Century Minstrelsy', *JEGP* 53 (1954), pp. 532–45; Tyrwhitt (1775) as quoted by Moore in the same article, p. 532, n. 3.

[11] *Sources and Analogues of Chaucer's Canterbury Tales*, eds Bryan and Dempster, p. 491. Loomis quotes from W. P. Ker.

stock rhymes, phrases and narrative devices when faced with the luminous poetic qualities of *Troilus and Criseyde*. Under the influence of New Critics and post-New Critics, most of us have internalised deeply the assumption that formulaic language is inartistic. What difference does it make if Chaucer uses the asseveration 'the sothe to seyne' or 'telle' twenty-three times in such a long and beautiful poem? And couldn't this and the many other asseverations be imitations of speech rather than borrowings from romance conventions? But when we note that twenty-one out of twenty-three instances of this phrase are used in rhyme, it seems much more likely that we are looking at a compositional habit or technique that Chaucer shared with the rhyming romances than at an imitation of colloquial speech. If we believe that Chaucer and his audiences were aware of the sources of this highly conventional and thus highly recognisable narrative manner, then we should be reluctant to dismiss its presence as inconsequential, as an authorial path of least resistance with no real implications for reception or interpretation. The point that borrowed language is never innocent, never leaves the borrower's own discourse as it was, could be made by recourse to a number of literary theorists. Language comes to us, Mikhail Bakhtin argues, 'shot through with intentions and accents'. Prior to its utterance by a new speaker,

> the word does not exist in a neutral and impersonal language (it is not, after all, out of a dictionary that the speaker gets his words!), but rather it exists in other people's mouths, in other people's contexts, serving other people's intentions: it is from there that one must take the word, and make it one's own.[12]

Although Norman Blake has argued that Chaucer considered English works 'insufficiently authoritative or fashionable to be worth quoting or alluding to',[13] Chaucer's adoption and transformation of romance language argues that he did take the risk of wrestling 'the word' away from verse that his culture was more likely to associate with *gestours* than with *auctors*. Rather than quoting or alluding to their work in the usual literary sense, he has done something more intimate: he has adopted some of their compositional methods along with their language.

Negative aesthetic and social judgments of the metrical romances have echoed for decades in critical writings, despite the lack of other evidence that Chaucer and his audiences shared the modern view of what constitute the 'defects of popular minstrelsy'. Do we have evidence that fourteenth-century audiences derided English romance for its 'bourgeois absurdities'? Did they deplore its 'rambling' and its 'want of plan', given the apparent difference in their preferences in regard to structure and length? Would Chaucer and his audiences share the same view of 'worn' or 'commonplace' language held by close-reading literary critics in a print culture?

---

12 'Discourse in the Novel', *The Dialogic Imagination*, ed. Michael Holquist, trans. Caryl Emerson and Michael Holquist (Austin, 1981), pp. 293, 294.
13 *The English Language in Medieval Literature* (London, 1977), p. 22.

The main evidence for Chaucer's endorsement of such judgments is of course *Sir Thopas* itself. But we seem to be in the midst of a gradual reinterpretation of Chaucer's parody, one that opens the way for a more positive assessment of Chaucer's reception of English romance in *Troilus and Criseyde* and elsewhere. Frequently in Chaucer we see self-consciousness shading into self-parody, and the first tale he gives to his fictional representative in *The Canterbury Tales* is such an instance. *Sir Thopas* is not only a parody of English minstrelsy, but, as Burrow saw, also an 'image' or 'cartoon' that represents 'many of the weaknesses and some of the strengths not merely of the hacks but also of the true poets of the age, including Chaucer himself'.[14] In Alan Gaylord's words, the target of Chaucer's parody is 'not the romances but the fancies and temptations of his own practice'.[15] The main evidence for these claims is, once again, the existence in serious contexts of many of the same stylistic mannerisms supposed to be derided as absurd or inartistic in *Sir Thopas*. Consistent with this idea that *Thopas* contains an element of self-parody is the suggestion that the *Thopas-Melibee* pairing depicts the extremes of Chaucer's own authorial role: 'his position as court entertainer, successor to generations of professional minstrels, is belittled in the self-mockery of *Sir Thopas*, but as the adviser to kings the author of the *Melibee* writes essentially without irony'.[16]

If we are willing to take *Sir Thopas* as a parody that includes among its targets one extreme of Chaucer's own poetic practice, rather than as an expression of his contempt for the minstrel style, we may now ask what purpose this style serves amid the impressive array of styles, conventions, and genres in *Troilus*. To take just one aspect of the minstrel manner in *Troilus*, let us look at Chaucer's use of formulaic phrases familiar from metrical romance. The prevailing view of formulaic poetry among those who study oral traditions is that oral genres and their near descendants in the realm of writing operate from a principle of metonymy, in which a given occurrence of a traditional phrase draws upon, or is contiguous with, all other occurrences. For an audience who knows the tradition, a formulaic expression can convey a wealth of associations carried over from previous contexts. John Miles Foley points out that in written works that derive from oral traditions, formulaic expressions can appear to be 'repetitive, mechanical structures' when looked at 'through the interposed lens of literary values and assumptions'.[17] But

---

14 J. A. Burrow, *Ricardian Poetry*, p. 14.

15 Alan Gaylord, 'The Moment of *Sir Thopas*: Towards a New Look at Chaucer's Language', CR 16 (1982), p. 320.

16 Richard Firth Green, *Poets and Princepleasers: Literature and the English Court in the Late Middle Ages* (Toronto, 1980), p. 143. See also Lee Patterson, ' "What Man Artow?": Authorial Self-Definition in *The Tale of Sir Thopas* and *The Tale of Melibee*', SAC 11 (1989), pp. 120–4, and Seth Lerer, ' "Now holde youre mouth": The Romance of Orality in the *Thopas-Melibee* Section of the *Canterbury Tales*', *Oral Poetics in Middle English Poetry*, ed. Mark C. Amodio (New York, 1994), pp. 185–99.

17 John Miles Foley, *Immanent Art: From Structure to Meaning in Traditional Oral Epic*

audiences competent in the tradition in question can reinstill these structures with a referentiality that contributes significantly to a poem's aesthetic
and emotional effect. In the British ballad, for example, a stock or formulaic
reference to a girl 'sewing and combing' in her bower almost always signals
her conscious or, more often, unconscious, longing for a lover. Plucking
flowers has similar sexual overtones, while an individual who is 'playing at
the ball' is likely to be singled out from a group for seduction or abduction.[18]
Ballads were transmitted both memorially and in writing, while *Troilus* was
very much a written creation in a literary tradition. But poets persisted in
using the referential power of certain stereotyped phrases even in increasingly textual environments such as fourteenth-century England because it
was still capable of importing into texts associations and meanings that were
otherwise inaccessible.[19] This kind of meaning is built up slowly in the minds
of poets and audiences as they become familiar with a particular tradition.
Thus, in thriving oral traditions, the formula becomes more meaningful with
use, a perspective strikingly different from the literate's assumption that
phrases *lose* their impact as they are repeated.

At least one ballad formula rich in connotative meaning is also present in
Troilus: the miracle of bells that ring 'without man's hand' is evoked in a
speech by Pandarus (III, 188–9). Flemming Andersen argues that this formulaic expression imports into a ballad in highly compressed form the significance of all the miraculously-ringing church bells in all manifestations of the
tradition with which the audience is familiar. I am suggesting that perhaps
some of the many romance formulas found in *Troilus* might also bear a more
potent meaning than we can easily recognise if we bring to the poem only a
modern aversion to formulaic language. I do not wish to exaggerate this
point: not every formulaic phrase in metrical romance or in Chaucer is ripe
with this kind of extratextual meaning, but we may well be missing some of
the power of those formulas that do mean in this traditional, rather than literary, way.

As a final example of Chaucer's use of traditional and formulaic English
phraseology, we might recall the appealing stanza near the end of *Troilus* in
which the poet-narrator apostrophises an element or an imagined aspect of
his audience as 'yonge, fresshe folkes, he or she' (V, 1835ff), urging that they

---

(Bloomington, 1991), p. xii. See also Alain Renoir, 'Oral-Formulaic Rhetoric: An
Approach to Image and Message in Medieval Poetry', *Medieval Texts and Contemporary
Readers*, eds Laurie Finke and Martin Shichtman (Ithaca, 1987), pp. 234–53.

18 These ballad examples are well documented by Flemming G. Andersen, *Commonplace
and Creativity: The Role of Formulaic Diction in Anglo-Scottish Traditional Balladry* (Odense,
DK, 1985). Andersen's understanding of the connotative functions of formulaic language
corresponds to Foley's concept of 'traditional referentiality'. Neither claims that this function of formulaic language is exclusive to orally performed narratives, only that it can be an
important part of an audience's reception of such works.

19 Foley, *Immanent Art*, p. 7.

... thynketh al nys but a faire,
This world that passeth soone as floures faire.

Much has been written about this stanza, which gives at least the illusion of drawing a moral from the poem's tragic outcome, but it is not always noted that its last two lines weave together two English commonplaces. Both are attested before and after Chaucer: 'life in this world is but a fair (or a cherry fair)' and 'to pass like a flower', often a flower in grass or hay – these expressions probably go back to Isaiah 40.6, and, even there, were instances of proverbial wisdom.[20] Although the mutability *topos* itself runs the whole spectrum of elite to popular texts, Chaucer's verbal formulation of it here is firmly rooted in English idiom.

That it is rooted in native English poetry as well is suggested by a related passage in *Kyng Alisaunder*. Near the end of his long poem and as a prelude to the sorrowful announcement that Fortune has turned away from his hero, the *Alisaunder*-poet writes:

> In this werlde falleth many cas,
> Gydy blisse, short solas! ...
> The leuedyes shene als the glas,
> And thise maidens, with rody faas,
> Passen sone als floure in gras;
> So strong, so fair, neuere non nas
> That he ne shal passe with 'Allas'.   (7820–30)[21]

The similarity to *Troilus* is intriguing. The context for both is reflection on the hero's death in the light of this 'false worldes brotelnesse', as Chaucer had put it in the preceding stanza. The 'yonge, fresshe folkes' whose life in this world 'passeth soone as floures faire' closely parallel the maidens who 'passen sone als floure in gras' in *Kyng Alisaunder*. *Alisaunder* was once part of the Auchinleck Manuscript, and thus Chaucer may have read it, but the whole complex of ideas is so deeply traditional that I see no reason to think in terms of direct literary borrowing. Rather, Chaucer's use in *Troilus* of these stereotyped phrases imports a wealth of meaning from other English contexts in which are lamented the world's transience, the passing of youth and beauty and the unreliability of Fortune.

If I have succeeded in suggesting that we might profitably reassess Chaucer's reception of the formulaic language of metrical romance, then perhaps too there is hope for his reception of its other conventions, including its 'long-winded and inconsequent stories', 'want of meaning' and – who knows – perhaps even its 'bourgeois absurdities'. The English metrical

---

[20] B. J. Whiting, *Proverbs, Sentences, and Proverbial Phrases* (Cambridge, MA, 1968), W662 and F326.
[21] Edited from MS Laud Misc. 622 by G. V. Smithers, 2 vols, EETS 227 and 237 (London, 1952, 1957).

romances had something to offer Chaucer that continental works could not – a narrative and poetic tradition in his own language and a stylistic norm from which he could vary. But this tradition came with a price, and that is why Chaucer's reception of it was so ambivalent – neither the scathing rejection traditionally ascribed to him, nor an uncomplicated advocacy, but a *quiting*, a weighing of strengths against limitations. We all recall the fictional Host's vehement response to *Sir Thopas*: 'Now swich a rym the devel I biteche! . . . Thy drasty rymyng is nat worth a toord!' (VII, 924, 930). But what inspired Chaucer to this vigorously voiced denunciation of minstrel-style verse? Virgile, Ovide, Omer, Lucan and Stace? The language of some real-life Harry Bailley? As Loomis pointed out long ago, both lines have close counterparts in that quintessential English metrical romance, *Guy of Warwick*.[22] The language of English romance is only one stream in the confluence of Chaucerian styles, but clearly it had its uses.

---

[22] L. H. Loomis, 'Chaucer and the Auchinleck MS: *Thopas* and *Guy of Warwick*', *Essays and Studies in Honor of Carleton Brown* (New York, 1940), pp. 148–9. The parallels are from the Auchinleck *Guy*: 'þe deuel biteche ich ʒou ichon' (5834) and 'þou nart nouʒt worþ a tord!' (3704).

'Redinge of Romance' in Gower's *Confessio Amantis*

JEREMY DIMMICK

A MANS, the hapless lover of the *Confessio Amantis*, has few sources of encouragement in his pursuit of a lady supremely indifferent to him, and his main recourse is fantasy. In Book VI, dedicated to Gluttony, he pleads innocent to the vice of Delicacy, describing his own meagre amatory diet: even if he were starving, his lady would not spare 'o goodly lok' to feed his heart.[1] Among the crumbs from love's table on which he survives are romances:

> Fulofte time it falleth so,
> Min Ere with a good pitance
> Is fedd of redinge of romance
> Of Ydoine and of Amadas,
> That whilom weren in mi cas,
> And eke of othre many a score,
> That loveden longe er I was bore.
> For whan I of here loves rede,
> Min Ere with the tale I fede;
> And with the lust of here histoire
> Somtime I drawe into memoire
> Hou sorwe mai noght evere laste;
> And so comth hope in ate laste,
> Whan I non other fode knowe.   (VI, 876–89)

This is the most explicit account Amans gives of what he likes to read, and what demands he makes of 'romance' (not a term Gower uses elsewhere in the *Confessio*): he reads to identify with the protagonists, and to appropriate their experiences as his own.[2] He does not make any particular distinctions among the stories of lovers – one title can stand for scores of others – and the

---

1   *Confessio Amantis*, VI, 715. All citations of Gower's works are from G. C. Macaulay, ed., *The Complete Works of John Gower*, 4 vols (Oxford, 1899–1902).
2   For an important account of the psychology of reading in the *Confessio*, setting out from this passage, see James Simpson, *Sciences and the Self in Medieval Poetry: Alan of Lille's*

125

generic definition is relatively minimal; romances here are tales of lovers from the distant past. If there is any more precise distinction being made, it may well be one of language rather than genre: Gower's only other uses of the word, in his Anglo-Norman *Mirour de l'omme*, refer to the French language or a work written in French, and the choice of *Amadas et Ydoine* as the one example to be named seems to confirm Amans's preference for Anglo-Norman romances of refined, chivalric love.[3]

Indeed, the choice of *Amadas* is wonderfully indicative of Amans's motives as a reader: he identifies with Amadas as one who was in his *cas*, and the chime of their names means that Amans's favourite romance is one in which he virtually appears by name. The *histoire* of Amadas and Ydoine provides the optimistic prospect of romance closure which Amans's own experience in love obstinately fails to reach. Initially Amadas, like Amans, succumbs to lovesickness when Ydoine resists him; however, she accepts his service, and the obstacles to their union are thereafter external. Though apparently insuperable – they include the forced marriage and apparent death of the heroine – the obstacles are of course finally overcome. Such a story-pattern offers obvious encouragement to Amans. If he can view his own story as destined for romance closure, he can interpret every hindrance as the deferral of an inevitable union. He is simply stuck in the first stage of the *Amadas* story, lovesick for a 'dangerous' mistress. The lady's total lack of interest in him may be identified as *danger*, and *danger* as the mere deferral of consent. In fact, Amans goes further in his procedure of reading as appropriation: both Amadas and Ydoine, not the hero alone, 'weren in my cas'. He collapses the distinction not only between himself and Amadas, but between hero and heroine, himself and his lady. All are in the same *cas*.

All these sources of hope turn out to be nebulous: Amans is not Amadas, and there are hints that he knows this well before Venus's eventual rejection of his suit on the grounds of his advanced age. The hope he derives from reading romances, Amans continues in his confession on Delicacy, is short-lived and imperfect:

> And that endureth bot a throwe,
> Riht as it were a cherie feste;
> Bot forto compten ate leste,
> As for the while yit it eseth
> And somdel of myn herte appeseth.   (VI, 890–4)

'Anticlaudianus' and John Gower's 'Confessio Amantis', Cambridge Studies in Medieval Literature, 25 (Cambridge, 1995), pp. 254–71.

3   'Romance' is paired antithetically with 'latin' at *Mirour de l'omme*, ll. 8150, 21, 775, 27, 476–7; cf. also 18 374. On the probable Anglo-Norman origins of *Amadas et Ydoine* (the one complete manuscript extant is continental), see John Revell Reinhard, *The Old French Romance of 'Amadas et Ydoine': An Historical Study* (Durham, NC, 1927), pp. 124–38; William Calin, *The French Tradition and the Literature of Medieval England* (Toronto, 1994), p. 71.

Amans is dissatisfied with the very narratives on which he is so dependent. The effect of his feeding on romance lasts only 'for the while', and the process must be repeated 'fulofte' (876) for him to be sustained by it.[4] This lurking dissatisfaction beneath his wishful identification of himself with his literary heroes gives Genius some crucial leverage in directing Amans's reading. If the *Confessio* existed solely as a collection of narratives calculated to feed his obsessive desire for hope, Genius would do no more than repeat the same story over and over again – a story whose sole narrative function would be to privilege and reward male desire, overcome or ignore female resistance. However, a different prospect is opened up by Amans's own unease with the prospect of such iteration, his occasional capacity to see through his and Genius's strategies of temporary subsistence on handed-down love stories. Amans's unease with both his reading-matter and his mode of reading provides Genius with the opportunity to modify and redirect them.

One alternative strategy to avoid this potentially endless iteration would be for Genius to repudiate Amans's preferred reading altogether, directing his and our notice to some alternative, antithetical discourse. The risk here is that the lover will refuse to follow him, dismissing as irrelevant any materials that so obviously fail to suit his own programme of reading. There are indeed times when Genius risks losing his attention completely, most notably at the end of Book VII, where Amans becomes the first of Gower's critics to respond to five thousand lines on the philosophy of Aristotle with distinctly muted enthusiasm:

> The tales sounen in myn Ere,
> Bot yit myn herte is elleswhere.   (VII, 5411–12)

Amans may show a sporadic and undirected sense of dissatisfaction with love-stories whose capacity to satisfy desire is so incomplete and so transient, but this wavering of commitment is a long way from being a positive transference of allegiance from the matter of love to Aristotelian philosophy and political morality. Rather than ignore this resistance, Genius accommodates it: he temporises with Amans's demands on him by taking his favourite reading-matter and working it into the *Confessio*'s larger design. One means by which Gower is able to develop long-term arguments over the course of the poem is the interrelationship of tales which share certain generic signals: their dialogue with one another, and with tales of different genres, cuts across the poem's static organising principle of exemplary illustrations for particular vices. We shall see that romances, though few in number, have an important function in the *Confessio*: they constitute a link between Amans's private preoccupations and Gower's broadest thematic concerns, and provide the poem's

---

4 This lack of confidence distinguishes him from the otherwise very similar lover in Gower's *Cinkante Balades* XXIV, who reflects on the story of Pygmalion, and derives 'graunt espoir de la comparisoun' that he will be 'certein/ De grace' (ll. 13–15).

most confident affirmations of moral, familial and social good. However much stress they are put under (and at times the pressure is extreme), the *Confessio*'s romances have a vital role to play in holding the work together.

II

The first of the *Confessio*'s romances, the 'Tale of Florent' (I, 1407–1861), seems at first glance to be a prime example of the kind of story which feeds Amans's desires – a wish-fulfilment disguised as an *exemplum*. Florent, as a young knight confronted with the prospect of a forced marriage to an aged 'loathly lady' (in outline the story is that of Chaucer's *Wife of Bath's Tale*) is a negative image of Amans as he is finally revealed – an old man getting nowhere in his pursuit of a desirable lady.[5] The resolution of Florent's predicament, with the transformation of old woman into young princess, reveals that the disjunction of age and desirability was an illusion. The hero's reluctance, mirror-image of the reluctance of Amans's lady, vanishes with her transformation, and the tale ends with the union of lovers which is Amans's prime narrative requirement. Such closure is certainly one of the generic constituents of Gower's romances – they are essentially optimistic narratives, and always give prominent place to sexual love – but it is only part of the picture. Even as Genius appears to fulfil Amans's demands on him to the letter, he quietly introduces a corrective to Amans's obsessive pursuit of love, while also anticipating motifs and narrative structures which will receive their fullest development in the *Confessio*'s two long, idealistic romances, 'Constance' and 'Apollonius of Tyre'.

Gower sets up his narrative with an initial flurry of generic signals:

> Ther was whilom be daies olde
> A worthi knyht, and as men tolde
> He was Nevoeu to themperour
> And of his Court a Courteour:
> Wifles he was, Florent he hihte,
> He was a man that mochel myhte,
> Of armes he was desirous,
> Chivalerous and amorous,
> And for the fame of worldes speche,
> Strange aventures forto seche,
> He rod the Marches al aboute.   (I, 1407–17)

Here are all the keywords of romance knighthood – Florent's worth, his might, his desire for fame and 'strange aventures', the court space from which he sets out. That he is presently 'wifles' is a broad hint that marriage is his

---

5   On the various analogues see Sigmund Eisner, *A Tale of Wonder: A Source Study of 'The Wife of Bath's Tale'* (Wexford, 1957); for Gower's telling see pp. 62–72.

destination in this tale: the ensuing narrative must bring Florent through adventure to honour, marriage and worldly establishment, unless it is wholly to contradict the generic expectations it has set up.

The bare outline of the story conforms to expectations: Florent's adventures prove him the best of knights, and reward him with the hand of a princess. Such closure conforms admirably to Amans's expectations of a romance, but the 'strange aventure' that brings Florent to this predictable conclusion is full of surprises. In the initial portrait Florent is presented in active terms as an autonomous, self-determining hero: he 'mochel myhte', he is 'desirous' and 'amorous' and he positively seeks out adventure. His own will provides the simple dynamism which sets the plot in motion. At once, however, Florent loses the initiative, and he never truly regains it. He is captured 'be strengthe' (1422) by a hostile family, and in the ensuing fight kills the family's son and heir, Branchus. At this point the plot meets up with its analogues as Branchus's grandmother proposes the riddle of 'what alle wommen most desire' (1481), as an alternative to death.

Throughout this narrative, the initial impetus of Florent's will, his desire to assert himself in the realm of love and arms, is dissipated. The knight who 'mochel myhte' is unable to fight his way out of trouble, and he confirms the turn away from military solutions which the narrative has taken, when he forbids anyone from his uncle's court to seek vengeance should he be killed. His submission to the loathly lady's will is gradual and somewhat reluctant – he briefly considers shutting her up 'in an Ile' (1578) after the wedding, since she cannot live long – but is eventually complete. Up until his final quandary, the choice of having his half-disenchanted bride fair by day or fair by night, the virtue of *trowthe* has ensured that he makes the right moral choices; Florent 'hath levere forto dye/ Than breke his trowthe' (1511–12), and this ethical core prevents what is already a lighthearted romance from descending into burlesque. Faced, however, with what is not a moral choice at all, he is finally paralysed: *trowthe* does not help him to rank the benefits of fame – a beautiful wife by day, capable of being displayed as a trophy – and love which he was seeking at the outset. He gives up the freedom of choice altogether, with, under the circumstances, a remarkably good grace:

> Thus grante I yow myn hole vois,
> Ches for ous bothen, I you preie;
> And what as evere that ye seie,
> Riht as ye wole so wol I.   (1828–31)

It is at this point, with the pacification of the knightly will complete, that the takeover of the story by its female characters likewise becomes complete. Florent was set his riddle by one old woman, and has been given his answer by another; he has just given up his 'hole vois' to the disenchanted lady – and she now reveals that she was transformed in the first place by her wicked stepmother. Florent set out seeking to impose himself on the world of knightly adventure, and has ended up being a passive centre in a narrative whose action is patterned by various female wills.

At this moment, however, the romance closure we were originally primed to expect returns with a vengeance: Florent, by giving up the freedom of his will, wins everything he could desire. He is proved to be the 'kniht that in his degre / Alle othre passeth of good name' (1848–9), winning the fame he initially sought, and he marries a beautiful princess. The mechanism by which he has reached this moment of self-establishment may be non-standard, but the outcome is just what Gower's initial generic signals promised us. The modification is not superficial, all the same: Florent has gained all he desires, but not by desiring it. In his last choice, giving away the freedom of choice, he recognises for the first time something which the virtue of *trowthe* does not require him to perceive: his own good (even his own moral good) is not the sole criterion of value. By yielding his 'hole vois' to his wife, Florent acknowledges that she is a narrative subject in her own right, is not merely an adjunct to his own desires or self-worth. Of course, it turns out that her choice conforms to the pattern of Florent's desires: the terms of her disenchantment are essentially that she must agree to become a romance heroine, winning the 'love and sovereinete' (1847) of the best of knights. To become the heroine of someone else's romance is the condition of her liberation from her own romance of exile and alienation.[6]

With its late revelation that the heroine has a history, an exile-romance whose closure cannot be achieved in isolation from that of Florent's quest-romance, the tale becomes a combination of two narrative paradigms. The quest romance, with its active, assertive male protagonist, is combined in 'The Tale of Florent' with the exile-romance as represented by the suffering heroine, who has become something more than a reflex of the hero, the object necessary to the subject's attitude of desire:[7] she becomes a secondary protagonist, operating in a different kind of romance, the romance of exile which is to be given its full development in the tales of 'Constance' and 'Apollonius'. The values of the exile paradigm win out: the reorientation of heroism in 'Florent', away from action to endurance, and finally to a new sense of oneself as operating in the context of other selves – in a society – is a tacit rebuke to Amans's self-isolating obsession with his lady as merely the object of his desire.[8]

In the *Confessio*'s distinctively social vision of ethics, the romances offer a means of saving sexual love from Amans's privatised conception, by

---

6   This pattern of alienation and restoration is explored at length in Northrop Frye, *The Secular Scripture: A Study of the Structure of Romance* (Cambridge, MA, 1976), pp. 97–157.

7   Here my phraseology is informed by Evelyn Birge Vitz, *Medieval Narrative and Modern Narratology: Subjects and Objects of Desire* (New York, 1989), pp. 1–10.

8   On this point see Kurt Olsson, *John Gower and the Structures of Conversion: A Reading of the 'Confessio Amantis'*, Publications of the John Gower Society, 4 (Cambridge, 1992), pp. 82–4.

reorienting narrative impetus away from the hero's will. In 'Constance' (II, 587–1603), sexual love is not seen in isolation, as a dominating passion which excludes all other considerations; instead it takes its place in a continuum of 'kindly' bonds of love, integrating the love of parents and children, husbands and wives, humans and God. At the nadir of Constance's fortunes, when she is put out to sea for the second time and lies in a dead swoon, 'he which alle thinges may/ Conforteth hire' (1063–4), and care for her infant son revives her will to live. Without explicitly underlining the echo of Mary and the Christ child in the tableau of Constance nursing her son, Gower presents the pair with delicate pathos, as an emblem of human love informed by the divine:

> And tho sche tok hire child in honde
> And yaf it sowke, and evere among
> Sche wepte, and otherwhile song
> To rocke with hire child aslepe:
> And thus hire oghne child to kepe
> Sche hath under the goddes cure.   (II, 1078–1083)[9]

The union of spiritual, sexual and parental love is a recurrent motif in 'Constance', a tale full of internal echoes of episode and motif. The conception of Moris is by dispensation of 'the hihe makere of nature' (916); when Allee sees his son for the first time, without knowing who he is, he feels an instant, non-rational bond of 'kindly' love, and his desire for Constance when he half-recognises her in Rome is compared with the longing of a soul in purgatory (1381–2, 1421–5). Where Amans habitually isolates sexual love as an all-encompassing obsession, 'Constance' aims to integrate sexuality into a broader pattern, both social and cosmic.[10]

Integration, indeed, is at the heart of Gower's romance mode in 'Constance'; its dynamic is the effort to reconstruct and enhance its heroine's identity in the final sequence of family recognitions and reunions. Her role as missionary is united with the roles of wife, mother and daughter, and takes on political dimensions too: her enforced wanderings define the boundaries of a Christian empire, assimilating England to Rome not only by converting the Saxons to Rome but by creating a dynastic alliance through her marriage to Allee. To the east and south, by contrast, she finds only hostility. The map of her journeys can be seen as creating a myth of origins for an imperial Christendom, while giving it an Anglocentric spin by making an English king the father of 'the cristeneste of alle' the emperors (1598). 'The Tale of Constance'

---

9   Chaucer renders the Marian analogy explicit: *Man of Law's Tale*, II, 834–54.
10   Here, as Winthrop Wetherbee argues, Chaucer's version differs radically, with its 'consistent refusal to grant its heroine a full measure of earthly existence', 'Constance and the World in Gower and Chaucer', *John Gower: Recent Readings*, ed. R. F. Yeager, Medieval Institute Publications, Studies in Medieval Culture, 26 (Kalamazoo, 1989), pp. 65–93 (p. 69).

unifies the spiritual and the secular at the level of empire as well as in the bond of mother and child. It integrates Gower's moral, familial and political preoccupations, as a narrative equivalent to the theoretical structure of philosophy which Gower offers in the Aristotelian terms of Book VII: the division of moral philosophy into ethics, economics and politics is presided over by theology, 'the conserve/ And kepere of the rem[e]nant' (VII, 54–5).[11]

The importance of 'Constance' in the Confessio's thematic and structural economy is reinforced when its design and many of its details are recapitulated and varied in the poem's last and longest tale, 'Apollonius of Tyre' (VIII, 271–2008). Just as 'Constance' itself is built, in typical romance fashion, around the elaboration of related motifs and episodes, so 'Apollonius' shares the same mode of internal construction, and also develops a set of echoes and resonances with 'Constance', over the gap of six intervening books.[12] The likenesses run from small details to the largest principles of design. Apollonius meets without recognising his only child, here his daughter Thaise: 'he hire loveth kindely,/ And yit he wiste nevere why' (VIII, 1707–8) just as with Allee and Moris: 'This child he loveth kindely,/ And yit he wot no cause why' (II, 1381–2). The recognition of an instinctive tie between those 'so sibb of blod' (VIII, 1703) precedes the recognition scenes which wind up both romances, and offers a redemptive inversion of the unnatural parental figures who are the villains in both, the two mothers-in-law in 'Constance', the incestuous Antiochus, and Thaise's treacherous foster-parents in 'Apollonius'; similarly, the reunion of husbands and wives relates back to the earlier threats of incest, rape or prostitution. Indeed, the entire narrative structures are almost identical, with their sequence of enforced but ultimately providential sea-voyages, initialised by abortive marriages (Constance's to the Sultan, Apollonius's suit to the daughter of Antiochus), and proceeding through a set of variations on the themes of establishment of and threat to family bonds: no sooner are the hero and heroine united than they are severed, until the final series of recognitions and reunions establishes them at the centre of an enlarged family, and with a wider and more secure political authority.[13] 'Apollonius' differs structurally

---

11 Macaulay's edition has the unmetrical 'remnant'; my emendation brings the text into line with the word's thirty-nine other occurrences in the Confessio, where it is consistently trisyllabic; see J. D. Pickles and J. L. Dawson, eds, A Concordance to John Gower's 'Confessio Amantis' (Cambridge, 1987), p. 499.

12 See Peter Goodall, 'John Gower's Apollonius of Tyre: Confessio Amantis, Book VIII', Southern Review 15 (1982), pp. 243–53; Olsson, John Gower and the Structures of Conversion, pp. 71–86. The Historia Apollonii, Gower's ultimate source, depends on the same structural principle: see Elizabeth Archibald, Apollonius of Tyre: Medieval and Renaissance Themes and Variations; Including the Text of the 'Historia Apollonii Regis Tyri' with an English Translation (Cambridge, 1991), pp. 12–13.

13 From the closeness of the connections, Archibald argues that the Historia Apollonii influenced the development of the Constance story: see Apollonius of Tyre, pp. 58–60, and 'The Flight from Incest: Two Late Classical Precursors of the Constance Theme', CR 20 (1986), pp. 259–72.

only in being the more elaborate, since it has more protagonists; separate plot-strands follow the wanderings of Apollonius himself, his wife and his daughter.

Variations in the middle of the narrative aside, there is a shared basic structure, convoluted in its disposition of reiterated or inverted episodes, but ultimately circling back to an optimistic and seemingly inevitable closure in which families are reunited and just political rule re-established. This is the single feature most definitive of 'romance' in the *Confessio* as I am using the term: though these tales can be seen as driven by arbitrary and meaningless coincidence at the level of individual incident and motivation, they gain (at least in retrospect) a deep structural predictability, enhanced by the fact that the *Confessio* uses that structure more than once.[14] I must stress that this generic definition is intended as a local rather than a universal one; 'romance' is, of course, a problematic label, because so many diverse kinds of definition have intersected on the one term, but it strikes me as comparatively unproblematic within the *Confessio*'s own spectrum of narrative kinds. In a single, stylistically homogeneous but generically various work such as Gower's, characteristic narrative motifs and their structural disposition are the chief determinants, though as we saw with 'Florent', Gower does borrow certain romance keywords as additional generic markers.[15] Structurally speaking, it is the romances' integrative tendency and reconciliatory trajectory which make them so useful to Genius as he tries to resist Amans's version of love without abandoning love-narrative as a vehicle for idealism. In the romances, Gower finds a narrative structure in which he can resolve ethical, sexual, familial and public thematic strands in parallel: a single recognition and reconciliation sequence simultaneously brings about the restoration of personal identity, the reunion of lovers and of parents and children, and the restoration of political security.

The romances are stories where sexuality provides the generating cell for larger social structures, and in which any threats to what the *Confessio* represents as normative and natural are eventually foiled; their urge towards the unification of diverse matter provides a narrative anchor for a poem which often seems inclined to fly apart at the seams. Their capacity for optimistic, morally- and socially-resolved closure is a powerful poetic resource, but it is not one which can become the *Confessio*'s own closure without serious

---

[14] Here I differ significantly from William Robins, 'Romance, Exemplum, and the Subject of the *Confessio Amantis*', SAC 19 (1997), pp. 157–81, an impressive article which appeared after I wrote this paper.

[15] For an approach to Middle English romances generally that combines structural with stylistic analysis see Susan Wittig, *Stylistic and Narrative Structures in the Middle English Romances* (Austin, 1978) and Carol Fewster, *Traditionality and Genre in Middle English Romance* (Cambridge, 1987).

opposition or qualification from other, more sceptical currents. Rather, they affirm a redemptive norm by which to control the violations that proliferate elsewhere.

III

The point at which the disruptive elements of the *Confessio* come into closest and most corrosive contact with its romances is in 'Jason and Medea' (V, 3247–4222). This is a romance which goes badly wrong, in part by going on too long: in reaching but continuing beyond its predictable, apparently secure, closure, the narrative enters much darker territory: 'Jason' strays from romance into the disruptive world of Ovid's *Metamorphoses*.

The tale opens, like 'Florent', by defining the circumstances and desires of its protagonist – which, indeed, are virtually identical to Florent's. Jason, too, sets out from his uncle's court, eager to see 'othre Marches'; he is a 'worthi kniht' who 'soghte worschipe overal' (V, 3285, 3256, 3261). The initial impetus of the plot comes wholly from his own will; in extracting and reshaping the story (primarily from Benoit de Sainte-Maure's *Roman de Troie*), Gower suppresses the plot of King Pelleus against his nephew.[16] His desire for fame and love, and Medea's desire for him, continue to impel the narrative – it remains much more closely tied to the quest paradigm than 'Florent' – and in their own private designs they arrive at what seems a classic romance closure. When Jason returns to Greece, successful in his quest and betrothed to the heroine, the story-pattern seems to have resolved itself in ideal fashion. What is missing, by comparison with the 'Constance'/'Apollonius' paradigm, is the larger family union which works the sexual love of the protagonists into a more capacious social design: Medea's family have been left behind, and rather than a closing sequence of reunions and recognitions, Oetes remains impotently angry in Colcos, and the last we hear of his wife is a laconic 'The moder wepte' (3911).

In confirmation that there is unfinished business here, Gower continues beyond the romance closure, with a sudden shift of generic gears. The source changes from the *Roman de Troie* to Ovid's *Metamorphoses*, and the portrayal of Medea also metamorphoses, transforming her from a resourceful romance heroine to something altogether more numinous and dangerous, the sorceress seeking magical herbs to bring about the rejuvenation of Eson, who 'glod forth as an Addre doth' (3967). To the transformation of Medea succeed those of Eson and of Jason who – unlike Florent – abandons his 'trouthe' (4191) to marry Creusa; Gower concludes with her vengeance on their two sons – a murder which goes unpunished. Crimes are rarely unpunished in the

---

16 See Linda Barney Burke, 'Women in John Gower's *Confessio Amantis*', *Mediaevalia* 3 (1977), pp. 238–59 (pp. 243, 255 n. 14).

Confessio, and the judicial loose end here contrasts forcibly with the precision with which the good are rewarded and the evil destroyed in 'Constance' and 'Apollonius'.

Instead, Gower continues by winding backwards to provide a prequel, 'Phrixus and Helle' (V, 4243–363): in response to a question from Amans, Genius explains how the Golden Fleece came to be in Colcos in the first place. The responsibility turns out to lie with another of the *Confessio*'s wicked stepmothers: Yno engineers the exile of her husband's children by his first marriage – they are put out to sea like Constance – one of whom survives to arrive at Colcos on the back of the golden ram. As in 'Florent', this act of family disruption which lies at the origin of the narrative is only revealed when the narrative is complete, but there is a darkness in the treatment of the motif in 'Jason', quite absent from the earlier romance's resolution. In 'Florent' the agency of the wicked stepmother only emerges when it can no longer do any harm: the princess has been restored to herself thanks to the hero's virtue, and her evil can be revealed precisely at the moment that it has been thwarted. The heroine is restored to her proper form, and the series of disruptions of family that began with her enchantment and continued with the feud between the families of Florent and Branchus is concluded.

In 'Jason', however, Medea ends up repeating and intensifying the crime of child-murder: the heroine, instead of redeeming and being redeemed from the cycle of family violence, perpetuates it. Medea's killing of her two sons by Jason, because of his abandonment of her for Creusa, turns out to be a repetition-with-variation of Yno's attempted murder of her husband's two children by his first wife. The addition of 'Phrixus and Helle' as a coda extends the principle of composite structure already apparent in the bipartite 'Jason and Medea'. The narrative structure of 'Constance' and 'Apollonius' is circular and unitary, its parts integrated by principles of subordination, repetition and variation, and resolved together in the final sequence of recognition scenes. The combined 'Jason' and 'Phrixus', by contrast, is linear and additive in construction, its closure uncertain and always susceptible of further addition as it is worked into a larger narrative cycle: the secure, optimistic closure of the non-cyclic romances seems to be possible only through their isolation from the great romance cycles, all of which tend towards the tragic. It is worth noting that Gower's 'Florent' is the only one among the English analogues not to be Arthurian in setting.

'Jason and Medea' cannot be isolated thus from its historical context; it contributes to an unredeemed, self-perpetuating cycle of unnatural crimes which forms part of the great tragic cycle running from the fall of Thebes to the fall of Troy.[17] The presence of that cycle is only hinted at here: that

---

17 Ruth Morse, *The Medieval Medea* (Cambridge, 1996), has a short but penetrating discussion of the cyclic affiliations of Gower's 'Jason' (pp. 220–4). 'Thebanness' is a *leitmotif* of Lee Patterson, *Chaucer and the Subject of History* (London, 1991); on its connection with Troy in Chaucer, see esp. pp. 98, 130–36, 152–53.

Jason's voyage to Colcos was the initial cause of the destruction of Troy is briefly pointed out, but immediately dismissed as 'noght to mi matiere' (3310). Genius tells us that Yno was the daughter of Cadmus, but describes him merely as another king of 'thilke daies' (4274); however, much earlier – in fact, in Genius's first tale, that of Acteon – he names him as the founder of Thebes. The cycle is first introduced, then, in the Confessio's first example of the destructive power of sexuality, and continues in isolated fragments throughout the poem, its own state of fragmentation mirroring the violence of the history. The chain of family crime will run through to the death of Ulysses at the hands of his son Telegonus; this is the point at which the Roman de Troie ends, and is retold by Gower in Book VI as the last tale before the introduction of Alexander, who is to be Aristotle's pupil in the philosophical instruction of Book VII. The narrative of Alexander's birth and upbringing shows that he, like Telegonus, becomes an unwitting parricide: the family crimes which the romances strive to redeem have a deep hold on some of the poem's central narratives.[18]

The prominent place and sheer bulk of 'Apollonius' help to suggest a narrow victory for the romances as Genius reaches the end of the inset tale-collection: by subordinating the punishment of unnatural love to the triumph of 'honeste love' celebrated in the reunion, extension and political establishment of Apollonius's family, the Confessio draws us to the end of Amans's confession with a tenacious optimism. The last of the exempla, however, is not the end of the poem, and the outcome of its own, complex closure is less clear-cut. Amans, so implausible a romance hero himself, does show a certain correspondence with the structure of romance in the resolution of his own narrative. In most respects, to compare Amans with Constance would be absurd, but he shares with her the temporary loss of name and identity, and their eventual recovery: as Constance is disguised as 'Couste', so Gower's lover-persona is eventually identified as 'John Gower'; his perception of his old age in the mirror given him by Venus is a kind of recognition scene. Yet the Confessio's romances have been social narratives above all, reconstructing an ideal society even as they reconstruct the full identity of their protagonists; by contrast, the leading motif in the resolution of Amans's narrative is severance. It is at the moment when his petition to Venus is rejected that Amans, fainting, has a vision of the great lovers, many a score, with whose experiences he has been wishfully identifying himself; his recovery prompts his permanent exile from love's court. Venus sends him home, 'ther vertu moral duelleth,/ Wher ben thi bokes' (VIII, 2925–6). Where Apollonius and Constance are finally surrounded by an extended family and something of an empire, we leave Gower on the margins of the poem's world, facing the metamorphoses of age and death. His society will consist of books and authors;

---

18 'Acteon' (I, 333–78); 'Ulysses and Telegonus' (VI, 1391–788); 'Nectanabus' (VI, 1789–2366).

thus (in the original version) he carries a message from Venus to her 'disciple' and 'poete', Chaucer, for Gower to deliver 'whan ye mete' (VIII, 2941*–2*).

Amans, then, can only fulfil part of the function of the romance hero; his identity remains too exclusively private. The *Confessio* has another, public protagonist in its closing moments, however – its dedicatee, Richard II. Gower presents his king as a new Apollonius, preserved from adversity by divine providence, in a passage praising Richard and referring delicately and in general terms to the crises of the mid-1380s. From the perspective of 1390 or 1391, when the original version of the *Confessio* was completed, Richard appears to have returned to lasting prosperity: that he was 'not infortunat' when beset by 'infortune', and now fosters 'love and acord' in his kingdom and abroad (VIII, 2999*–3000*, 3018*), is the poem's final testimony to the optimistic vision of its romances. Of course, Gower's celebration of Richard's virtue and security turned out to be premature: his presence in the *Confessio* is fragile, for within two years Gower rewrote the end of the poem, omitting all praise of the king in favour of anxious political meditation. The events of the end of Richard's reign, as Gower was to chronicle them in his violently hostile *Cronica tripertita*, show as clearly as 'Jason and Medea' how readily an apparently secure romance closure can collapse into metamorphosis.

The *Ide and Olive* episode in Lord Berners's *Huon of Burdeux*

ELIZABETH ARCHIBALD

THE Middle English *Ide and Olive* (with its French sources) offers a unique variation on the story of the Flight from an Incestuous Father, a popular theme – disturbingly popular, we might think – in the later Middle Ages; versions in Latin and in every western European vernacular were produced over the period from the twelfth century to the sixteenth.[1] This text combines two themes which have become much discussed both in scholarly circles and more widely in the western world today: cross-dressing and incest. A recent book review was headed 'Cross-dressing for success' and subtitled 'The author, about to become a nun, became a conquistador instead'; a recent newspaper article entitled 'The lust that dare not speak its name' discussed Kathryn Harrison's startlingly frank and controversial account of her affair with her father.[2] In this essay I shall consider the effects of combining these two themes, and discuss a number of special aspects that distinguish this version from its analogues.[3]

The earliest version of the story of Huon of Bordeaux occurs in a thirteenth-century French verse cycle attached to the Charlemagne cycle.[4]

---

[1] For discussion of these stories see Margaret Schlauch, *Chaucer's Constance and Accused Queens* (New York, 1927; rptd. AMS Press, 1973); Archibald, 'The Flight from Incest: Two Late Classical Precursors of the Constance Theme', CR 20 (1986), pp. 259–72; and also *Dangerous Propinquity*, my forthcoming study of the incest theme in medieval literature.

[2] *Lieutenant Nun, the memoir of a basque transvestite in the new world*, ed. Catalina de Erauso (Boston, 1995), reviewed in the *Times Literary Supplement* of 17 March 1996; Kathryn Harrison, *The Kiss* (London, 1997), discussed in *The Independent* of 17 April 1997.

[3] I know no other medieval narrative which combines the two themes, but it seems to have survived in oral tradition, for a version of the story including both the incestuous father and the final sex change was recorded in Quebec in 1951; see Catherine Velay-Vallentin, *La Fille en garçon* (Carcassonne, 1992), pp. 199–215 (I am indebted for this reference to Mme Danielle Régnier-Bohler).

[4] For the French metrical text see *Esclarmonde, Clarisse et Florent, Yde et Olive: Drei Fortsetzungen der Chanson von Huon de Bordeaux*, ed. Max Schweigel, *Ausgaben und Abhandlungen aus dem Gebiete der romanischen Philologie* LXXXIII (Marburg, 1889), pp. 152–62. In his introductory synopsis Schweigel indicates variations in the French prose text, which is generally very close to the metrical source. For the Middle English text, a very close rendering of

The hero, Huon, kills the emperor's son, and in punishment is dispatched on a hopeless mission to Babylon. Helped by Oberon, king of the fairies, he accomplishes the mission, marries Esclarmonde, the emir's daughter, is reconciled with Charlemagne, and eventually succeeds Oberon as king of Fairyland (to the annoyance of Arthur, who apparently wanted this throne himself – an amusing instance of French/English one-upmanship). One of the continuations deals with the adventures of Huon's daughter Clarisse (Claryet in Berners), and her eventual marriage to Florent (Florence), heir to the throne of Aragon. The next continuation tells the story of their daughter Yde (Ide); the nineteenth-century editor comments gloomily 'here the imagination of the author assumes very repulsive features'.[5]

> Queen Claryet dies in childbirth; King Florence adores their only daughter, Ide. When she is fifteen he tells his lords that he will marry again, and has found a woman who resembles his dead wife: Ide. The barons are horrified, and so is Ide when she is told. She disguises herself in male clothing and runs away. She rides through Aragon and Lombardy into Germany; being short of money, she takes service with a German. He is killed in a Spanish ambush; she survives, only to meet robbers from whom she escapes with difficulty.
>
> She arrives at Rome and offers her services to the emperor. Everyone admires her, especially princess Olive, whose servant Ide becomes. Ide distinguishes herself in battle against the king of Spain. The emperor makes her first chamberlain and high constable. As a reward for further service, the emperor invites Ide to marry his daughter. Ide is horrified; she tries to excuse herself on the grounds of her humble birth, but the emperor is angry and she has to agree. On the wedding night she tells Olive that the marriage cannot yet be consummated, but after some days confesses the truth to her.
>
> The devoted Olive is prepared to accept the situation, but a spy informs the emperor, who is furious and threatens to burn them both if a public bath reveals Ide to be a woman. She begs him for mercy, but he orders the fire to be prepared. Then a voice from heaven warns him not to touch Ide: God will change her into a man as a reward for her virtue, and she and Olive are to succeed the emperor on his death, which is imminent. Ide is transformed, and that night their son Croissant is conceived; a few days later the emperor dies. Some years later messengers from Florence summon Ide and Olive to visit him: since Ide's flight he has been ill, and also contrite. The visit goes so well that Ide and Olive stay with him, leaving Croissant to rule at Rome.

The subsequent adventures of Croissant were added to the original cycle, as was the story of Huon's son Godin.

A prose version of this cycle was produced in 1454 for three nobles at the

the French prose version, see *The Boke of Duke Huon of Burdeux*, ed. S. L. Lee, 2 vols, EETS ES 40, 41, 43, 50 (London, 1882–7); the *Ide and Olive* episode appears in vol. II, pp. 690–737.

5 Lee, Introduction to *The Boke of Duke Huon*, I, p. xxxv. The heroine is named Yde in the French version and Ide in the English version; I shall use Berners's English forms of names throughout, unless I am referring specifically to the French text.

court of Charles VII of France (some parts were omitted, including the adventures of Godin). No manuscript of this version survives, but it was printed at Paris in 1513, and was soon translated into English by Lord Berners (who also translated Froissart's *Chronicle* and *Arthur of Litell Britayne*, and the Spanish texts *The Castell of Love* and *The Golden Boke of Marcus Aurelius*). According to the colophon of the 1601 edition of *Huon of Burdeux*, Berners translated it for the Earl of Huntingdon; Blake has argued that this was Francis Hastings, the second Earl, and that *Huon* was produced relatively early in Berners's career as a translator, about 1515.[6]

The *Ide and Olive* episode fits in well with the view that late medieval prose romance tends to deal with matters of fact rather than fancy, reducing the supernatural in favour of realism, and emphasising didacticism.[7] It is part of the Charlemagne cycle, which seems to have been particularly popular in later medieval England. It is pious, if not didactic, in that the heroine's virtue, demonstrated in her very proper flight from her incestuous father, is finally rewarded by God who rescues her from the crisis of her impossible marriage to another woman. While no overt moral about incest or indeed anything else is offered at the end of the episode, it is clearly implicit. Early in the story much is made of the horror of the courtiers, as well as Ide, at the prospect of the incestuous marriage. Sorbar, a converted Saracen who had helped Florence and Claryet earlier, exclaims that incest is 'worse than bogery [heresy]' (p. 694). At the end Florence's penitence brings about a reconciliation.

Adventures in love and in battle are generally taken to be the central subject matter of medieval romance; very often deeds of martial prowess help the hero to win the hand of the heroine. Both themes appear in the story of Ide, but given the gender of the protagonist and the nature of the plot, both are treated in unusual ways. When Ide flees from home, the narrator remarks 'of her iorneys and adventures I wyll make no mencyon, because she founde no thynge by the way to let her' (p. 702). She does serve a considerable apprenticeship as a knight.[8] In Germany she runs out of money and has to sell her horse and travel on foot; she is taken for a squire, and enters the service of a German, telling him that her previous master died in Aragon. On the journey to Rome Ide and her companions are attacked by Spaniards; she alone survives (by running away) and then meets a band of robbers, whom

---

6   N. F. Blake, 'Lord Berners: A Survey', *Medievalia et Humanistica* n.s. 2 (1971), pp. 119–32.

7   See Derek Pearsall, 'The English Romance in the Fifteenth Century', *Essays and Studies* n.s. 29 (1976), pp. 56–83; Paul Scanlon, 'Pre-Elizabethan Prose Romances in English', *Cahiers Elisabéthains* 12 (1977), pp. 1–20.

8   Jacqueline de Weever, discussing the French metrical version, comments on this apprenticeship aspect, and on the unusual fact that Yde serves in turn as squire, knight and general; on the other hand, as she notes, Yde herself remarks that as Florent's daughter she certainly should have 'prouece et hardement' (this comment is omitted by Berners). See 'The Lady, the Knight, and the Lover: Androgyny and Integration in *La Chanson d'Yde et Olive*', *Romanic Review* 81 (1991), pp. 371–91 (pp. 372 and 378–9).

she asks for food and drink. They attack her, so she attempts to pacify them in a very unchivalric way: 'Syrs, why make ye that haste to sle me/ lytel shal ye wynne therby nor lese, hold here my sword, I yelde me into your handes, and I praye you in the honoure of our lorde Iesu chryst gyue me some mete and drynke . . .' (pp. 704–5). When she refuses to join the band and 'lerne to be a thefe and a murdrer', the chief insists on wrestling with her: she throws him against a rock, knocking him out, and manages to escape, killing five of the thieves in the process (pp. 706–7). As she rides off she addresses them in a style we might now call 'in your face' as 'horson thefes'.[9]

Ide proves more conventionally chivalric when she gets to Rome, and fights for the emperor against the king of Spain. She does great deeds in battle, culminating in the capture of the Spanish king, and it is this 'hye prowesse' that makes the emperor's daughter Olive fall in love with Ide. This love is increased by Ide's peacetime activities, which remind one of Chaucer's Griselda – diplomatic skills are as important as martial ones here:

> . . . she dyd so moche by her wyt that all dyscordes and debates that were in the empyre betwene lordes or neybours, she set them in peas and acorde, wherfore the emperor louyd her in such wyse that without her he dyd nothynge / and the emperour's doughter Olyue loued her in such wyse that she coude not lyue one day without ye syght of her, she was so taken with loue, thynkynge that she neuer sawe so goodlye a yonge man . . . (p. 720)

The princess's overwhelming love for her father's champion is a conventional motif in romance, but, not surprisingly, Ide does not reciprocate this passion.

Such love between two women was not without literary precedent. It would have been well known to medieval readers from Ovid's story of Iphis, a possible source for *Yde et Olive*.[10]

> Ligdus, a Cretan, tells his pregnant wife Telethusa that if she bears a girl, he will have it killed. In a dream Isis orders Telethusa to raise the child whatever its sex; it turns out to be a girl, so Telethusa raises her as a boy named Iphis. Ligdus arranges for Iphis to marry the charming Ianthe, who is much in love with 'him'. Iphis loves her too, but despairs of ever being able to enjoy this love. Telethusa delays the wedding for as long as possible; at last she appeals to Isis for help. Immediately Iphis becomes a boy, and the lovers are happily married.

Iphis laments that she feels passionate love for Ianthe, but has no hope of satisfying it;[11] the narrator emphasises the frustrating and unnatural nature of

---

9 These incidents and remarks may seem typical of late medieval popular romance, but in fact they are all found in the original French metrical version.

10 *Metamorphoses*, ed. and trans. F. J. Miller, 2 vols, Loeb Classical Library (Cambridge, MA., 1951), 9.666–797; see Nancy Vine Durling, 'Rewriting Gender: *Yde et Olive* and Ovidian Myth', *Romance Languages Annual* 1 (1989), pp. 256–62.

11 *Metamorphoses* 9.726ff. Iphis remarks that her unnatural love has no parallel in the

this love in the phrase 'ardetque in virgine virgo' (l. 725: a virgin burns for a virgin). Ide feels no such fatal attraction: she is appalled by the situation she finds herself in, and has to use her diplomatic skills to avoid disaster. On the wedding night she locks the door and tells her bride 'my ryght swete loue, god gyue you good nyght/ for as for me, I can gyue you no good/ for I fele suche a dissease, the which greueth me sore' (p. 724). It is a situation reminiscent of the unhappy marriage of Tristan and Isolde Blanchemains. The luckless Olive replies generously that she loves Ide so much that she is quite willing to wait fifteen days to do 'ye thynge, the whiche of right ought to be done bytwene man and woman', though eventually she becomes so unhappy that Ide tells her the truth.

At no point does Ide express any love for Olive, not even after her dramatic transformation, which is passed over very hurriedly.[12] In Ovid's story Iphis leaves the temple of Isis and begins at once to walk with longer strides, and to become darker-skinned, stronger and shorter-haired (786–90): but in *Ide* no sooner has God's messenger announced the miracle to the angry emperor than the narrative moves swiftly to the following night during which Croissant is conceived (p. 729). Nothing is said about Ide's feelings for Olive at any point, except that when she first notices the princess's interest in her, she 'prayed to our lorde Iesu chryste that he myght so dele that she be not acused nother of man or woman' (p. 711). Ide does go so far as to kiss and embrace Olive once they are married – but there is none of the frustrated passion that causes Ovid's Iphis to lament 'Oh, what will be the end of me, whom a love possesses that no one ever heard of, a strange and monstrous love?' (726–8). Later in the sixteenth century – the second *aetas Ovidiana* – Ovid was to become widely available in English translation, and extremely influential;[13] but Berners, dutifully following his prose source, did not imagine the complex and transgressive emotions suffered by Ovid's Iphis.[14]

---

animal world (731–4). This contrasts with the comment of Myrrha in the next book of the *Metamorphoses*: she desires her own father, and envies what she sees as the freedom of the animals, who can mate incestuously without criticism (*Metamorphoses* 10.323–31).

[12] Diane Watt argues that *Ide* is a lesbian romance: see 'Read My Lips: Clippyng and Kyssyng in the Early Sixteenth Century', *Language, Gender and Sexuality*, eds Anna Livia and Kira Hall (New York, 1997), pp. 167–77.

[13] Arthur Golding's translation was published in 1565–7. George Sandys added a note to the story of Iphis in his 1632 version recording several historical examples of women transformed into men, one reported by Montaigne; see Ann Rosalind Jones and Peter Stallybrass, 'Fetishising Gender: Constructing the Hermaphrodite in Renaissance Europe', *Body Guards: The Cultural Politics of Gender Ambiguity*, eds Julia Epstein and Kristina Straub (London, 1991), pp. 80–111, esp. pp. 84–5 (I am indebted for this reference to Dr Judith Mitchell).

[14] Nor, however, did Berners or the earlier French prose writer follow the lead of the *Ovide Moralisé* in verse (composed in the late thirteenth and early fourteenth century, and adapted in a prose version by Pierre Bersuire, whose text was in turn translated by Caxton); there Iphis's father is interpreted as God calling for the eternal damnation of the sinful soul (the female nature), and her mother as the church which strives to save the souls of her children:

If the story of Ide and Olive can be seen as anti-chivalric, the same might be said of the standard plot of the Flight from the Incestuous Father narratives, familiar to us in Middle English from *Emaré* (and also, in a modified form, from the *Man of Law's Tale*).[15] In some versions it is introduced as an exemplary story: Beaumanoir says in the prologue to his *Manekine* that he wants to tell a tale that will be profitable to his audience, and at the end he insists on his moral, that however sinful we are, we should put our trust in God like his heroine.[16] *Emaré*, on the other hand, begins with a conventional prayer, and ends without any moral. The story usually stands alone, but *Ide and Olive* belongs to a small subgroup of versions which form part of a larger narrative unit in which chivalry plays a much larger part. Ide's incestuous father was in fact the hero of the previous section of the *Huon* cycle, the courtship of Claryet and Florence. After their marriage, Huon returns to fairyland, Florence inherits his father's crown, and Claryet dies in childbirth. At this point Florence, up till now an unimpeachably honourable and virtuous hero, suddenly turns into an incestuous father. The adventures of the dynasty continue after the resolution of Ide's crises with her son Croissant as hero (and in the French metrical version her half-brother Godin too). I know no English counterpart to this structure, but there are several analogues, not identical, but comparable, in French.[17]

There are a number of significant points of comparison and contrast between *Ide* and *Emaré*, the only other extended Flight from the Incestuous Father narrative in Middle English. In neither text does the father promise his dying wife not to marry again unless he finds a woman who resembles her (this promise appears in many other versions of the plot). In *Emaré* the king appears to fall in love with his daughter only after he has been presented with a magnificent cloth woven by an emir's daughter and decorated with images of famous pairs of lovers (ll. 109ff), which seems to ignite his incestuous desire.[18] In *Ide* the king, like everyone else, admires and loves the beautiful young princess, but there is no particular moment when he falls in love with

---

Ovide Moralisé, ed. C. de Boer et al., *Verhandelingen der Koninklijke Akademie van Wetenschappen te Amsterdam, Afdeeling Letterkunde*, nieuwe reeks, 30 (1931–2), 9, ll. 3190ff.

15 *Emaré*, ed. E. Rickert, EETS ES 99 (London, 1908; rptd 1958); Chaucer, *Man of Law's Tale*. On the role of incest in Chaucer's story of Constance see also Archibald, 'The Flight from Incest' (note 2 above), and Carolyn Dinshaw, 'The Law of Man and its "Abhomynacions"', *Exemplaria* 1 (1989), pp. 117–48, reprinted as ch. 3 of *Chaucer's Sexual Poetics* (Madison, 1989), pp. 88–112.

16 *La Manekine*, ed. H. Suchier in *Oeuvres Poétiques de Philippe de Rémi, Sieur de Beaumanoir*, 2 vols, SATF (Paris, 1884), I, 3–263 .

17 See *Lion de Bourges*, eds W. W. Kibler, J.-L. Picherit and T. Fenster, 2 vols (Geneva, 1980); here too an apparently admirable hero suddenly becomes an incestuous father, and the story of Joieuse's vicissitudes is preceded and followed by chivalric adventures starring her father, future husband and future father-in-law. *La Belle Hélène de Constantinople* describes the adventures not only of the persecuted heroine but also of her twin sons; see A. H. Krappe, 'La Belle Hélène de Constantinople', *Romania* 63 (1937), pp. 324–53.

18 *Emaré* takes this cloth with her in her exile, and the text frequently suggests that it

her. He announces to his barons that he intends only to marry a woman who resembles his dead wife – then stuns them by identifying this bride as his own daughter, and threatens to execute anyone who objects. They think this decision must be inspired by the devil (p. 694). In *Emaré* the king obtains the pope's permission for this marriage. No one speaks out openly against it, though it is implied that the court is shocked (236–40). When Emaré refuses to marry her father, he orders that she be dressed in the magical cloth and set adrift. This is the father's reaction in many versions of the story, but in others the heroine takes the initiative and runs away, like Ide who is aided and abetted by an old lady-in-waiting and by Sorbar (who suggests the disguise of male clothing).[19]

Emaré has a series of adventures which emphasise her vulnerability and defencelessness – and indeed the vulnerability and defencelessness of women in general. She is taken in by a kind lord, married to a king who has fallen in love with her, then slandered and set adrift again through the machinations of a jealous mother-in-law.[20] Ide, on the other hand, has a splendid career as a knight, apparently at no disadvantage because of her feminine physique, and is loved and admired by all. Emaré lives quietly in her final refuge at Rome until her father and her husband happen to come there to do penance for their sins. Although she has been so passive up to this point, it is she who orchestrates the recognition scenes, and she returns joyfully to her proper status as a king's daughter, a king's wife and mother of a male heir. For Ide, also at Rome (a secular Rome, with no mention of the Pope), feats of martial and diplomatic prowess bring an unwelcome reward in the form of marriage to the emperor's daughter; this is the conventional happy ending for a male hero, but of course not for Ide. The revelation of her true identity comes after her inappropriate marriage, and it brings a new and even more dreadful crisis, which only God can resolve.

In the stories of Emaré and her fictional sisters, the final recognition scene is a happy one; once the heroine's identity is established (through her own efforts), her ordeals are over, and she is joyfully restored to her proper status as

---

enhances her beauty and desirability. Mortimer J. Donovan sees it as a fairy object and compares it to Cinderella's dresses; see 'Middle English *Emaré* and the Cloth Worthily Wrought', *The Learned and the Lewed*, ed. L. D. Benson (Cambridge, MA, 1974), pp. 337–42. For a differing view, see Amanda Hopkins' essay in the forthcoming volume of essays from the 1998 Cambridge conference on Romance in Medieval England, edited by Judith Weiss.

19 Cross-dressing is rare in this group of stories. It does appear in the Y*storia Regis Franchorum et Filie in qua Adulterium Comitere Voluit*, ed. H. Suchier in 'La Fille Sans Mains: II', *Romania* 39 (1910), pp. 61–76; but there the heroine reverts to female clothing as soon as she finds refuge in a nearby town.

20 Such problems clearly also arose for women who had not had to flee an incestuous father. Christine de Pizan reminds her readers that a married woman is alone, without family and friends around her, and is likely to be slandered and plotted against by the jealous family and retainers of her husband: see *The Treasure of the City of Ladies*, trans. Sarah Lawson (Harmondsworth, 1985), pp. 70–1.

a princess and queen, a wife and mother, and to the protection of her husband. In the story of Ide, on the other hand, the quasi-recognition scene is most unwelcome; it introduces a threat to her life, and returns her to the vulnerable state in which she left her father's court. She looks after herself very effectively for most of the story, while she is cross-dressed; her victories in battle are not attributed to her faith in God, and it is clear that she has real ability as a warrior. The most serious danger she encounters comes at the very end, when her life and her honour are both seriously threatened by the emperor, and it is only then that God intervenes. To counter the disastrous revelation of her true gender, He warns the emperor not to harm Ide, and gives her a new shape and identity: in effect He confirms the identity she has assumed, that of a man. Thus Ide is able to consummate 'her' marriage and acquire a new status, as emperor of Rome.

Ide's cross-dressing turns the conventional narrative pattern of the Flight from the Incestuous Father inside out. Let us now consider some implications of this unusual combination of incest and cross-dressing. It creates a symmetrical pattern in the story: at beginning and end Ide must contend with a tyrannical father. At first her virtue and her happiness are threatened by inappropriate endogamy, her father's attempt to keep it all in the family; but at the end the crisis is caused by inappropriate exogamy, the emperor's perfectly reasonable attempt to marry his daughter to his new champion, which unknown to him threatens to be a union just as sterile and dangerous for his lineage as incest. The problem of the emperor of Rome (the equivalent of the persecuting mother-in-law in the analogues) is resolved by Ide's transformation, and by his speedy death. The birth of a son to Ide and Olive completes the restoration of order and stability (whereas in the analogues it is the birth of a son which triggers the jealous mother-in-law's attempt to destroy the heroine). It is only at this stage that Ide encounters her own father again, as a sort of epilogue. There is no need for a recognition scene, since Florence knows what has happened to Ide. When she returns to her home to make her peace with him, they meet not as father and daughter, as in other versions of the story, but as equals: both are or have been kings, husbands, fathers and warriors. Rather than returning to Rome, Ide stays at her father's court and succeeds him, since she is now his male heir.

The two father figures share the same problem, that their only heir is a daughter. Nancy Vine Durling argues (in relation to the French metrical version) that the crisis in Yde's life is placed in a very public, political context. She comments that 'the introduction of the incest theme . . . allows the poet to problematise such issues as legitimacy, genealogical succession and the role of women' (p. 262).[21] Durling concludes that Yde's disguise and

---

[21] She also argues that 'there is a consistent undercutting of female presence': the mother dies in childbirth, the daughter cross-dresses throughout the story, there is no miraculous intervention by the Virgin (as in some other Incestuous Father stories) and eventually the heroine is turned into a man.

146

metamorphosis permit 'a regendering of the narrative – a reorientation of the cycle along the axis of male power and patrilineal continuity' (p. 262). Yde's father informs his assembled lords of his decision to marry her before he tells her. This is also the case in many other Incestuous Father stories; what is different here, of course, is that by becoming a man at the end of the story, and then begetting a son, she assures the patrilineal line of descent.[22]

Patriarchy and patriliny are clearly important issues in these stories. In all Incestuous Father (and also Accused Queen) stories, the exiled heroine has a son (sometimes two, but never a daughter), who will ultimately inherit not only his father's kingdom but often his grandfather's too.[23] Durling comments:

> Yde's disguise and ultimate change of gender allow a restitution of non-transgressive sexuality, culminating in natural, patrilineal succession and assuring the stability not only of Huon's line, but also the continuation of the cycle itself ... Whereas the transvestism theme alone would have merely been an appropriate response for a sexually threatened female character, the theme of gender change allows a resolution of the public dimension of the incest threat through a public demonstration of approved sexuality. (p. 259)

Claude Roussel in his seminal article on the Incestuous Father theme agrees that the birth of a son 'conjure definitivement les fantasmes incestueux', but he takes a rather grimmer view of the transformation: 'la virilisation de l'heroïne, confirmée et complétée par le miracle, constitue d'abord une protection contre les convoitises masculines' (p. 56).[24] The only reliable way for a woman to avoid unwelcome advances, from her father or anyone else, is to become a man.

This motif of sexual transformation may well have been inserted into the Flight from the Incestuous Father plot under the influence of Ovid's *Metamorphoses*. As has been pointed out by Durling (p. 257) and others, Ovid places the story of the transvestite Iphis immediately after the story of Byblis, who loved her own brother incestuously, though unrequitedly (and shortly before the story of Myrrha, who arranged to sleep with her own father). It may well have been the proximity of these narratives which prompted the story of Ide – the only medieval narrative known to me where incest and cross-dressing are combined.[25] Women who dress as men are found in medi-

---

[22] *Apollonius of Tyre*, an early and influential version of the Incestuous Father theme in which all the dominant males have only daughters, ends in the same way: after the family reunion, Apollonius and his long-lost wife produce a son and heir. See Archibald, *Apollonius of Tyre: Medieval and Renaissance Themes and Variations* (Cambridge, 1991), pp. 15–18.

[23] This is emphasised in *Emaré*, for instance, where her son is explicitly said to succeed his grandfather as emperor of Rome (ll. 1024–5).

[24] 'Aspects du père incestueux dans la littérature médiévale', *Amour, mariage et transgressions au moyen âge*, eds Danielle Buschinger and André Crepin, Göppinger Arbeiten zur Germanistik 420 (Göppingen, 1984), pp. 47–62.

[25] I have found one brief classical narrative which combines the two, but in an even more

eval literature in romance and fabliaux, where the disguise is usually temporary and brief, and in hagiography, where the disguise may last for many
years.[26] I shall discuss here only the romance narratives known to me in
which cross-dressing by the heroine plays a significant part in the plot (they
are all French): the *Estoire Merlin*, written about 1230, in which the
enchanter reveals the true identity of Grisandole, a young girl who has won
much esteem at court disguised as a knight;[27] the thirteenth-century *Aucassin
et Nicolette*, in which the ever-resourceful heroine travels disguised as a minstrel to find her beloved and undeserving Aucassin;[28] the late thirteenth-
century *Roman de Silence*, in which the royal heroine is raised as a boy because
in her country girls cannot inherit the throne;[29] and the fourteenth-century
Tristan de Nanteuil, in which the hero's wife, the converted Saracen Blanchandine, is separated from her husband, reluctantly marries a love-smitten
sultan's daughter, and when threatened with exposure chooses to be turned
into a man.[30] Earlier in the *Huon* cycle Claryet, Ide's mother, cross-dresses
very briefly at the suggestion of a villainous suitor who then abducts her, but
her disguise has no problematic consequences (II, pp. 608-15). In the Anglo-
Norman and Middle English versions of *Bevis of Hampton*, the hero's wife
Josiane does at one point disguise herself as a pilgrim and minstrel; but no
details are given, and the episode is very brief.[31] Cross-dressing, which is quite
common for heroines with problems in Renaissance narratives (and can
create further problems comparable to Ide's, as in *Twelfth Night*), is relatively

unusual form since the two women involved are long-separated sisters who do not recognise
each other; see *The Myths of Hyginus*, CXC, trans. Mary Grant (Lawrence, Kansas, 1960),
pp. 146–7. But it seems unlikely that this story would have been widely known in the Middle
Ages, and the plot is very different.

[26] For a valuable survey of cross-dressing by women in medieval literature and history, see
Valerie R. Hotchkiss, *Clothes Make the Man: Female Cross Dressing in Medieval Europe* (New
York, 1996). See also John Anson, 'The Female Transvestite in Early Monasticism: the
Origin and Development of a Motif', *Viator* 5 (1974), pp. 1–32; Michèle Perret, 'Travesties
et transsexuelles: Yde, Silence, Grisandole, Blanchandine', *Romance Notes* 25 (1985), pp.
328–40; Vern L. Bullough and Bonnie Bullough, *Cross Dressing, Sex and Gender* (Philadelphia, 1993), esp. ch. 3; and Elizabeth Castelli, ' "I Will Make Mary Male": Pieties of the
Body and Gender Transformation of Christian Women in Late Antiquity', in *Body Guards*
(see note 12 above), pp. 29–49. Regrettably, Margery Garber ignores the Middle Ages in her
splendid study *Vested Interests* (New York, 1992).

[27] Ed. H. O. Sommer, *The Vulgate Version of the Arthurian Romances*, 7 vols (Washington,
DC, 1908–13), II, 281–92.

[28] *Aucassin et Nicolette*, ed. M. Roques, CFMA (Paris, 1954).

[29] Heldris de Cornüälle, *Le Roman de Silence*, ed. and trans. Sarah Roche-Mahdi (East
Lansing, 1992); for bibliography see the recent special issue of *Arthuriana* devoted to *Silence*,
vol. 7:2 (Summer 1997).

[30] *Tristan de Nanteuil*, ed. K. V. Sinclair (Assen, 1971); see also A. H. Krappe, 'Tristan de
Nanteuil', *Romania* 61 (1935), pp. 55–71, and Sinclair, *Tristan de Nanteuil: Thematic Infra-
structure and Literary Creation* (Tübingen, 1983).

[31] *Bevis of Hampton*, ed. E. Kölbing, EETS ES 46, 48, 65 (London, 1885–94; rptd as one vol.
1975), ll. 3893–3948.

rare in medieval literature, where heroines separated from male protectors are more often presented as passive victims who endure a series of undeserved vicissitudes.

These romances which include cross-dressing can be divided into two groups, in relation to the story of Ide. In the *Roman de Silence* and in the *Estoire du Merlin*, when the cross-dressed heroine is finally revealed as female, she marries the king – the conventional happy ending. In *Aucassin et Nicolette* the heroine restores herself to her true female appearance once she has ascertained that Aucassin still loves her, and they are married. In *Tristan de Nanteuil*, however, as in the story of Ide, recognition provokes a new and potentially fatal crisis. Like Ide, the cross-dressed heroine is loved by a king's daughter and has, albeit reluctantly, gone through a marriage ceremony with her; she is then threatened with highly embarrassing exposure. In each case God resolves the crisis by transforming the embarrassed heroine into the man she has been assumed to be. In *Tristan de Nanteuil* an angel gives Blanchandine the choice of being a man or a woman; believing her husband Tristan to be dead, she decides to be a man so that she can avenge him and remain faithful to his memory. In *Ide*, however, the voice from heaven addresses the emperor, informing him that he should not punish Ide who is about to be transformed into a man, and also that he only has eight days to live; he is to make Ide and Olive his heirs, and is to take comfort in the knowledge that they will have a son within a year, who will have painful adventures in his youth, but later 'ioy and welth ynough' (p. 729).

Why was cross-dressing less common as a narrative strategy for heroines in medieval literature than it was in the Renaissance? There has been much discussion of cross-dressing by scholars of Renaissance literature. Of course the fact that female dramatic roles were played by boys makes cross-dressing a more visible problem in this period. We know that there was considerable anxiety about the effect of these theatrical practices on public morality.[32] There are also records from the later sixteenth century of the indictment of women on charges of cross-dressing. Jean Howard argues that anxiety about cross-dressing depended on the sense that outward appearance was crucial to hierarchical distinctions of status as well as gender, and that the theatre was a place which blurred these boundaries.[33] Such anxiety seems to have been present in the Middle Ages too, though less has been written about it.[34] Deuteronomy 22.5 explicitly forbade cross-dressing for both men and women, and so did medieval law codes; but the Bulloughs point out that a double standard was in operation. Since to be female was widely seen as a state of inferiority, there was greater tolerance of female cross-dressing: 'That a

---

[32] See for instance the first chapter of Lisa Jardine's *Still Harping on Daughters* (Brighton, 1983).

[33] 'Cross-dressing, the Theatre, and Gender Struggle in Early Modern England', *Shakespeare Quarterly* 39 (1988), pp. 418–40.

[34] See the comments in Bullough and Bullough, pp. 64–6.

female might desire to be a male, in fact, seemed to be a healthy desire, a "normal longing" not unlike the desire of a peasant to become a noble.'[35] This attitude is clearly reflected in the stories of women disguised as monks.[36] For men to cross-dress was more disturbing, since it involved taking on lower status, and also raised suspicions of seduction plots.[37]

No less an authority than Hildegard of Bingen explains that dress should show men's characteristically masculine courage, and women's characteristically feminine weakness (the ban on dressing in male clothing is also adduced here as the reason why women cannot officiate as priests). But if a man is in danger of death, or a woman of loss of chastity, cross-dressing is permitted, as long as the subject is suitably humble about it, and God's mercy is assured.[38] The heroines in the romances where cross-dressing occurs are all vulnerable and trying to protect themselves. It is striking that in two of these texts, Merlin and Silence, the finale includes the unmasking of cross-dressed men at court who are the lovers of the unchaste queens shortly to be replaced by the virtuous heroines. Acceptable and unacceptable cross-dressing are thus explicitly contrasted. Here again Ide and Olive offers an unusual variation: Ide is a threat to the princess, and thus to the emperor, because she is not a man – it would be much better if she were in fact the princess's male lover.

Recent articles on medieval texts involving cross-dressed women have insisted on the threat they pose to patriarchy and patrilineal descent, what Sharon Kinoshita has called 'the politics of lineage'.[39] Anson argued that for monks the prospect of a cross-dressed woman in their midst would have been titillating, a sensational fantasy (p. 5). For kings without sons, however, the discovery of cross-dressing at court could be a nightmare. In the stories of Silence and Grisandole, the king can achieve a solution unaided: he executes his adulterous queen and her lover(s), then marries the refrocked heroine. In the stories of Blanchandine and Ide, where the heroine is married to the princess before her identity and gender are revealed, the only way to restore dynastic stability is by miraculous metamorphosis – for Ide this conveniently has the added effect of conclusively removing the threat of incest with which her story began.

---

35 Bullough and Bullough, p. 67; and see Castelli. This patronising but benign interpretation was not applied to the case of Joan of Arc; cross-dressing was one of the major charges brought against her (see Hotchkiss, pp. 49–68).
36 See Hotchkiss, Anson and also Castelli.
37 Bullough and Bullough, p. 46. For a fascinating case of male cross-dressing in London in 1394, see Ruth Mazo Karras and David Lorenzo Boyd,' "Ut cum muliere": A Male Transvestite Prostitute in Fourteenth-Century London', Premodern Sexualities, eds Louise Fradenburg and Carla Freccero (London, 1996), pp. 99–116.
38 Scivias, ch. 77, ed. A. Führkotter with A. Carlevaris, 2 vols, Corpus Christianorum, Continuatio mediaevalis, 43–43A (Turnhout, 1978), II, p. 291. Thomas Aquinas allowed the same exception to the rule for women in danger: see Hotchkiss, pp. 55–6.
39 'Heldris de Cornuälle's Roman de Silence and the Feudal Politics of Lineage', PMLA 110 (1995), pp. 397–409.

As de Weever points out in relation to the French metrical version, Yde is simultaneously lady, knight and lover, the constituent elements of medieval romance. De Weever argues that Yde's achievements constitute 'a criticism of literary romances, showing that a woman can achieve the heroic rewards reserved for men' (p. 388). But the ending of the story presents a problem. The cross-dressed heroine generally reverts to conventional female behaviour when she reverts to female dress and marries. But in the case of Ide, whose story began with the particularly horrible threat of an incestuous marriage to her own father, God intervenes to solve her problem by making her apparent masculinity real and permanent.[40] De Weever rejects Perret's view that this is a reinforcement of the status quo, and argues that the story 'criticises and deconstructs the whole estate of knighthood . . .' (pp. 388–9). It would be nice to think that this was so, that the story of Yde/Ide is indeed 'a subtle plea for toleration', as de Weever puts it; but I am not persuaded. Roussel's pessimistic view that 'virilisation' is the only way for her to evade incest may be too extreme; after all, the threat of incest disappears once she leaves home. But in the story of Ide and Olive, the moral seems to be that even if a woman can beat the men, it is better for her to join them.[41]

[40] Blanchandine's case is rather different, since her main problem is the apparent death of her husband; as she discovers too late that he is still alive, her transformation could be seen as an unnecessary tragedy, whereas Ide's life as a man is entirely happy and successful.
[41] I am grateful to the medievalists who heard an earlier version of this paper at the Fifth Biennial Conference on Romance in Medieval England for their useful comments, and to my colleagues Judith Mitchell and A. S. G. Edwards for their help with a later draft.
   An interesting study of the French *Yde* came to my attention too late to be included in this discussion: Robert L. A. Clark, 'A Heroine's Sexual Itinerary: Incest, Transvestism and Same-Sex Marriage in *Yde et Olive*' in *Gender Transgressions: Crossing the Normative Border in Old French Literature*, ed. Karen J. Taylor (New York, 1998), pp. 89–105.

The Strange History of *Valentine and Orson*

HELEN COOPER

R OMANCES, like insects, recurrently evolve new species from a limited
number of archetypes; and, like insects, once they have evolved they
rarely become extinct. Most romances survive predominantly in copies made
one or two centuries after their first composition,[1] and many acquired a
further lease of life through the new technology of printing, which gave them
a breadth of currency in the early Renaissance which they could never have
known in a manuscript age. Even when the original texts began to go out of
fashion, many of the stories evolved new life-forms to survive. Many metrical
romances, both French and English, were rewritten in prose in the fifteenth
century; and as reprintings of the medieval versions ceased during the course
of the next century, the stories reappeared as plays, ballads or chapbooks.

There is an assumption that the changes involved in these processes were
the opposite of Darwinian evolution: that they mark not progress, but degeneration. Editors of French or Anglo-Norman romances rarely look forwards to
Middle English adaptations of the texts for comparative material, still less for
critical enlightenment. Few editors of those medieval English romances that
make the transition to print give the fact a mention, and they are still less
likely to use early printed editions as textual witnesses – usually, it has to be
acknowledged, with good reason.[2] The prose romances that emerged in the
fifteenth and early sixteenth centuries must have a claim to be the most
rarely read generic corpus within English literature: for every person who has
read *King Ponthus*, there must be a hundred who have read its original metrical

---

[1] Derek Pearsall describes the fifteenth century as 'the great age of fourteenth-century
romance', in his 'The English Romance in the Fifteenth Century', *Essays and Studies* NS 29
(1976), pp. 56–83 (p. 58); other English romances of apparently medieval composition are
preserved only in copies from as late as the mid-seventeenth century, whether in manuscript
(the Percy Folio) or print (the earliest text of *Roswall and Lillian* was published in Edinburgh
in 1663). The French prose Arthurian romances likewise reached their height of copying in
the fifteenth century, and their widest dissemination in print at the start of the sixteenth.
[2] The most detailed exploration of what can happen to a single text through such lengthy
processes of transmission is by Nicolas Jacobs, *The Later Versions of Sir Degarre: a study in
textual degeneration*, MÆ Monographs 18 (Oxford, 1995).

version, *King Horn*; and the ratio of those familiar with the Oberons of *Huon of Burdeux* and of *Midsummer Night's Dream* must rise to credit-card-number proportions.

This paper starts from a premise of neither evolution or regression, but simply of historically conditioned change. The different periods at which romance texts were copied, or the different forms taken by the core stories, mark different moments of historical understanding; the recopying of the same text in a later century, or the adaptation of a metrical romance into prose or a prose romance into a chapbook, represents a cultural shift that the reappearance of the text or the story can serve to decode. The discussion here offers a case study of a single story, *Valentine and Orson*. It is not possible to write the full history of the romance, since the record of its mutations, vast as it is, is incomplete: its very earliest version can only be conjectured from translations and adaptations; some of its later metamorphoses, most particularly its English Renaissance dramatisations, are known of only through casual references; and the dozens of later versions surviving in single copies imply a further hinterland of popular editions that were read to pieces.[3] Among these many versions, the early Tudor prose rendering stands out as very peculiar indeed; but it is that version on which the whole tradition pivots.[4]

The original, metrical version of *Valentine* was almost certainly written in French in the early fourteenth century.[5] That text no longer survives, but it can be largely reconstructed from adaptations surviving in various other European languages: some fragments in Middle-Dutch verse, perhaps of the late fourteenth century; a Low-German metrical version recorded in manuscripts of around 1500; a German prose version of 1465; and a sixteenth-century Old-Swedish prose retelling.[6] The Low German poem specifically

---

3   This article does not attempt to give a complete bibliography of the metamorphoses of the work (George Keiser, who is working on a bibliographical history of both the texts and illustrations of *Valentine*, has noted some two hundred editions from both sides of the Atlantic). The material on the English printed versions that follows is derived from the holdings (including microfilms) of the Bodleian Library, Oxford, and the Cambridge University Library, supplemented by the widely varying information supplied by *A Short-title Catalogue of Books printed in England, Scotland, and Ireland 1475–1640*, compiled by A. W. Pollard and G. R. Redgrave, 2nd edn revised and enlarged by W. A. Jackson, F. S. Ferguson and Katharine F. Pantzer, 3 vols (London, 1976–91; hereafter *STC*); *A Short-title Catalogue of Books printed in England . . . 1641–1700*, compiled by Donald Wing, 2nd edn, 3 vols (New York, 1982–94); the electronic *English Short-title Catalogue* of books printed before 1800; and the British Library catalogue.
4   All quotations are from *Valentine and Orson*, ed. Arthur Dickson, EETS OS 204 (London, 1937).
5   The fullest study of the ancestry of the work is by Arthur Dickson, *Valentine and Orson: A Study in Late Medieval Romance* (New York, 1929), pp. 3–27.
6   The verse and prose German versions and the Dutch fragments are edited by W. Seelman, *Valentin und Namelos. Die niederdeutsche Dichtung. Die hochdeutsche Prosa. Die Bruchstücke der mittelniederländischen Dichtung*, Niederdeutsche Denkmäler IV (Norden and

mentions a French source, and there is no reason to doubt its existence.[7] The common derivation of all these versions is indicated, not only by the fact that the story they share fulfils the requirements of a happy ending in rediscovery, marriage and due succession, but also by the distinctive name – or lack of it – given to its second protagonist: not Valentine and Orson, as in the prose version and its descendants, but Valentine and Nameless.

The episodes that make up the story of *Valentine and Nameless* almost all sound thoroughly familiar: it was composed late enough in the tradition for the author to have worked by raiding other romances magpie-fashion. It starts with the marriage of the sister of King Pepin of France to the King of Hungary. Her mother-in-law, jealous of the new queen, steals her twin sons at birth and exposes them, then has her falsely accused of infanticide and banished together with her loyal supporter Blandemer. He, however, is abducted and imprisoned, and the queen finds her way to the court of the King of Araby. The twins, meanwhile, have been rescued, one (the future Nameless) by a she-wolf, the other (Valentine) by King Pepin's daughter, who comes to love him as he grows to adolescence. In due course Valentine overcomes the wild man Nameless, and taking him as his companion sets out to seek his parents. They rescue, first Blandemer, then the queen, though they do not yet realise who she is. Nameless then proceeds to rescue a maiden named Rosemund from the attentions of a giant, and himself lies with her and marries her. The brothers travel on to Hungary and help the king overcome the enemy Saracens. They then encounter a maiden called Rosilia who has been told by a serpent who the brothers are, where their mother is, and that the still inarticulate Nameless can be given speech by the cutting of a vein under his tongue. Rosilia and Valentine fall in love; the brothers rescue their mother from a giant (brother of the one previously killed by Nameless); she is reconciled to her husband, and the original villains are put to death. Valentine and Rosilia marry, and they all return to Pepin's court, where his daughter, realising that she could not have married Valentine anyway since they are related, settles for Blandemer instead. Nameless's lady Rosemund meantime has set out disguised as a minstrel to find him; and all the happily married heroes finish up as rulers, the particular disposition of kingdoms varying according to the text in question.[8]

Even such a bare outline of the story is enough to indicate its generic centrality as romance, whether in dynastic terms (the sons recovering their parents and inheriting kingdoms), innocence vindicated (in the story of the falsely accused queen) or love (with its typical romance culmination in marriage). It is the kind of story that accords with spirit-level accuracy to one's

---

Leipzig, 1884). The Swedish is edited in parallel with the Middle Low-German verse text by Werner Wolf, *Namulös och Valentin* (Uppsala, 1934).

[7] See Seelmann, *Valentin*, p. xxiv.

[8] This account is based on the summary given by Dickson, *Valentine: A Study*, pp. 13–21.

horizon of expectation for romance.[9] God and human virtue combine to reaffirm the rightful line of descent, defeat pagans and villains, and ensure the victory of (most) young love over all the impediments laid in its path. Romance of this kind has something of the effect in the secular world of saint's life in the religious: it insists that God will protect both the accused innocent and the true heir, that ideals of love and chivalry can be attained, that a happy ending is achievable not only in the next world but in this.

The metrical romance was reworked into French prose, as *Valentin et Orson*, in the late fifteenth century, probably not long before its first publication in 1489; there are no surviving manuscripts. It was translated into English by Henry Watson and printed by Wynkyn de Worde in the first decade of the sixteenth century.[10] At first glance, the prose version of the story looks like the same kind of confirmation of romance expectations as is found in the metrical version, only here run riot. It adopts all the key structural elements and a good many of the incidental ones too, adding for good measure a 'Green Knight', an angel that appears to the hero in a dream, a talking brazen head, a magician, a flying wooden horse operated by turning a pin, and twelve peers of France, though a different set from those of the Charlemagne romances (Charlemagne himself figures as a child in the story). For four-fifths of its considerable bulk, almost every conceivable expectation that one might have of romance is fulfilled. They are set up, however, not to affirm a generic faith in the attainability of secular ideals under God, but in order to be systematically destroyed at the end. The structure of the plot symmetrically undoes all the earlier achievements of the story, and brings down with those the whole ethos of the genre. The prose *Valentine* is a story of thwarted expectations – of personal and political treachery and disaster: the very opposite of what its baroque elaboration of romance motifs had promised.[11]

---

9   The term derives from Hans Robert Jauss, 'Theorie der Gattungen und Literatur des Mittelalters', *Alterität und Modernität der mittelalterlichen Literatur: Gesammelte Aufsätze 1956–76* (Munich, 1977), pp. 76–138 (p. 110).

10 The earliest surviving fragment of the de Worde edition is dated to 1502 by Lillian Hornstein (*Manual*, p. 155), and c.1510 by the *STC*, 24571.3. Dickson dates the translation variously between the two (*Valentine and Orson*, pp. xiv, xvii), and conjectures that it may have been made from the third (1505) edition of the French. For the printing history of the French prose version see Brian Woledge, *Bibliographie des romans et nouvelles en prose français antérieures à 1500* and its *Supplement* (Geneva, 1954, 1975), no. 188.

11 The degree to which it contradicts expectations is indicated by the reluctance even of modern scholars to credit what it is saying. Its editor, Arthur Dickson, insists in his Introduction, contrary to the plain evidence of the text, that its heroes are 'constant in love' (p. x), with a footnote to explain away the difference to the effect that 'the author was led astray by the temptation to include one more story'; and he sums up the work as 'an epitome of chivalric character and adventure' (p. xi). Kathryn Hume, in her study 'The Formal Nature of Romance', *Philological Quarterly* 53 (1974), pp. 158–80, categorises *Valentine and Orson* as one of her 'Type A' romances, that show the restoration of order after testing – which is a fair description of *Valentine and Nameless*, but not of the prose. Similarly, Velma Bourgeois Richmond finds the romance unproblematic, *The Popularity of Middle English Romance* (Bowling Green, OH, 1975), pp. 105–18.

The reasons for this shift in the French lie beyond the scope of this paper; *Valentin et Orson* is one of dozens of metrical works that make the transition into French prose, most of them in the fifteenth century, and it is one of several that fail to fulfil normal romance expectations. English made a much more hesitant start on the prose romance only in the second quarter of the fifteenth century, and a markedly high proportion of those produced in the first sixty years or so of the tradition – those that precede *Valentine and Orson* itself – show the same tendency as *Valentine* towards transgression of expected structures and their accompanying ideology. Many of these works seem to be written with a full awareness of that generic pull towards the happy ending almost universal in metrical romance, the restoration of order both for the protagonists themselves in their personal and emotional lives and at large in the body politic, as rule is duly handed down from father to rightful heir despite the worst machinations of usurpers and invading Saracens; but they do not carry that awareness through to fulfilment. Instead, their dominant content is of polities tearing themselves to pieces in civil war, kin-killing and the irrecoverable disruption of orderly lineal descent, in the most extreme instances by the transgression of the father in incest, or the transgression of the son in parricide; on some occasions, all at once.[12]

The earliest such works are also the earliest prose writings to be designated as romances in modern studies.[13] They include expositions of Classical material such as *The Siege of Thebes* and *The Siege of Troy*; three prose renditions of the matter of France; and, most famously, Malory's *Morte Darthur*. The latest work to show these strongly anti-romance tendencies is *Valentine and Orson* itself.

The obvious reason for most of these texts to disrupt the expectations of romance, in its simplest definition of secular stories of love or chivalry set far away or long ago, is that they emerge from various discourses that lie outside the genre, in a way that makes the modern generic label somewhat factitious. The *Sieges* of Thebes and Troy derive ultimately from the archetypal tragedy and epic, *Oedipus Rex* and the *Iliad*. The original stories of Arthur and Charlemagne long predate the emergence of romance in the West, and carried no expectation of a happy ending. All the fifteenth-century prose redactions of such works might therefore have acquired their association with romance back-handedly or obliquely, and indicate nothing about contemporary expectations. But the case is different with *Valentine and Orson*, which locates itself unequivocally within the romance mode through its extensive use of just those motifs and conventions that give the genre its distinctive mark, yet

---

[12] For a study of the full range of such works, see Helen Cooper, 'Counter-Romance: Civil Strife and Father-killing in the Prose Romances', *The Long Fifteenth Century: Essays for Douglas Gray*, eds Cooper and Sally Mapstone (Oxford, 1997), pp. 141–62.

[13] E.g. *Manual*; George R. Keiser, 'The Romances', *Middle English Prose: A Critical Guide to Major Authors and Genres*, ed. A. S. G. Edwards (New Brunswick, 1984), pp. 271–84, with a supplement to the listings given in the *Manual* on pp. 284–6; and Pearsall, 'The English Romance', pp. 72–83.

which ends with disaster for its protagonists. *Valentine* is therefore the test case for establishing whether this association of disaster with the English prose treatment of romance material is a real one: whether the gradual entry of prose as a medium for romance-type stories in the fifteenth century did indeed bring with it a change of focus that marks its products as generically distinct, that governs the *choice* of prose over verse as the preferred medium for telling stories of disaster even when they also recount chivalric and amatory material, and that invites the *selection* of such stories for prose adaptation or translation into English.

It is just the first and longest, more 'romance', section of the prose *Valentin* and its English translation that seems to be based on the metrical text, though with the addition of a great many additional minor adventures. The basic shape of the metrical version is still clearly visible: the marriage of Pepin's sister, here called Bellisant, to the Emperor of Greece; the false accusation of unchastity (made in this case by a lustful archbishop after she has rejected his advances); the birth and separation of Valentine and Orson, Orson being raised, as his name indicates, by a bear; their eventual discovery first of their mother, then of their father; the love of Pepin's daughter, here named Eglantine, for Valentine; and Orson's winning and wedding of his lady Fezon, though the suitor from whom he saves her is a pagan Green Knight who is converted to Christianity rather than a giant (though he is allowed a giant brother). Interspersed with these are a number of major new plot strands. The cast of villains is reinforced by Pepin's two illegitimate sons Haufray and Henry, who are born through a process of trickery and deceit parallel to the accusation of Bellisant. Valentine and Orson are assisted in their later adventures by a dwarf magician Pacolet, who can get them out of the most life-threatening situations. Valentine encounters and overcomes not only a great many more Saracens than in the original, but a dragon as well. Such quintessential romance elements set up strong expectations on the part of the reader for a happy ending, fulfilled in the original metrical version, but increasingly and aggressively thwarted in the prose.

The destructive processes start within the first part of the story. Valentine's initial urge to find his mother gradually turns into an obsessional questing that is never satisfied even when he has found the ostensible objects of his desire, first his mother, then his father: 'desire' indeed becomes an insistent repetition in the text. His determined initial search for identity is superseded by an eagerness to assume new roles and disguises that ultimately bring disaster. The history of Orson's relationship with Fezon is a variant on this perpetual reaching for more. In the first part of the work, it is not enough for him to have won her heart even when he is still in the shape of a wild man without speech: he goes on to test her faithfulness, since, he claims,

> women were of suche a nature that for a lytell thynge they chaunged theyr thoughtes and promyses, and broke theym falsly. (p. 163)

Orson is unaware of how closely the romance idealisation of women is related to the discourses of misogyny, but it seems that the author is fully conscious of the connection. Fezon passes the test unscathed, fully living up to her passionate assertions of fidelity and stability:

> Aboue al other I loue one and hym wil I loue and kepe faith and loyalte as I haue sworne vnto hym, nor neuer for other wil I chaunge him nor forget him;
> (p. 164)

but Orson, having married her, goes on to fail the very standards that she has set. In the final section of the work, he seduces the maiden Galazye on the poor excuse that 'he knewe not whether Fezon was dead or not' (p. 300). Only after Galazye has become pregnant does he inform her that he cannot marry her because he is married already. She retreats into a convent; the plot impasse is resolved by Fezon's conveniently dying of grief when she hears of her husband's unfaithfulness. Valentine's own record in faithfulness is little better. He initially promises marriage to Pepin's daughter Eglantine so long as his birth proves him worthy of her:

> For by the fayth of my body if God will that I be of a place come that is any thyng worth or of valoure of extraction for to haue you. I shall neuer haue to spouse nor wyfe other than you. (p. 85)

He appears never to think of her again, however, instead falling in love with another lady, Clerimond, spending most of the romance pursuing her, and eventually marrying her. Eglantine, unlike in the metrical version, is given no alternative husband. Other major characters are given unexpectedly violent ends. The faithful magician Pacolet is stabbed to death by one of the Saracen kings he has tricked; Valentine inherits his magic tables, 'in whych was wryten all the secretes of hys arte' (p. 282), but that does not prevent him from the entirely natural catastrophe that forms the climax of the work: having completed his quest for his parentage, he goes on to kill his father.

Valentine's killing of the Emperor is in fact a chivalric act that goes wrong: both are disguised as Saracens in the crucial battle. Orson, who had been fighting alongside the Emperor, realises from hearing Valentine's battle-cry

> that it was his brother that hade slayne his father, so he threw downe his shelde and hys spere, and lyfte up hys helme. After he cryed in weping, brother Valentyne euill prowesse have you doone, for to daye you haue slayne the father that engendred you. (p. 308)

From this moment on, there is no question of this story's being just an unusually capacious romance: it has turned into something actively opposed to the genre. Nearer the start of the work, the plots of the bastards Haufray and Henry had been frustrated; at the end, they too kill their father Pepin, and his queen – by poison, a form of murder that was regarded in the Middle Ages

159

with particular abhorrence as being close to witchcraft.[14] Valentine perceives his access to Pacolet's magic as equally tainted, redefining it as a 'dampnable' evil to be renounced and suggesting that his killing of his father may be retribution for his sin in 'playing' with 'such art' (p. 310). It is notable, however, that there is no narratorial comment to endorse this idea of disaster as divine punishment for sin. The passage reads much more like Valentine's own attempt to find some reason or justice in an event that has destroyed the whole generic basis of the story in which he is an actor.

Elsewhere, much of the force of the rediscovery of parents by children is to enable a smooth succession in the passing on of the throne from father to rightful heir; here, that process of right inheritance is impossibly compromised. Valentine does indeed take on the rule of the empire, but he soon abandons it to Orson and embarks on a life of penance. Only a few pages after he has married Clerimond, and with no child conceived, he breaks in half their wedding ring – ostensibly to serve as a recognition token, but she never knowingly sees him alive again. Part of the penance prescribed for him by the Pope is that he is not to speak for seven years: just as the wild Orson, at the start of the story, had been unable to speak, so Valentine must now commit himself to dumbness as punishment for sin. His penitence finally brings the reward of a pious death. The story had opened with the empire threatened with being left without heirs when the Emperor casts off his wife; the birth of twin sons, even in the forest, would seem to promise, within the world of romance, a double insurance against a problematic succession. Yet Orson too abdicates as emperor to become a hermit in the woods, so retreating to the wilds into which he was first born. Both the empire and the realm of France are thus left in jeopardy at the end of the story, in the hands of regents while the infant heirs are incapable of government – perhaps the most unstable of all political conditions. The fate of the empire is indeed elided within the summary vision of the future in the closing sentence of the narrative:

> And the grene knyght gouerned [Orson's] chyldren so that they finisshed their dayes gloriouslye and wente vnto the blysse that neuer shall haue ende, to the which he bryng vs all that suffered deathe for vs on the crosse. (p. 327)

Such a commitment of not only the protagonists but also their descendants to the bliss of heaven is somewhat unusual in romance, and emphasises a further oddity of the ending here: that the happy endings found in other romances orchestrate a providential ordering within *this* world. *Valentine* moves more towards the patterns of hagiography, where God's will is made manifest only in a rejection of secular values and ideals, and anything resembling bliss is excluded from the worlds of time and space, or of chivalry and love.

Valentine and Orson are not, of course, the first romance heroes to

---

14 See Richard W. Ireland, 'Chaucer's Toxicology', CR 29 (1994–5), pp. 74–92, esp. pp. 75–82.

become hermits. Guy of Warwick, the most famous example, had returned to his own home, concealed his identity, and begged alms from his wife, as Valentine does; but the wife Guy had abandoned does at least arrive at his deathbed in time to receive a final kiss from him, whereas Clerimond arrives only after her husband has died.[15] Guy, moreover, acknowledges a continuing role for the ethos of heroism as an element of his penance; and although *Guy of Warwick* is a dynastic romance (the point of it is to construct a legendary origin for the earls of Warwick), Guy himself was not reneging on any political responsibilities comparable to those of Valentine and Orson. In the *Morte Darthur*, Lancelot's retreat to a life of piety after Arthur's death has in it a strong penitential element, like Valentine's, but it functions as a kind of epilogue after the extinction of the Arthurian political and chivalric order. Valentine's years of penance are an integral part of the narrative, and his final canonisation (p. 326) insists that his act of parricide is fully compensated for; but the consequences of the deed remain, and so, in the reader's mind, does the force of his curse on himself when he discovers what he has done:

> I am a boue all the other the moost cursed, vnhappy, and euil fortuned. Alas death where arte thou that thou comest not and take me for I am not worthy that the earthe susteyne me, nor that none of the elementes lende me nourisshinge whan that I haue commytted suche a dede before god detestable, and to the men abhomynable . . . it is not reason that I live ani more vpon the earth, nor that I be put in the nombre of knightes. (pp. 308–9)

The character whom the start of the romance has trained the reader to think of as the epitome of chivalry has been betrayed by that same ethos into an act of 'euill prowesse' that casts him as a parricide, like Edippes, the Oedipus of *The Siege of Thebes*; and as with Edippes, that act means that he cannot accept his place in the system of patrilineal descent approved and confirmed by God that provides the stable core of the metrical romances.

It is misleadingly easy to assemble hypotheses as to why late fifteenth-century England should have privileged such stories: appeals to the *Zeitgeist* may be suggestive but can never carry proof. Social changes may underlie some of the alteration of detail, such as that Bellisant's champion, who challenges and overcomes the wicked archbishop, in the prose version becomes a merchant. The political history of England in the fifteenth century can itself be represented as a series of disasters: the breakdown of the lineal succession with the Lancastrian usurpation of 1399 and the ensuing rebellions; the loss of the English conquests in France; civil war; the further usurpations of Richard III and Henry Tudor. Even that one supposedly stable point in all earthly trouble, faith as represented in the beliefs and daily rituals of the Church, was

---

15 *The Romance of Guy of Warwick: The second or fifteenth-century Version*, ed. J. Zupitza, EETS ES 25–6 (London, 1875–6), ll. 10655–68; the story is the same in the earlier versions, and in the fifteenth-century French prose redaction.

under threat at the start of the fifteenth century from Lollardy and at the start of the sixteenth from the Reformation. The prose *Valentine*, with its visionary angel and pious ending, is certainly neither heretical nor sceptical, though it has its thread of ecclesiastical satire in its lustful and malicious archbishop; but in contrast to the providential ordering of most romances, it does portray God as absent from the crucial moment of the story, a moment, moreover, that connects with the specifics of fifteenth-century history. The Saracens of *Valentine* are the Turks, who had captured the Eastern centre of Christianity, Constantinople, in 1453, and who three years later had been turned back from Belgrade, then on the borders of Hungary, only by the raising of the siege by a Christian army under Friar, later Saint, Giovanni da Capistrano – an event recorded in the English metrical romance *Capistranus*. In the prose romance, history is kept at bay and Constantinople saved. Hungary gives its name to both the country and the city of Angory in the romance; and it is while fighting in defence of that city that Valentine kills his father. The city may be held for the Christians, but the action brings with it Valentine's curse on himself, not the *Capystranus* poet's celebration of God's miraculous support of His knights in the modern day as in the days of Charlemagne.[16] The prose *Valentine* and its context in similar English works make it clear that fifteenth-century readers did not look to chivalric romance merely as a form of escapism into a moribund ideology. The story insists rather that chivalry is not enough: that a will towards good is no guarantee of right action, that God does not always preserve the political order, and that evil can sometimes win without remedy in this world.

That removal of providence from the world allows for the possibility of some fairly drastic generic realignments, not least towards tragedy. *Valentine and Orson* never describes itself as a tragedy, even in the medieval and Elizabethan sense of the fall, usually deserved, of the great man from Fortune's wheel.[17] Valentine's sense of being 'euil fortuned' goes beyond that, as his association with Edippes indicates: both are unwitting father-slayers who have to pay the price. The tragic elements of the work come into a much sharper focus if it is thought of as an early Renaissance composition rather than a late medieval romance. The secular focus of Renaissance humanism was needed before writers dared to imagine a world in which humankind was left to act independently of divine control, but *Valentine* is making a first gesture in that direction. Despite its piety, it takes a step towards the scepticism more usually associated with texts such as Marlowe's *Dr Faustus* or Shakespeare's *Hamlet*: that is, it presents a world in which God exists, but where He does not intervene – where providence is absent from the crucial

---

16 STC, 14 649, c.1515; *Middle English Romances*, ed. Stephen A. Shepherd (New York, 1995), pp. 391–408, ll. 34–57.

17 This is the non-dramatic definition that came to be associated with stories of the kind found in Boccaccio's *De casibus virorum illustrium*, and given in Chaucer's *Monk's Tale*, Lydgate's *Fall of Princes*, and *The Mirror for Magistrates*.

moments of the action.[18] Shakespeare made his own contribution to the process of turning romance into sceptical tragedy in his rewriting of the play of *The True Chronicle History of King Leir*: the source play has a Christian setting and a happy ending in which father and daughter are reconciled and Leir restored to his throne, but *King Lear* turns it inside out to become a tragedy set in a pagan world where the gods are absent.[19]

Such a realignment for *Valentine*, however, is at odds with the bulk of the work, and the powerful gravitation of the story towards the more predictable forms of romance reasserted itself in the course of the sixteenth century, to turn it back into something much more like the metrical *Valentine and Nameless* from which it originated. The prose romance continued in existence, with reprints surviving from c.1555 and c.1565, and a somewhat abbreviated (but still substantial) text replacing it in the seventeenth century,[20] discussed further below. Alongside those, however, there appeared alternative versions: a pageant for Edward VI's coronation celebrations, at least two plays in the 1590s, and a verse narrative of around the same date. The pageant presumably did no more than present the first part of the story: one plate-armoured and one hair-covered man would have been enough to recall the woodcuts accompanying Watson's translation.[21] The metrical version, preserved in the Percy Folio and entitled *The Emperor and the Child*, decisively deletes the disasters of the prose romance.[22] Its brief story – it runs to only 184 lines, a ratio of one and a half lines for each chapter of the prose – preserves the calumniated queen, the birth and separate upbringing of the children, their recovery of their mother, Valentine's marriage, and the restoration of wife and children to the Emperor. It therefore corresponds remarkably closely to the kind of romance that became popular on the Jacobean stage: *The Winter's Tale* would be a prime example, a play that, like *Valentine* (but unlike its source, Green's *Pandosto*), even associates its lost baby with the brief appearance of a bear.

Although the dramatic versions no longer survive, it seems likely that they too abandoned the catastrophe of the prose romance for the simpler and more

---

18 Without wishing to get embroiled in the infinite criticism of *Hamlet*, I take it that most readers and spectators do not infer from the prince's remark on there being a special providence in the fall of sparrow that the whole action is to be regarded as under the direct control of God.

19 For a collection and discussion of the earlier versions of the Lear story, including *King Leir*, see *Narrative and Dramatic Sources of Shakespeare*, ed. Geoffrey Bullough, vol. 7 (London and New York, 1973), pp. 269–402. The 'historical' Lear of the Geoffrey of Monmouth tradition long predates the Christian era.

20 STC, 24 571.7, 24 572, 24 573. The sparsity of copies surviving of each of these (one, or one and some fragments, of each) suggests that there may well have been other editions that do not survive.

21 Dickson, *Valentine: A Study*, p. 286.

22 *Bishop Percy's Folio Manuscript: Ballads and Romances*, eds John W. Hales and Frederick J. Furnivall, 3 vols (London, 1868), II, 390–9. The dating (c.1600) is based on the evidence of its vocabulary and versification.

predictable happy ending, both because of greater ease of staging and because of their association with other romance-type works.[23] Richard Hathwaye and Anthony Munday, to whom Henslowe made a payment of £5 in 1598 for 'a Boocke called vallentyne & orsen', also dramatised another story of a calumniated and vindicated queen, Chaucer's tale of Constance; and Munday was the translator of the great chivalric prose romance *Amadis de Gaule*. Three years earlier, 'an enterlude of Valentyne and Orsson, plaid by hir maiesties Players' had been licensed to Thomas Gosson and Raffe Hancock; this is probably the same text as was licensed to William White in 1600, as 'a famous history called Valentine and Orsson played by her maiesties Players'. This play figures in the records of the Queen's Men alongside other romance-related texts such as *Sir Clyomon and Sir Clamydes* and the original happily ending *King Leir*.[24] Some of the playbooks of the Queen's Men passed to the Chamberlain's Men for Shakespeare to rewrite them later;[25] it is possible that the haul included not only the text but the bearsuit of *Valentine*, so allowing the bear of the *Winter's Tale* a more literal association with the romance than intertextuality alone.[26]

There is no evidence that Shakespeare knew the prose *Valentine*, though it would be entirely possible that he did. The plays, or a version of the story such as the *Emperor and the Child*, would have been enough to provide all the elements that the *Winter's Tale* has in common with the romance. The end of the *Emperor* is indeed as decisive an assertion of restored order (for the exonerated wife and the rediscovered heirs) and happiness (for the penitent husband) as is found in Shakespeare's play, though the phrasing is as summary as the rest of the narrative:

> and soe att lenght, in spite of ffortunes happ,
> they lived in ioy, and ffeared noe after clappe.

A comparable couplet ends Nahum Tate's adaptation of *King Lear*, spoken by Edgar as he is about to marry Cordelia:

[23] See Dickson, *Valentine: A Study*, pp. 287–8, and E. K. Chambers, *The Elizabethan Stage*, 4 vols (Oxford, 1923), III, 333, 448, IV, 403–4.

[24] Chambers, *Elizabethan Stage*, III, 333, 448; Andrew Gurr, *The Shakespearian Playing Companies* (Oxford, 1996), p. 210.

[25] Gurr, *Shakespearian Playing Companies*, p. 209.

[26] An intermediate moment in this hypothetical history of the bearsuit may be provided by *Mucedorus*, where a bear has a very similar run-on part in the second scene ('Enter ... being persued with a beare', *Mucedorus*, ed. C. F. Tucker Brooke, *The Shakespeare Apocrypha* (Oxford, 1908), p. 107 (Act I scene ii, opening stage direction). The play was first printed in 1598, but may well be older. It may have belonged, like *Valentine*, to the Queen's Men, but had passed to Shakespeare's company by the time of its third quarto of 1610 (see Brooke's Introduction, pp. xxiii–v, and Chambers, *Elizabethan Stage*, IV, 36). This would bring it close to the date of the *Winter's Tale*, on which see the edition by Stephen Orgel (Oxford, 1996), pp. 79–80, and *William Shakespeare: The Complete Works*, eds Stanley Wells and Gary Taylor (Oxford, 1986), p. 1241, for rival dates from 1609 to 1611.

Whatever storms of fortune are decreed,
That Truth and Virtue shall at last succeed.[27]

The misrepresentation of the tragedy of *Lear* in those lines is comparable to the misrepresentation of the prose romance by *The Emperor and the Child*. Both stories had moved once from romance to tragedy, and both revert to their original much safer and more comfortable trajectories. The closing couplets of the *Emperor* and the Tate *Lear* represent attempts to reimpose romance endings onto texts that insisted on something diametrically different.

As this proliferation of versions suggests, *Valentine and Orson* should not be thought of as only, or even primarily, a medieval text. Although the last surviving copy of the full-length version of the prose romance belongs to the edition of c.1565, the work was licensed to Thomas Purfoot in 1586 and transferred to his son in 1615.[28] No printed editions survive relating to these entries, but in 1637 Thomas Purfoot jr. published an abbreviated version that reduces Watson's 118 chapters to 52: the compression, interestingly, happens almost entirely after Valentine has been reunited with his father – after the initial, expected shape of the romance is complete. This text had an even more extended life than Watson's own, being reprinted every few years through the seventeenth and eighteenth centuries, often with the same

---

27 Quoted from the 1771 edition. Tate wrote his version in 1681, and it continued to be the standard form of the play on stage until the 1840s – interestingly, a chronological range very close to that of the first miniaturisations of *Valentine and Orson* to its final Victorian stage extravaganzas, discussed below. The earlier *King Leir* likewise puts its final twenty lines into couplets that summarise the happy ending of the story (Bullough, *Narrative and Dramatic Sources*, VII, 402).

28 Edward Arber, *A Transcript of the Registers of the Company of Stationers of London, 1554–1640* (vols 1–4, London, 1875–7; vol. 5, Birmingham, 1894), II, 453, III, 576. *Valentine* is associated with *The Twelve Peers of France* and *Paris and Vienne* in the 1586 entry, and with *The History of the Seven Wise Masters of Rome*, *Huon of Burdeux* and 'the Abridgement of Frozards [Froissart's] Chronicle' in 1615. The phrasing of the entries ('the old booke of Valentine and Orson', 1586; 'copies . . . which were the copies of Master Thomas Purfoote his father deceased', 1615), strongly suggests that both refer to the Watson text, notwithstanding the assumption made by the STC in its entry for 24 573 that they refer to the abridged text. The 1637 'Printer to the Reader', however, describes the history of the work as having been 'translated out of French into English about 100 years agoe, by one Henry Watson, and since that time it hath by him bin Corrected, and put into a more plyant stile, & so followed on to the Presse till this present Edition'. There is no supporting evidence for the revision being Watson's. Most (but not all) later reprints of this edition bear the same title as the 1637 original, *Valentine and Orson. The Two Sonnes of the Emperour of Greece, Newly Corrected and amended, with new Pictures lively expressing the Historie*. The spelling is modernised over the years, but 'newly' remains. It was not until the eighteenth century that the prefatory material was updated, with Watson being put two hundred years in the past: the earliest edition I have seen is *The History of Valentine and Orson* (Belfast, 1782), in which the woodcuts are at last also recut.

woodcuts as appear in the 1637 edition. The introductory 'Printer to the Reader' is similarly reprinted, with its commendation of the work:

> Here may the Princely Mind see his own model; the Knightly Tilter his martial atchivements, and the amorous Lady her dulcet Passages of Love . . . The History for the strangenes, may well bear the title of Courtly contents, for indeed it is a garden of courtly delights.

The 1637 text keeps the full outline of the prose romance, but censors some of the problematic sections. The antifeminist explanation for Orson's testing of Fezon is cut; rather than making Galazye pregnant on their first meeting, he performs a year's funeral solemnity after his first wife's death before marrying her. Henry and Haufray's killing of Pepin is much abbreviated, and Valentine's life history from his penitential visit to the Pope to his sanctified death is rendered as Protestant as is reasonably possible. The final sentences of the story, taken out of this world to the next by Watson, are decisively returned to where they belong:

> So [Orson] taking his way toward a Wood he there spent the remainder of his daies. The Green Knight after so gouerned his Children, that they carefully spent their time on earth, and followed their Father to his Grave.

Further abbreviations, and further censorship, followed. The 'twenty-first edition' of 1708, entitled *The Famous History of Valentine and Orson*, reduces the format and brings the text down to thirty-three chapters, removing along the way Valentine's vows to Eglantine, and cutting down Orson's testing of Fezon still further. In a move parallel to the 1637 text's greater abridgement after Valentine has rediscovered his father, the print here goes into a smaller font after Bellisant has been reconciled with her husband. One effect of the original prose is intensified, however, when the abbreviation puts into successive paragraphs Henry and Haufry's poisoning of their father and Valentine's killing of his.

The Famous History of Valentine and Orson is a misleading title for this work: it usually designates the smallest version of the story yet, that written by Lawrence Price around 1673, which runs to nineteen very small pages of text in six chapters.[29] This gives an even briefer story than the *Emperor and the Child*, and removes all the problematic elements, including all the women except Bellisant herself. Even the wicked archbishop becomes a wicked arch-priest, perhaps because bishops were considered an endangered species in the wake of the Commonwealth. Yet another version, midway in length between the 1637 text and Price, appeared around 1700 as *The Famous and Renowned History of Valentine and Orson*, 'newly Printed and Abbreviated for the Benefit and Recreation of young Men and Maids, whose Impatience will

---

[29] Still shorter are the chapbooks published from c.1680 – just twelve pages in length.

not suffer them to read the larger Volume'. Here again, the sexual improprieties and the Catholicism disappear. Valentine dies, and is

> interred with all Honour due to so noble a Warrior: Orson lived long after with his wife the fair Lady Galazy (whom he married after [the] Death of the Lady Fezon) administering Justice; and was greatly beloved of all his Subjects.

Uncomplicated martial valour, marital propriety and political well-being thereby rule supreme.

A comparable process happens with the French prose *Valentin*, but it is interestingly different in the detail of its censorship. It too was reprinted in an abridged version closely based on the fifteenth-century original, and for even longer than in Britain: the last known edition dates from the 1870s.[30] Like the later English versions, this shows some anxiety over the problematic elements – the heroes' betrayal of their first loves, the father-killing – but the degree of anxiety created by each is in inverse proportion to the English: it is the father-killing rather than the sexual misdemeanors that receive the sharpest abridgement. Early in the romance, therefore, Valentin is allowed to make his full declaration of faith to Eglantine. In an extraordinary abbreviation of much of the most problematic action, however, in the course of a single chapter (LIII), Orson's seduction of Galazye is removed; Valentin fights and overcomes the pagans; apparently in mid-battle, the infant Charles succeeds to the throne of France, but without Pepin's ever dying, let alone being poisoned; and when the corpses are identified after the battle, the emperor is found to be among them. There is no attempt to tie up the loose ends that all this creates: the story goes on as before with Valentin's declaring his repentance for the death of his father (whom he has not, in this version, killed), and with Fezonne's death over Orson's unfaithfulness (even though he has not apparently been unfaithful).

The history of the story in England in the nineteenth century shows even greater diversity in the forms it takes. A version printed in 1804, of twenty-two small pages, follows the sexually puritan pattern by cutting one woman from each hero's life – Eglantine and Galazye both disappear – but it does keep the death of Valentine's father, and with that a sober, if thoroughly platitudinous, verse ending:

> Thus, reader, you may see that none withstand,
> Tho' great in valour, or in vast command,
> The mighty force of death's all conquering hand.[31]

More commonly, the resistance to the unhappy ending of the story reasserted itself with more verbal conviction than ever before. Also in 1804, Thomas

---

30 *Histoire de Valentin et Orson* (Épinal, n.d.).
31 *The Famous History of Valentine and Orson* (unlocated, 1804); the pages are numbered to 24, but 18 and 19 do not appear.

Dibdin turned the story into 'A Romantic Melo-drama' in two acts, a reworking popular enough to be reprinted c.1830;[32] this is so fantastic a production that one would think it had lost contact with its roots in the prose romance entirely, if it were not that extracts from the 1637 'Printer to the Reader' still reappear in the preface. This version ends at the same point as the original metrical version or the *Emperor*, with the brothers' discovery of their mother, and their marriages to their brides Eglantine (a convenient composite of Valentine's first love's name with his second love's role) and Florimonda. The Finale to the play takes the kitsch of the *Emperor* to new heights:

> Moment of triumph! virtue's power,
> Resplendent rising, gilds the day,
> Surmounts misfortune's clouded hour,
> And drives each wint'ry storm away.
> > Thrice happy day!
> > Huzza! huzza!

The nadir was reached in the 1840s, with *Valentine and Orson: A Singularly Original and Touching Extravaganza*,[33] based on Dibdin, but with the addition of fairies, some appalling puns, and up-to-the-minute references to railways. The final lines in this version are spoken by Pippin, the suitably undignified variant of Pepin:

> And since to marry each has made his mind up,
> In one 'grand blaze of triumph' let us wind up.

The sharp contrasts between the various endings of *Valentine* epitomise equally sharp differences in cultural responses to romance itself: they measure the changing horizons of generic expectation. The changes are only partly a matter of chronology. *Valentine and Nameless* attached a value to the archetypal happy ending such as could still be replicated in *The Winter's Tale*, with its recycled bearsuit; the achievement of desire in those carries a weight it is never accorded in either the escapist wish-fulfilment of the *Emperor* or Price's *Famous History* or Dibdin's Romantic Melo-Drama. The prose romance did not bring such values into disrepute; but the rewriting of the climax of *Valentine and Orson* as disaster does mark a symbolic moment more usually dated to the high Renaissance, when writers brought themselves to imagine what a world would look like in which providence does not always intervene.

---

32 Thomas Dibdin, *Valentine and Orson: A Romantic Melo-Drama* (London, 1804 and ?1830).
33 Written by A[lbert Richard] Smith, C[harles] Kenny and J. Taylor. I quote from the fourth edition (London, ?1845).

Index

169

Index

Index